SLINKYS AND SNAKE BOMBS

Non-Fiction Titles by the Author
The Busy Person's Guide to British History
The British Empire in 100 Facts
Deus Vult: A Concise History of the Crusades
The Romans in 100 Facts
Forgotten History: Unbelievable Moments from the Past
The Napoleonic Wars in 100 Facts
The American Presidents in 100 Facts
The Sultans: The Rise and Fall of the Ottoman Rulers and
  Their World

Historical Fiction Titles by the Author
Silent Crossroads
Echoes
And God Watched
Edge of Life

SLINKYS AND SNAKE BOMBS

Weird but True Historical Facts

Jem Duducu

AMBERLEY

For My Darling L12

First published 2021

Amberley Publishing
The Hill, Stroud
Gloucestershire, GL5 4EP

www.amberley-books.com

British Library Cataloguing in Publication Data.
A catalogue record for this book is available from the British Library.

ISBN 978 1 3981 0299 6 (paperback)
ISBN 978 1 3981 0300 9 (ebook)

Typeset in 11pt on 15pt Sabon.
Typesetting by SJmagic DESIGN SERVICES, India.
Printed in Great Britain.

Contents

Introduction

Over the years I have written a variety of history books. Of all of these, historical fiction is the most liberating; it's nice to make things up when it suits the plot. However, that sort of thing tends to be frowned on in non-fiction titles (the clue is in the genre title), of which this is my ninth. But the thing I love about history, where it beats fiction hands down, is that some truly bizarre events really happened. No need for embellishment. There are actual moments in our past that in a fictional story would cause readers to roll their eyes and say, 'No way, that's completely impossible.'

History is everything that has happened to humanity right up to the start of this sentence. So why do we keep writing about the Romans or the Second World War or the Tudors? These are all important, but history shouldn't have hidden alleys filled with centuries of stories. It's almost like there are ghettos of lost topics and eras, some of which we can't even guess at because they are so little known – or completely forgotten.

That's not to say that this missing information can't be rediscovered. A famous incident recently was the discovery of the remains of King Richard III in a Leicester car park. Up until then, there had been genuine debate about whether he was a hunchback. It made sense that the new dynasty (the Tudors) would vilify and distort the last Plantagenet ruler … until we were able to see that Richard's skeleton, even after a cursory inspection, clearly had a twisted spine.

Some facts will never change: the Battle of Hastings will always have happened in 1066, but we may yet find the bodies of some of the key players, such as Harold Godwinson, which would add another chapter to our existing knowledge on the topic. I mention this because I have written this book in good faith and with plenty of research, but it would not surprise me if, say, in five years, a few of these facts change as new information comes to light.

Like *Forgotten History: Unbelievable Moments from the Past*, this is a collection of articles (edited and enlarged) from my *History Gems* Facebook page. I find readers' comments fascinating. Sometimes people get very upset over something that happened centuries ago. Others make weird leaps in time from, for example, a story set in the Middle Ages with a comment like, 'Well, our government is the same now.' It isn't, it really isn't. Sometimes I engage with the comments, other times I ignore them, but my favourite posts are always something like, 'I never knew that' or 'Thanks for digging that up.'

Sometimes people accuse me of making things up or challenging received wisdom. The very first person I ever banned was a man who got *very* angry when I dared to say that Robin Hood was a legend. With around 98K likes on a Facebook page that's been running for over eight years, only banning about a dozen people shows there is more good than bad out there.

So, to the doubters out there, some of these facts may sound bizarre and a few may sound unbelievable, but they have all been fact-checked. Also, most of them are a summary of a bigger story which I have distilled. Want to know more? Get a book on the subject or do a Google search. There's almost always more. My intent here is to summarise, inform and entertain, but never to the point of distorting the facts.

This book is a culmination of years of digging around some of those bigger stories, when a footnote has a stranger tale to tell than the main body of text. Or when a documentary makes a passing reference to something that makes me think, 'There's more to that.' The result is a collection that will take you to a time before the story of humanity, all the way up to the tail end of the twentieth century. This book will transport you back to ancient civilisations, across deserts, into the oceans and beyond. I am particularly proud of all the women included in these stories. There's an undeniable bias in old chronicles towards men, so this is a chance to show how brave, intelligent and sometimes wicked women have been through the millennia.

Finally, as in *Forgotten History*, I have ordered all the information so it's roughly chronological, with the book split between four loose eras: ancient history, from prehistory to around AD 550; the Middle Ages, from 550 to 1500; the Early Modern, from 1500 to 1900; and the modern era, comprising the twentieth century. Would an Indian recognise Shah Jahan as an Early Modern ruler or a Mayan understand the concept of the Middle Ages? No, but it's a structure to stop the reader getting lost in the information. Saying that, there's no through-line. This is the perfect book to pick up when you want to just flip to a random page and read.

In summary, I hope you have as much fun reading this as I did researching and writing it.

Ancient

The Most Terrifying Predator That Ever Lived

The largest dinosaurs and largest animals to ever walk the earth are the slightly disappointing sauropods, giant plant-eaters. (Additional fact: the largest animal in all of world history is the blue whale.) These plant-eating sauropods are cool but, let's be honest, not as cool as the predators.

However, the largest recorded arthropod (an invertebrate with an exoskeleton, a segmented body and paired, jointed appendages – or, as you and I would most likely call them, bugs) is the extinct *Jaekelopterus*, whose common name is the sea scorpion. If you find an image you can see that … well, it was terrifying. Its body length was thought to average around 240 cm (about 8 feet) and that was just its body. The claws were over 40 cm (more than 6 inches) and thought to be capable of crushing a man's arms had we coexisted, but the *Jaekelopterus* lived during the Middle Devonian period, roughly 390 million years ago. To put that into context, that's more than 100 million years before the first dinosaurs.

It is thought that this arthropod was more of a freshwater scorpion rather than one found in the sea. Its enormous size was possible only because it lived underwater; exoskeletons crush internal organs when they get too big, which is why modern insects rarely grow bigger than the size of adult male's hand. Also, the oxygen content was far richer in the earth's atmosphere then, meaning the breathing holes on the scorpion's body could draw in enough oxygen to survive. Today, it would suffocate.

The *Jaekelopterus* is thought to have been an apex predator, meaning once it had matured there wasn't anything in its habitat that could kill it. The main fossils of the creature were found in western Germany, which is an area of great beauty and charm today; 390 million years ago, however, it was home to these giant sea scorpions – so not a great destination for a beach holiday.

The Time It Rained … a Lot

It's only human to complain about the weather. If it's hot for too long, we complain about the heat; if it's cold for too long, we complain about the cold. If the weather changes too often, we complain about how changeable it is. When it comes to the weather, we are never happy, but we should be grateful we didn't live through the Carnian Pluvial Event. This occurred about 230 million years ago when it rained a lot. How much, I hear you ask. Guess.

In the biblical story of the Great Flood, it rained for forty days and forty nights. The entire globe was covered with water in an apocalyptic event that would wash the earth of the sins of man. Whether that was a fable or not, it is peanuts compared to the Carnian Pluvial Event. For it to show up in the geological records it had to go on for a significant period, but how long? A thousand years would be silly, wouldn't it? Well … Mother Nature is capable of the strangest things, and in this case, it rained for (approximately) *2 million* years!

No, that is not a typo; it does say '2 million'. This event changed the world's geology and, of course, the life forms on the planet. High extinction rates occurred, bizarrely, mainly among marine animals such as ammonites and conodonts (sort of early eels). Unsurprisingly, after this huge deluge, major evolutionary innovations followed. The two most notable were the first occurrences of dinosaurs and corals.

So let's be happy with the weather we have because 2 *million* years of rain changes everything.

Lake Turkana, the Gift That Keeps on Giving

Lake Turkana in Kenya is remarkable for a number of natural records: among others, it is the world's largest permanent desert lake as well as the world's largest alkaline lake. Furthermore, it is the site of some of the most significant anthropological finds in the world. The first came in the 1970s when a 2-million-year-old skull was found. It was originally thought to be *Homo habilis*, but it was later proven to be a different species of hominid, so *Homo rudolfensis* was created (this was a time when the lake still had its old British imperial name of Lake Rudolph). Hominids are proto-humans; they were formerly known as 'ape-men', but this term is problematic and is no longer used.

Then, in the 1980s, the remains of a 4-million-year-old hominid was found. It should be noted that when we are talking about remains of such extreme age, an entire skeleton is never found; most often it's a piece of a limb or a section of the skull. In this case, it was a piece of mandible that was eventually assigned to the Ethiopia-based hominid species *Australopithecus afarensis*. This was an incredible find. About a decade or so after that, a further skull was found to be 3.5 million years old.

It should come as no surprise that Lake Turkana is near the Great Rift Valley, the area still thought to be the location where our species originated. We will never know if all these remains were once on land and eventually submerged by the lake or if we are looking at the remains of clumsy ancestors. In any case, with this collection of finds, the lake became one of the most important sites of Palaeolithic archaeology in the world.

Then, in 2015, Lake Turkana revealed another sensational find: a stone hand axe, essentially a piece of rock crudely sharpened on one edge. It is as basic a stone tool as can be found, and it threw the world of Palaeolithic archaeology into a frenzy. Up until then, it had been thought that hominids first started using tools around 1.4 million years ago, but this tool was 1.76 million years old. That doesn't sound like a lot in this context, so let's put it in perspective: 360,000 years ago there were no *Homo sapiens* in Europe because the continent was still largely under ice. Mammoths roamed the world and Neanderthals were still a huge proportion of the world's population. So yes, 360,000 years is a big deal. This tool was the stealth bomber of its age, and if our ancestors hadn't worked out how to manipulate their environment to better themselves ... well, you wouldn't be reading this right now.

It seems that every decade or so, the lake reveals yet another amazing find that sends shock waves through the world of archaeology. Who knows what else lurks in its depths?

Mysterious Ruins Part 1

Marine archaeology is often overlooked when it comes to the study of the past, and yet, despite its inherent difficulties, it provides some of the most interesting discoveries. Digging and surveying under water creates unique challenges, but quite often thick muds and silts just off the coastline act as amazing preserving agents – leading to hot debates.

Take for example the finds in the Gulf of Khambhat, just off the coast of India. In May 2001, India's Union Minister for Human Resource Development reported that sonar had detected the ruins of ancient structures off the coast of Gujarat. A follow-up marine excavation began in November of the same year and in October 2002 unearthed evidence of microliths (tiny stone tools), the basic outlines of structures, some wood that could be radiocarbon dated and the remains of constructions using wattle and daub (a building material of wood and mud).

The problem comes from the radiocarbon date of the wood, which places it at around 7,500 BC. This staggeringly ancient date shows the power of the preserving layers of mud, but it also led to more questions than answers. We know that India had an ancient civilisation, the Harappan, but it began around 4,000 BC and was located much further north. Also discovered were tiny flakes of what some thought were pottery, while others claimed they were such tiny fragments as to be natural metamorphic deposits. Even if it was pottery, it wouldn't be the world's oldest, which is about 20,000 years old from Jiangxi province in China, but it would be the oldest pottery in India.

And so the fight began. One reasonable argument runs that a piece of wood is not necessarily part of the ruins; it could simply be from an ancient tree. Or it could have floated there at a different point in time. At the other end of the spectrum, some argue that because this is likely the oldest town on earth and it's now under water, it must be Atlantis, the cradle of all civilisations. What isn't disputed is the fact that there is a unique and amazing archaeological site on the bottom of the Gulf of Khambhat. So now, over to you; you have four options:

1) These are old but explainable ancient ruins;
2) The wood's old but the ruins are far more recent;
3) We've found Atlantis!
4) Aliens, got to be aliens ...

Mysterious Ruins Part 2

Occasionally archaeologists stumble across something truly mysterious. Tel Aviv University had been carrying out some fairly routine surveys of the seabed in the Sea of Galilee. Quite unexpectedly, they found a huge, previously unknown structure on the sea floor. The underwater photo showed that the structure is a cone-shaped monument made of basalt boulders, approximately 70 metres (230 feet) in diameter, 12 metres (39 feet) high and weighing an estimated 60,000 tons.

Initial findings indicated that the structure had to have been built on dry land, and as the Sea of Galilee formed 6,000 years ago, the structure is at least that old. If it was built before the Sea of Galilee formed, it would be significantly smaller but thousands of years older than the Pyramids – and far more complex than Stonehenge. Of course, a find of this age is prehistoric (that is, it occurred before writing was invented), so there can be no record of which civilisation built it and why.

Like the previous mysterious ruin, the fact that it became submerged over time probably saved it from destruction. Basalt was not going to wear away in 6,000 years, but locals have a habit of repurposing the building materials of ancient sites, so a large pile of handy blocks would have meant that over the millennia they would likely have been broken down until there was no evidence of the site ever existing.

The origins of the site remain a mystery. This was a colossal endeavour made by peoples unknown for reasons unknown, highlighting the frustrations that often occur in Neolithic archaeology.

Gold!

We humans are fascinated by gold, probably because it is both rare and shiny. It was one of the earliest metals to be mined by humans because it is soft and easy to shape. The very earliest gold objects come from modern-day Bulgaria and are about 6,500 years old, predating even the Bronze Age. It is the first metal humans manipulated.

Relative to other elements, gold is rare, and the reason for this has to do with physics. All the elements up to the size of iron ($Fe26$) were created in the Big Bang. All atoms larger than iron (so cobalt, $Co27$, onwards) were created in other, later astrological events. Basically, the larger the atom, the more force required to hold the subatomic particles together. Gold is such a large atom ($Au79$) that it can only be made in the dying hours of a star going supernova. When a star explodes, in one of the most destructive events in the universe, it spreads its component atoms across the galaxy. The gold we have today is the fallout from long-dead supernovas that exploded in other solar systems. It is stardust that has fallen on our planet and worked its way into the earth's crust. No chemical reaction on planet earth makes it, nor is it recycled by natural events. So that explains gold's rarity.

Gold retains its shine because it doesn't react chemically to almost anything under natural circumstances. As such, compared to more common metals such as silver, it does not tarnish over time; it is this permanent lustre that makes it an attractive metal for adornment, both personal and otherwise. So, in conclusion, gold is rare, malleable and shiny. Maybe we are all magpies at heart.

Opium Has Been Part of Our Medicine Cabinet for a Long Time

The first signs of possible opium use are the poppy seeds found in a Spanish cave burial site dating back to (approximately) 4,200 BC. What's interesting about this is that poppies aren't common in Spain, although it is unclear whether they were more prevalent in the Neolithic. Deliberate cultivation of the opium poppy started around 3,200 BC in central Asia; it has been growing in what is now Afghanistan for over 5,000 years.

The ancient Egyptians included opium in their legends, and its ability to dull pain made it useful to Egyptian doctors in many medical procedures. Several Greek gods (perhaps the most famous being Demeter who, according to legend, was the creator of the poppy) associated with dreams or health were sometimes shown with poppy wreaths. It has been a fundamental part of many civilisations since ... well, since the dawn of civilisation.

Recreational use of the opium poppy seems to have started in the Islamic world (where alcohol was banned but opium was not) around the fourteenth century but was never widespread due to cost. In China, the use of opium began in the seventeenth century. Opium dens became the stuff of legend in the West, but it was the British who took it to a whole new level. To create favourable trading terms with traditionally closed-off China, Britain flooded the Chinese market with opium to cause an epidemic of addiction and generate a surge in demand. While it was technically a legal substance in both Britain and China, this was a shocking display of British imperial cynicism and led to the so-called Opium Wars with China. Britain won these easily, but more punitive settlement terms were not sought because Parliament had an unusual pang of conscience and recognised that the Chinese had only been trying to stop a flood of cheap narcotics into their territory – and that they were right to do so.

It wasn't until the late nineteenth and early twentieth centuries that opium became a controlled substance, which is where Bayer, a German pharmaceutical company, becomes part of the story. Many modern drugs are based on naturally existing ones, and Bayer attempted to enhance the pain-killing effects of opium by creating a synthetic version which they dubbed Heroin. Of course, it was copied and became the highly addictive narcotic that is trafficked across the globe today. Bayer no longer stake a claim to the brand name.

The History of Pregnancy and Periods

If there's one thing we've got in common it's that we've all been born. Although being able to understand when a woman is pregnant is a complex process, somewhat counterintuitively, pregnancy tests have been around for a long time. Some of the early ones were surprisingly good. For example, the first record of a pregnancy test comes from ancient Egyptian sources. Records describe a test that required a potentially pregnant woman to urinate on barley and wheat grains over a few days. If the seeds sprouted, she was pregnant. It turns out that this test is 70 per cent accurate. Not bad, but there was still a healthy margin of error, and the results weren't exactly quick or practical.

The first test with a high level of accuracy was devised thousands of years later in the New World at the University of Pennsylvania in 1931. Maurice Friedman and Maxwell Lapham came up with what was later called the rabbit test, although their initial trials were conducted with mice. They injected the urine of a potentially pregnant woman into a rodent. If the woman was pregnant, the animal's ovaries would react to the high levels of the pregnancy hormone (human chorionic gonadotropin, hCG) and enlarge. It was 98 per cent accurate, and as only pregnant humans produced hCG, it was about as good a test as could be devised.

Unfortunately, not only is this an unpleasant example of animal testing, but even worse is the fact that checking the animal's ovaries required it to be killed and dissected. These tests were extremely common in the Western world into the 1970s, which is a lot of rabbits. But there is some good news. A later alternative to the rabbit test, known as the Hogben test, used the African clawed frog. This time, the results were confirmed without the need for dissection (although the frogs did spend most of their lives having human urine poured over their backs).

It is the telltale hormone hCG that is relevant to all of the tests above, including the ancient Egyptian one, and is still the cornerstone of pregnancy tests today. Modern home-testing kits are now more than 99 per cent accurate. Of course, if you're not in a hurry, you could always wait nine months and see what happens. That test is 100 per cent accurate.

Menstruation, I think all women agree, is not much fun. I know that women today have many aids that help to make periods more comfortable: pads, tampons, painkillers, etc., but I wanted to find out how women coped in the past. What I discovered made me think.

Research has shown that the average woman living today in a modern society will menstruate 420+ times in her adult life. But it has been estimated that during our hunter-gatherer phase (when *Homo sapiens* evolved), a woman would have about fifty periods in her entire adult life. Some of this is explained by a shorter life span, but it gets more interesting. Contraception was, shall we say, limited in the Palaeolithic era, which meant women were likely to become pregnant much more often than in a modern urban setting. Also, infant mortality was high, so people needed to keep breeding to keep the tribe going; an heir and a spare simply weren't going to cut it. Women rarely have periods when they are pregnant, so this greatly reduced the amount of times an early *Homo sapiens* woman would menstruate. Then there's breastfeeding, another time when women rarely menstruate, but that stage now lasts about six months, whereas the average in the past was more likely to be three years.

Linking breastfeeding with pregnancies means that menstruation was comparatively rare, maybe on average a couple of times a year in a woman's adult life. Indeed, there is speculation that the arrival of menstruation might have been seen as the all-clear to try for another baby. It's theoretically possible that some of these early women might not have had a period for years or even a decade. This means that the women of the past weren't regularly dealing with cramps and other side effects of menstruation as is often the case today. Even just 100 years ago, it is estimated that women had about a third of the number of periods that a modern woman has. Better health, longer life and reliable contraception have made significant differences in the reproductive lives of women today.

Shang China

There is a saying that goes, 'Chinese and Russian history is easy; it's the same as everyone else's, just a lot more people die.' It's a pithy summary and a reminder that China has quite a lot of history, with archaeological records stretching back further than most countries. Even getting the different dynasties straight can be daunting for a Westerner.

Most of us in the West have heard of the Ming dynasty and possibly the Han or Qing dynasties, but the longest-running dynasty was the Shang dynasty, which lasted more than 500 years from (roughly) 1600 BC to 1046 BC. Yes, this was a working dynasty and administration 500 years before the Persians met the Greeks at Thermopylae and centuries before Rome was even a village. It is, however, disingenuous to think of this dynasty as ruling the same territory we know as China today. While it is true that the Shang dynasty ruled a large area, it may have been about a fifth of the present Republic of China. Also, there were several periods, centuries after the Shang, when China was a region of warring nations and dynasties. No brotherly love going on there. With those caveats, the archaeology associated with the Shang is impressive. Work at the ruins of Yin (near modern-day

Anyang in eastern China), identified as the last Shang capital, uncovered eleven major royal tombs, the foundations of palaces, and ritual sites containing weapons and remains from both animal and human sacrifices. Tens of thousands of bronze, jade, stone, bone and ceramic artefacts have been unearthed. The workmanship on the bronzes attests to the high level of sophistication this civilization achieved. The sheer quantity alone shames the likes of Tutankhamun's tomb.

The Anyang site has yielded the earliest known body of Chinese writing, not histories or official court documents but mostly divinations inscribed on oracle bones. Various words and symbols were etched into animal bones, which were ceremonially dropped or burnt and, depending on the resulting patterns, would give the shaman hints about the future. These discoveries give us a glimpse of the mindset of the people of this long-dead civilisation. More than 20,000 bones were discovered in the initial scientific excavations during the 1920s and 1930s, and over four times as many have been found since.

Di Xin was the last Shang ruler, but he was mad, suffered a series of military defeats and committed suicide, all of which resulted in the dynasty's decline. In its prime, however, the Shang was perhaps the most advanced culture in the world.

The Cat God

The Egyptians had many deities, some of which are better known than others. I believe the time has come to reveal the lesser-known goddess Bastet, a (domestic) cat god and one of the oldest of all the gods. The earliest evidence of her divinity is found during the Second Dynasty (2890 BC), a time on the very edges of any historical records, and she predates the unification of the Egyptian throne (when the kingdom was split between the Upper and Lower Nile).

In her earliest known incarnation, Bastet was a goddess of war, portrayed as a lioness. Later, she got a demotion (arguably) as she evolved into the cat goddess familiar today. Greeks occupying ancient Egypt toward the end of its civilization (and thousands of years later) changed her into a goddess of the moon. As a protector of Lower Egypt, she was also seen as a defender of the pharaoh and, consequently, of the later chief male deity Ra. Along with the other lioness goddesses, she would occasionally be depicted as the embodiment of the Eye of Ra, and she has been portrayed as fighting the evil snake Apep, an enemy of Ra.

Bastet was a local deity whose religious sect was centred in a city located in the Nile Delta near what is known as Zagazig today. That city was Bubastis and, yes, *Watchmen* fans, that's where Ozymandias's great cat's name comes from. In another pop culture reference, the Marvel superhero Black Panther comes from the fictional African country of Wakanda, which has a panther god called Bast. This could be a coincidence but it's remarkably similar to Bastet.

But back to Egypt where Bastet was important enough to have her main temple described by Herodotus:

> Save for the entrance, it stands on an island; two separate channels approach it from the Nile, and after coming up to the entry of the temple, they run round it on opposite sides; each of them a hundred feet wide, and overshadowed by trees. The temple is in the midst of the city … and bordered by trees reaching to heaven.

The elaborate design and prime location attest to her importance in Egyptian culture.

Bastet was both an important and much-loved deity, which probably goes a long way towards explaining why there are numerous examples of cat mummification; owners presumably wanted to have their favourite pet for company in the afterlife or as a guide in the underworld (who better to hiss at random shadows?).

In the words of Terry Pratchett, 'In ancient times cats were worshipped as gods; they have not forgotten this.'

The Oldest Story

Cuneiform is the most ancient form of writing in the world. It's a little over 4,500 years old and comes from ancient Babylon, now Iraq. The interesting thing about it (apart from its age) is that the clay tablets on which it survives were not recording important events or the deeds of kings but something far more mundane and yet far more important.

It seems that the ancient Babylonians were accountants before they were storytellers. The very earliest cuneiform tablets are lists of grain stores or records of payments to labourers (so we know the going rate for various jobs 4,500 years ago). This is more informative than myths about monsters because while myths tell us something about the social concerns of the times, the tablets reflect the beating heart of an economy that existed more than four millennia ago. A few centuries later and we get the world's first (extant) literary epic in *The Epic of Gilgamesh*, a poem that has the same narrative qualities we would expect to find in an epic tale today. We humans like a story of good overcoming evil, and if this is attached to adventure, so much the better.

The Epic of Gilgamesh was written in the city of Uruk, part of the Sumerian civilisation, and the origin of the modern name Iraq. The first half tells the story of Gilgamesh, King of Uruk, and Enkidu, a wild man created by the gods to stop Gilgamesh from persecuting his people. Enkidu challenges the king to a fight, which Gilgamesh wins, but eventually the two become friends and set off together on an adventure. Among many other events, the story tells of a great flood, more than a millennium before the one described in the Bible. After the two slay various monsters, the gods decide to kill Enkidu, leaving the king heartbroken. In the second half, Gilgamesh agrees to undertake a dangerous journey to discover the secret of eternal life, but he eventually discovers that there is no such thing: being human means we all face mortality.

This is a very brief summary, but even from this we can see its echoes in later stories such as King Arthur's search for the Holy Grail and, more recently, the same narrative DNA of mismatched buddy cop comedy-dramas. Gilgamesh shows that the foundations of a good story are timeless and universal. The irony is that these tablets were not meant to last. They were made of clay and were fired only when they were burned in an accidental fire or during an enemy attack. It was these acts of destruction that preserved them for millennia to come.

Have You Heard of Luristan?

And before you start thinking, please, no, *not* another rogue state, this is still a history book.

Luristan is first mentioned around 4,000 years go and would now be a large part of southern Iran. It doesn't become an area of archaeological interest until the first millennium BC when it was the epicentre of production of beautiful bronze artefacts, the oldest in the world, some of which date from the very first mentions of the region. By this time Luristan was part of the Persian Empire and was able to distribute its work across the biggest empire the world had ever known.

The most beautiful pieces are from about 800–600 BC and surpass anything else produced for millennia. Unfortunately, it was shortly after this period that the area came under attack from Alexander the Great, followed almost a millennia later by the Islamic Caliphate, then the Mongols and then Tamerlane. So, it's unsurprising that little of that ancient culture exists in anything other than the archaeological record.

Before the twentieth century, the majority of the inhabitants of the area (called Lurs) were nomadic herders, with an urban minority living in the city of Khorramabad. There were several attempts by early twentieth-century Iranian governments to forcibly settle the nomadic segment of the Lur population, but they were largely unsuccessful until after the Second World War. Today the Lurs number some 5 million and are concentrated in the west and south-west of Iran where they maintain their language and traditions.

Hatshepsut the Pharaoh

The title of this article is deliberately inaccurate. The term 'pharaoh' (which can be translated as 'great house') is a male-only title, a sign of the patriarchal nature of ancient Egypt. However, that didn't stop Hatshepsut from taking both the title and the throne and making them her own. She was the daughter of Thutmose I (the third pharaoh of the Eighteenth Dynasty) and his chief consort Ahmose, making her as high-born as a woman could be; this is reflected in her name, which means 'foremost of noblewomen'. As was often the case in this ancient civilisation, Hatshepsut married a close relative, in this instance her half-brother Thutmose II, the son of her father's secondary consort. They ruled together for a short time until Thutmose II died of natural causes in 1478 BC.

As a woman, Hatshepsut should not have become pharaoh, but due (likely) to a combination of ambition and a feeling that she had the better claim to the throne, she installed herself in the power vacuum left by her husband and became one of Egypt's most successful rulers. In theory, she was regent to her stepson Thutmose III, but in reality, she was the boss (and was most likely the power behind the throne during her husband's short reign, too).

Because her ascent to the throne broke taboos, records show that over the years there was what we would now call a PR campaign to show that she was a worthy exception to the rule. According to revised records, she was no longer the daughter of Ahmose but was now the result of divine intervention! Not only that but Thutmose I had planned ahead and declared Hatshepsut to be his heir, an historical revision that, in essence, erased the brief reign of her husband Thutmose II from the records. The spin doctors were at work even in ancient Egypt.

What all of this demonstrates is that Hatshepsut was a master manipulator. She was sensitive to the traditions of her time and bent them to her will to make an unusual situation appear far more palatable than it otherwise might have been. Perhaps the strangest effort was the alteration of some of her images created before her reign to show her as male. She even went back to older pharaohs and deliberately used feminine words to blur the idea that pharaohs had always been men (there had been a few women who had ruled briefly before, usually amid dynastic turmoil and regencies). As one inscription put it, 'She is served, Egypt bows the head.'

It is not with a little irony that what Hatshepsut did to other rulers she had done to her. Toward the end of the reign of Thutmose III and into the reign of his son Amenhotep II, an attempt was made to remove Hatshepsut from historical and pharaonic records. It wasn't subtle either, with her cartouches and images being crudely hacked off some stone walls. The problem with this lack of subtlety is that it quickly becomes obvious what has been destroyed, and the damage left Hatshepsut-shaped gaps in her material representations.

Whether it was a resentful Thutmose III who sought to erase signs of his powerful stepmother (she stopped him from ruling for twenty years), or his son Amenhotep II who wanted to break away from everything that had gone before him in the Eighteenth Dynasty, we'll never know. What is fortunate is that the desecrations and erasures were far from thorough or complete. Only the most obvious statues or carvings on only the most accessible monuments were ever defaced. It was almost as if nobody had the heart to undo the twenty years of constant building that marked Hatshepsut's reign. The final irony was that Thutmose III repurposed Hatshepsut's buildings rather than building his own. He was one of the first royal family members to be buried in the Valley of the Kings in what can only be described as an underwhelming tomb. His own monuments and inscriptions paled in comparison to those of his stepmother.

And inscriptions and monuments were definitely her thing. The Pyramids may have already been built, but she triggered one of the greatest periods of construction in Egypt's long history. Deir el-Bahari existed before Hatshepsut, but she turned it into the marvel that still exists today. It is a mortuary temple, merging a place of worship with a burial site, its colossal size rivalled only by the Pyramids and the Sphinx. It was a sign not only that Egypt was renewed, but that the woman at the top had immense power that dwarfed anything human. It's telling that Deir el-Bahari follows in the architectural traditions of the nearby (and earlier) complex of the Temple of Mentuhotep, except Deir el-Bahari outdoes it in every possible way. It is larger, with more ornamentation, and inside are grand depictions of all the things Hatshepsut wanted people to believe, such as her divine birth. This linked her to the holy temple and reminded everyone that she was no ordinary woman. It is not surprising that this complex is where she had her own mortuary temple constructed (although when the time came, she was buried elsewhere). Called Djeser-Djeseru, it translates as 'Holy of Holies'.

While Deir el-Bahari was the jewel in her crown, she also used Egypt's expanding power to remind everyone that she was in charge everywhere, from urban hubs to the very peripheries of the empire. To prove the point, she built a temple to Horus (later moved to a museum before the area was flooded to create an artificial lake) at the fortress of Buhen in Nubia. It was unusual for a pharaoh to build anything of significance at such a distant and unfashionable location, but Hatshepsut was out to amaze and impress. Similarly, there's a modest shrine carved into a mountain in the Sinai Desert, a site that would have rarely been visited and almost certainly never by the Egyptian elite, but to the local Bedouins it would have seemed as if the gods themselves had arrived and planted it there.

But it wasn't all about building. Over Egypt's long history, the country had expanded, contracted and been invaded. While the Eighteenth Dynasty was a time of recovery and consolidation, it hadn't yet reconnected some of its trade routes. In an attempt to rectify this, Hatshepsut sent a trade delegation to the Land of Punt. Historians and Egyptologists still debate exactly where the Land of Punt was, but it is mentioned on numerous occasions by a multitude of Egyptian sources. The consensus is that this kingdom was somewhere on the Horn of Africa.

Hatshepsut sent five ships and more than twenty representatives to reinvigorate the trade between the two countries. The expedition was a huge success and, according to records, included a number of firsts. Thirty-one live myrrh trees, the roots of which were carefully kept in baskets, were brought back to Egypt in what is the first recorded relocation of foreign trees. The Egyptians also returned with the first recorded cargo of frankincense. Punt was famous for both, and now Egypt could enjoy these luxuries again. (Frankincense, a resin, was ground down and turned into the dark eyeliner that we associate with Egyptian cosmetics.)

Trade brings wealth and it was undoubtedly profits from these new trade routes that helped pay for Hatshepsut's massive construction plans. Another benefit was that Egypt now had more luxuries on the market, a state of affairs that would keep the prosperous and powerful happy. Despite her supposedly tenuous grasp on power, Hatshepsut was never seriously challenged at any time throughout her reign. Even

Thutmose III didn't dare start unravelling her legacy until late into his reign.

Hatshepsut's record of accomplishments is outstanding by the standards of any ruler. However, the one area that hasn't been mentioned is war. It was under her father Thutmose I that Egypt saw considerable aggressive expansion by military means, but mentions of war under either Thutmose II or Hatshepsut are limited. There were minor campaigns in Nubia and into the Middle East, but nothing that could be described as major.

The reasons for the lull in hostilities are complicated and include the fact that Egypt's neighbours were licking their wounds after Thutmose I's campaigns. They were in no shape to launch a sustained attack against Egypt's huge stockpile of resources. As all the comments about trade and construction indicate, Egypt was wealthy and stable at this time. It would have been a formidable foe, and Hatshepsut seemed to be content to grow her power by means other than military aggression.

Because she put all her efforts into building and maintaining her authority, it is reasonable to assume that Hatshepsut felt she had nothing to prove by going to war. Military campaigns are famous for their unpredictable outcomes, and one major defeat could have spelt potential ruin, so it seems she fought the campaigns that needed fighting and no more.

Because of the attempts to erase her from the history of the day, there are gaps in Hatshepsut's story. Sometimes archaeology reinforces historical theory; other times the gaps in our knowledge of the era can be logically filled in with her reign, but we are talking about times that are on the very edges of history. To put it into context, she was living about 800 years before the foundation of Rome and about 1,000 years before the Persian Wars with Greece. What cannot be in any doubt, however, is that she showed both guile and intelligence and was a hugely powerful ruler in her day.

Getting exact dates this far back in history is notoriously difficult. It seems that Hatshepsut ruled for twenty-one years and lived into her early fifties. She died of natural causes, and if recent research is correct, her mummified remains have been found (although this is debated). The female mummy in question shows signs of diabetes, but it seems that what killed her was bone cancer which had spread throughout her body. Hatshepsut suffered from a skin disease and a carcinogenic salve was found at the burial site. It could be that in an attempt to treat a skin disorder she ended up killing herself with a toxic cream. I am not pausing on her death to be morbid but, instead, to pay tribute to modern forensic archaeology. This work is testimony to the expertise that allows us to assess a 3,500-year-old body and work out two separate illnesses from the remains. The woman also showed signs of worn-down teeth (common for the time as sand regularly got into food), and in 1903 a missing molar was found in a canopic box by Howard Carter (the same archaeologist who discovered Tutankhamun's tomb).

If these remains have been correctly identified, Hatshepsut was the first pharaoh to have been buried in the Valley of the Kings. It seems that she ordered the original tomb designed for her father to be enlarged. He may have been *a* ruler of Egypt, but she was *the* ruler of Egypt, and she needed a tomb of appropriate proportions to reflect her splendour.

Hatshepsut was a ruler who had to usurp the throne to gain power, and she spent a large portion of her reign maintaining that position. Over two decades she was able to grow Egypt's treasury, establish peace on the country's borders and create some of the most beautiful and impressive structures ever built. By any stretch of the imagination, she was a formidable and highly effective ruler.

The History of Circumcision

Many cultures have rites of passage to adulthood. One of the most common is male circumcision (this article is not about the abhorrent practice of FGM), the removal of the foreskin on the penis, carried out on boys who are close to puberty in places as diverse as modern-day Kenya and Turkey. It is traditionally practised by both Jews (who circumcise infant boys) and Muslims but is not exclusive to these faiths.

The practice goes back a long way in history. There is an engraving from Ankhmahor, Saqqara, Egypt, a place nearly 4,400 years old, that predates any of the monotheistic religions by about 1,000 years (at the very minimum), which is estimated to be from 2345–2182 BC and shows an adult circumcision in which the participants are smiling (I'm confident their smiles didn't last long). As an adult, the male would be able to remember the occasion and its significance, and even in the modern world the pain is part of the process. Avoidance of local anaesthetics is a common theme that stretches across races and cultures. 'Taking the pain' and 'being a man' are integral parts of the circumcision rituals in the cultures where it is practised. One member of my family had to have it done *twice* because it was inadequately done the first time and not, as he likes to joke, because he's such a man it (the foreskin) grew back!

Although Jews continue to circumcise infants, the practice today is otherwise usually seen as a rite of passage from childhood to adulthood. It's fascinating that in some African traditions the boy takes his severed foreskin and casts it into a nearby river as a way of saying goodbye to his childhood, both literally and physically. Other traditions required that a man was given a knife and sent off into the wilderness to remove the foreskin himself; he was shunned until he did so. Some would take hours; others took years. In circumcising African cultures, an uncircumcised man is seen as immature and unattractive to the opposite sex.

Even in the West, particularly in America, circumcision has been regarded as the 'clean' option despite there being no evidence for this. The writer is, for the record, neither condoning nor condemning the practice, merely reporting the facts.

That's it; the history of circumcision is over. You can uncross your legs now.

The Greek Gods ... There Were Loads of Them

While some Greek gods are still famous (Zeus, Mercury, Nike anyone?), many lesser-known ones have fallen into obscurity. However, these lesser gods still offer a good story and an insight into the culture of the ancient Greeks. One such example is Hecate. She is associated with witchcraft, potions, showing the way at crossroads (she is often shown carrying two torches) and dark magic such as necromancy (communicating with the dead).

Like all Greek gods, Hecate has an origin story. Hers is that she was the only child and daughter of Perses and Asteria, a star goddess, and was blessed by Zeus with many gifts. Although knowledge of her has not entirely disappeared (she gets a mention in *Macbeth*, where she is, of course, linked to the witches), she is on the very fringes of the overall mythology.

Hecate was popular in her day and was often associated with the home, where she was seen as a protector. Indeed, her need for vision in every direction meant that she was often depicted as having three heads, a kind of holy trinity half a millennium before the Christian concept emerged. In her prime, the cult of Hecate could be found, with many local variations, all over Greece and western Anatolia. There are examples of her own dedicated temples as well as spaces in temples for other gods where her followers were given room to pray to her, indicating that she was one of the more important deities. Perhaps critically, she was linked to the concept of the 'world soul', the connection believed to exist among all living things. This would make her one of the most important gods in ancient Greece – and yet she is barely remembered today.

Hecate's association with the natural world and witchcraft has led to her resurrection among Wiccans and neo-pagans. In this context, she is associated with the mother goddess or crone, and she sits well within the framework of this more modern mythology. Thinking of her original worshippers as witches would be wrong; this is a classic example of a new religion repurposing the deities and stories of an older one.

The Bible Backs Bald Men

The Bible is easily one of the most debated, dissected and discussed texts in history – and in the world. Some of it is unambiguous – 'Thou shalt not kill' – whereas other parts are steeped in the politics of the age or very heavy on symbolism (for example, the Book of Revelations). It is a large, dense and diverse collection and, occasionally, some bits are... well ... hard to explain. Take 2 Kings 2:23-25 (New International Version):

> From there Elisha went up to Bethel. As he was walking along the road, some boys came out of the town and jeered at him. 'Get out of here, baldy!' they said. 'Get out of here, baldy!' He turned around, looked at them and called down a curse on them in the name of the Lord. Then two she-bears came out of the woods and mauled forty-two of the boys.

I am not taking this out of context nor am I paraphrasing. There are a few variations in the translations, but the core story is the same. Elisha is mocked for being bald, so he prays to the Lord who promptly delivers bear-shaped revenge and blood is spilt. These two verses have created a very niche cottage industry of debate. First off, it's good to know that God is on the side of those who have male-pattern baldness (I have a vested interest in this). Saying that, attacking a bunch of children with bears for calling someone bald does seem something of an overreaction even by the standards of the Old Testament. The result is some breathtaking literary gymnastics to turn this story from what it is into something more acceptable.

My favourite spin on this is that Elisha had cut his hair in this way as his homage to God. So really, the passage is saying that God is displeased with those who do not show him respect. That *could* be the meaning, but it is a long way from a bunch of kids mocking a slap-head and then getting mauled by she-bears (why the bears are specifically female also leads to much debate). This is a microcosm of what all historians face. An ancient text is just the start of the story, not the end, and all kinds of meanings can be attached to mere words.

Now, over to you. What do you think the above verses mean?

The Ponytail Has a Long History

The term 'ponytail', used to describe the popular hairstyle, only came into common use in the 1950s, but the style itself goes back a long way. This is hardly surprising since it's a convenient way for both men and women to get long hair under control; pulling back the hair and securing it seems to be a natural thing to do. But let's consider the impact of the ponytail on culture and history.

The earliest images of ponytails come from about 1600 BC in ancient Greece, where it was a hairstyle of high-born women. Fast-forwarding a few millennia, we come to the 'queue' (French for tail) or 'cue' hairstyle worn by men in seventeenth-century China. When Manchuria conquered the rest of China and created the Qing dynasty (1644–1912), the new rulers required the style, consisting of a single, braided plait, to be worn by all male subjects (they shaved the front of their scalps and grew their hair from the crown of the head) as a sign of submission. Cultivating the cue was a matter of honour as well as necessity, and failure to comply was punishable by death. In this instance, the style was associated with men rather than women and lasted right up to the end of China's imperial era in 1912.

In the eighteenth century, both French and British soldiers had long hair which they pulled back, but the British Army banned it in 1800 in favour of shorter hair as long hair was felt to be unkempt and difficult to maintain. In later eighteenth-century Europe, men often had long hair which they wore in a ponytail tied with a ribbon. By contrast, the hairstyle was deemed too childish for women, so ponytails were typically seen on young girls but never on women at that time.

The ponytail, both as a name and as a fashionable hairstyle came into its own in the twentieth century, when women reclaimed the ponytail for themselves. At first regarded as an informal style, it was highlighted as 'modern' when the first-ever Barbie doll appeared with it in the 1950s. It was made famous by Hollywood films and its stars, especially the girl-next-door Sandra Dee, who helped to make it the height of fashion.

It took the sexy French actress Brigitte Bardot and her tousled version of the ponytail to kick it into the 1960s and make it a style for cool girls. It was reinvented again by Madonna, who made it a symbol of female empowerment on her famous 1990 Blonde Ambition tour. By this time, men who wanted to appear rebellious or artistic or edgy were adopting the style, which has grown in popularity since the latter part of the twentieth century.

Hairstyles today seem to rely more on the dictates of fashion than on gender stereotypes, and the ponytail has achieved equality by being readily adopted by both men and women. Has it peaked as a hairstyle? Based on the evidence of centuries, it is likely to be continually reinvented.

The Cyclops Was Real

The skull of a mammoth or an elephant looks nothing like the animal. The large hole where we might presume there would be an eye is where the musculature of the trunk is anchored, but unless you know this, it's easy to believe that the skull belongs to a giant of a monster with one eye, right? This is where the concept of the Cyclops is believed to have originated.

Many stories grew up around the Cyclops, who were believed to be blacksmiths, builders or, in the case of Homer's *Odyssey*, your typical man-eating bad guy. These giants were useful to explain the otherwise inexplicable in the ancient Greek world. For instance, when they found the enormous dressed blocks used in Mycenaean masonry, the early Greeks concluded that only the Cyclops had the combination of skill and strength to build in such a monumental manner.

But the ancient Greeks were wrong. It was humans all along, and it is this false belief that shows not everything was at its peak during the Hellenic era (roughly 700 BC). In the time of the Parthenon, it was considered impossible that ordinary humans could have built the mighty Mycenaean structures a thousand years earlier – only giants could have done it.

Kali Is a Fascinating Eastern Deity

Kali first appears in Hindu holy scriptures (the Mundaka Upanishad, written around 1200 BC) not explicitly as a goddess, but as the black tongue of the seven flickering tongues of Agni, the Hindu god of fire. This is the reason why she is often shown sticking her tongue out; she is showing one of her many forms. Her mention in the Upanishad means she has been around as long as Zeus or Thor, but unlike them, she still has millions of followers. She has undergone a huge amount of revision over the millennia and is associated with two major religions, Buddhism and Hinduism.

Kali's name means both the 'dark one' and the 'fullness of time', and she became a fully fledged goddess around 600 BC. So, while she is a goddess of war, violence and blood, she is simultaneously seen as a creator and protector in the cyclical nature of creation. What exists is destroyed and a new reality is brought into being which, in turn, is brought down by war and destruction – and so on and so forth until the end of time. At one point in the stories around the Hindu gods, she appears from another goddess's forehead to protect her from two demons (which she, of course, slays), and in another battle, she defeats an entire clone army by drinking their blood, including that of the god who led this army. Hindu stories are so uniquely colourful that everyone should read at least a few of them.

Kali is portrayed mostly in two forms: the popular four-armed version and the more powerful ten-armed Mahakali version. Just talking about evolved forms shows how this transformation or elevation of the gods' abilities has seeped into Eastern culture, influencing even something as silly as the anime series *Dragon Ball Z*, where heroes and villains are forever evolving into bigger and more powerful forms, with different hairstyles, numbers of arms and skin colours. Kali is described as black in both of her forms but is most often depicted as blue in popular Indian art. Her eyes are described as red with intoxication and rage; her hair is dishevelled and sometimes she is represented with small fangs.

During the time of British colonial rule in India, there were numerous reports of Thugees (the origin of the English word for 'thug'), bands of roving groups of Kali worshippers who robbed and murdered. That these bands acted in the name of Kali has been widely disputed in more recent times. While there can be no doubt that there were roving bands of bandits in India in the nineteenth century, there is no evidence they were committing their acts of robbery and violence for a specific deity. Is it possible that some of these men gave some of their ill-gotten gains to a Kali temple? Almost certainly. Kali was a popular god and it would be odd if no offerings were made to her, but that's not the same thing as saying the cult of Kali was behind such acts of violence.

Temples erected in Kali's honour are common on the subcontinent, but her followers are not murderers and they do not worship a blood god with sacrifices. It seems counterintuitive that a god associated with such extremes as fury, anger and violence is quietly prayed to in the temples of both Hindus and Buddhists.

Hydna the Great Swimmer

When you mention women and the Battle of Salamis (480 BC), most minds turn to Artemisia, a Greek queen who fought on the Persian side of the battle (and was immortalised by Eva Green in *300: Rise of an Empire*). However, there was another Greek woman who played a significant role in determining the ultimate outcome of the conflict.

Prior to this critical naval battle with the Persians, Hydna and her father Scyllis volunteered to assist Greek forces by sabotaging the nearby Persian fleet. Hydna was well known locally as a strong and able swimmer, having been trained by her father, a professional swimming instructor, from a young age. The Greeks needed as much time as possible to prepare their fleet and get into position, so Hydna and her father were to delay the Persian fleet.

After defeating the Greeks at Thermopylae, the Persian king Xerxes I had moored his ships off the coast of Mount Pelion to wait out a storm ahead of the coming Battle of Salamis. Tucked away in the bays and inlets of the coast, the huge fleet was safe from attack from the sea, but these positions left them vulnerable to attacks from the shore. Any advantage in the Battle of Salamis hinged on positioning. The Greeks were severely outnumbered, so they had to find a way of neutralising Persian fleet numbers. They chose the Saronic Gulf, located between the peninsulas of Attica and Argolis, a prime position for inflicting maximum damage because the gulf is essentially a bottleneck where the ships of the Persian fleet would either crash into each other or come at the Greek force in waves rather than all at once.

Hydna was known for her ability to swim long distances and dive deep below the surface. On the night of the attack, father and daughter swam 10 miles through choppy waters to reach the fleet. Then they swam silently among the ships, cutting their moorings and dragging away the submerged anchors. Without these, the ships crashed together in the stormy waters. As a result, most of the ships sustained considerable damage and a few sank. This effective delaying tactic allowed the Greek navy the time it needed to prepare and, ultimately, to secure an emphatic (and unexpected) Greek victory.

The Vergina Sun

Symbols are hugely important to humans, but they can be hijacked and used in ways the originators never envisioned. Perhaps the most famous example is the swastika, which has been used as ornamentation by many civilisations over the millennia. In Hindi traditions, it is used as a sign of strength and good fortune. However, the symbol's use by the Nazis for more than a decade has indelibly tainted its use in the West (for the full story do read *Forgotten History* by the same author).

A less well-known example of so-called symbol hijacking is the Vergina Sun, and its history is just as interesting. This rayed solar symbol was discovered in the 1970s in the tombs of Alexander the Great's family in northern Greece. Before this, the symbol had been seen as a standard example of Macedonian ornamentation. Interesting, yes, but obscure to be sure. However, now the symbol was associated with one of the most impressive military leaders in history and everyone wanted a piece of it.

The symbol went through a renaissance, appearing on Greek coins in the 1980s. The Greek region of Macedonia (where Alexander was born and grew up) adopted it as their prefecture flag and became a shoulder patch for Athenian police for a time. However, in the 1990s, when Yugoslavia broke up, Slavic Macedonia (which is not the same as the ancient Greek Macedonia) selected the symbol to be used as its national flag. Greece was incensed that another country had 'stolen' its symbol.

It was one of many grievances that erupted between the two nations and continues to create bad blood to this day. Greece tried to get the symbol trademarked as a Greek creation and succeeded in getting the Macedonian national flag banned from some events, including the Olympic Games. Eventually, the Slavic Macedonians changed their national flag to something a little less ... well ... Vergina Sunny. So Greece won that round. It is quite extraordinary that one nation can apply so much pressure on another that it is forced to change its national flag. Saying that, it is still a bone of contention, and I'm not getting involved or picking a side!

Musical Celts and the Terrifying *Carnyx*

The word *carnyx* comes from the Gaulish *carn*, meaning horn or antler. The *carnyx* was a metal trumpet which, rather than projecting away from the player's mouth, projects straight up and ends in a fanciful animal head. A hoard of six such horns was found in Tintignac in France, and every one of them has a stylised animal head – most of them a boar – in which the sound comes out of the animal's mouth at the top of the instrument. The *carnyx* was a war horn that looked ferocious and could be heard over the noise of battle. Whether they were a way of rallying the Celtic troops, scaring the enemy or possibly giving basic orders (like a trumpet in the nineteenth century) is a matter of conjecture, but the multiple references to them by their enemies indicate that they were an important part of Celtic warfare.

Contrary to popular belief, the Celts were not solely indigenous to Ireland and the British Isles. In fact, the term covers loosely similar tribes that in the Iron Age stretched from Ireland to parts of Anatolia (modern-day Turkey). Celts tended to be based north of the Alps, so the Mediterranean areas had their own civilisations distinct from the Celts. That said, it shouldn't come as a surprise that examples of Celtic culture have been found in places as varied as Scotland, Romania and Switzerland.

Diodorus Siculus, from the first century BC, made this observation in his histories: 'Their trumpets again are of a peculiar barbarian kind; they blow into them and produce a harsh sound which suits the tumult of war.'

Of course, Diodorus was a Roman, so he might have been biased.

Cynane of Macedon

Cynane of Macedon is not a well-known name, and yet she lived in a very famous time and had a very famous half-brother. She was the daughter of Philip II of Macedon (now northern Greece and not the Balkan country), the one-eyed king of supreme Greek military power in the fourth century BC.

Macedonia was not loved by the rest of the Greek city-states and was often mocked for being borderline barbaric. It did not have the illustrious history of places like Athens or Sparta, but that didn't change the reality of power politics at the time. Macedonia under Philip developed a heavy infantry that was incredibly effective despite its small numbers. In essence, it was a phalanx on steroids, with smaller shields but longer spears, so that even more ranks could bristle with sharp points as they faced the enemy.

It was this effective fighting force that Philip's son and Cynane's half-brother, Alexander III, would inherit. It was with this pre-built conquering machine that he would undertake the eight-year campaign that shattered the Persian Empire and earned him the title of Alexander the Great. It was Cynane's mother Audata, an Illyrian princess, and Olympia, Alexander's mother, who convinced Alexander that Philip wasn't his father, but that he was, in fact, the son of a god. So, it's safe to say there would have been robust sibling rivalry.

Cynane was trained in the martial ways of Macedonia and grew up to be a fine warrior in her own right. She not only fought on the front lines, but even killed the Illyrian queen Caeria in battle (remember that she was half-Illyrian herself), thus proving that her martial skills were not just for show. She had a daughter (out of wedlock with an unknown man) whom she named Eurydice and raised to be a warrior. Later, she schemed to have her daughter marry her half-brother, Philip Arrhidaeus, the new king of Macedonia, after Alexander's death in Babylon.

When asked on his deathbed in 323 BC who should inherit his empire, Alexander famously replied, 'Kratos' (the strongest). This led to an immediate fragmentation of his territories and a vicious war as his generals attacked each other in the power struggle that emerged. It was a staggeringly arrogant and downright stupid way to ensure an orderly succession.

Cynane became a victim of this civil war and was assassinated by a rival in the year of Alexander's death. Philip Arrhidaeus did marry Eurydice, but both were murdered on the orders of Olympia before they could produce an heir to claim the various titles vacated by Philip and Alexander. Thanks to the machinations of this seriously dysfunctional family, all that Alexander had so famously achieved was lost.

Mausoleum of the First Qin Emperor

What exactly is a mausoleum? It's a structure built as a monument, containing a burial chamber. In other words, it's a fancy tomb. And the fanciest mausoleum in the world has to be one in China. Qin Shi Huang was the first emperor of China and a man who was both feared and respected. He didn't quite unify all of China, but Chinese history often starts with him because he was the first to identify himself using the term 'emperor', which stuck for the next 2,000 years as the official title of China's ruler.

Qin was a warlord who unified territories under the threat of potential or actual violence, but he was also a builder. He constructed an extensive road network and restructured the administration to unify the disparate lands he conquered. All of this led to the foundation and standardisation of all the dynasties of China that were to come after him.

While he is famous in China for both his life and his death, it is his death in 208 BC that has more recently caught the world's attention. When he died, he was buried in a colossal funerary mound containing his tomb. This mausoleum is so full of riches (and traps to keep out robbers) that all of the contemporary chronicles gushed about the fabulous contents buried with him. Indeed, the descriptions were so extreme and, frankly, so outrageous that they were dismissed as hyperbole, and the exact location of the tomb was forgotten over the millennia.

None of the chronicles bothered to mention the terracotta army built to protect the emperor's resting place, and that's why its discovery in the 1970s stunned everyone. Quite simply, nobody knew it was there. It turned out that a hill behind a farmer's field was not part of the natural landscape but the only visible sign of the extensive burial site of the first emperor.

So, the question then becomes, if no one at the time thought the terracotta army was impressive enough to report, what lies in the still undisturbed tomb? There is one story of a jewel-encrusted map of the world, with all the seas and rivers in liquid mercury (recent soil samples from the top of the tomb show high levels of mercury). Nobody has disturbed the tomb and there are no plans to do so. This is because the Chinese have a deeply held respect for ancestors, and as Qin Shi Huang is seen as the father of the nation, it would be incredibly disrespectful to disturb his rest.

If I could choose to witness anything in history, I would travel back in time to survey Emperor Qin's tomb before it was sealed; that's my number one historical wish. This has to be the closest thing to an Indiana Jones moment that I can imagine.

The Trial of a Courtesan

Phryne of Thespiae was a famous (infamous?) courtesan in Athens in the early 300s BC. Her real name was Mnesarete, meaning 'commemorating virtue', which was obviously the wrong name for a 'working girl'. Phryne was the Greek for toad, common slang for courtesans, but as this particular Phryne had an unusual brownish/yellowish complexion, it could be that she was nicknamed for that. However, as Phryne was a highly sought-after courtesan, it's obvious that neither her name nor her unusual skin were putting anyone off. She was also known as Hetaira, which indicates a high-class courtesan, someone suitable to escort on a night out. Such a woman would be witty, charming and socially adept, skilled in the fine arts as well as those of a baser nature.

Stories of Phryne's great beauty travelled far and wide; she was the scandalous celebrity of her day. Legend has it that the sculptor Praxiteles, who was also her lover, used her as the model for the statue of the Aphrodite of Knidos, the first nude statue of a woman from ancient Greece, a statue that is still in existence today.

Despite all of this, it is for a court case that she is primarily remembered. Ancient Greek legal cases were the foundation of Roman law, which in turn is the basis for most of the laws in the democratic West. There was a presiding judge, a jury and lawyers for both the defence and the prosecution. In this case, Phryne of Thespiae was prosecuted for impiety and was defended by the orator Hypereides (who – guess what – was another one of her lovers). The speech for the prosecution was written by Anaximenes of Lampsacus. When it seemed as if the verdict would be unfavourable, Hypereides removed Phryne's robe and bared her breasts before the judges to arouse their pity (and/or possibly something else). According to the legend, her beauty filled the judges with superstitious fear, and they could not bring themselves to condemn 'a prophetess and priestess of Aphrodite' to death. In other words, they decided to acquit her out of pity.

This has to be one of the most insane courtroom stories ever. I suggest that if you are ever on trial, don't deploy nudity as a defence as you are likely to be held in contempt of court. However, the writer Athenaeus provides a different account of the trial as reported in the *Ephesia of Posidippus of Cassandreia*. He simply describes Phryne as clasping the hand of each juror, crying and pleading for her life, with no mention of disrobing. This makes a lot more sense, and juries can sometimes be swayed with a convincing sob story. But, perhaps unsurprisingly, it's the first version that has captured the imagination and gone on to inspire paintings and statues.

Ancient Chinese Technology

Images of medieval mariners navigating the seas might show them using an exotic-looking instrument called an astrolabe. Using the stars in the night sky, the astrolabe enabled them to calculate their location to a relatively high degree of accuracy. The assumption that follows from this is that the compass had yet to be invented. This is not true. The compass was invented around 200 BC in Han China and was made of lodestone, a naturally magnetised ore of iron. Unfortunately, the compass was not then used for navigation, but fortune-telling. It would take more than a thousand years for the Chinese to work out the other, more practical and reliable use of the compass.

An early astrolabe was invented in ancient Greece by Apollonius of Perga, between 220 and 150 BC, so in a similar era to the invention of the compass. However, again, rather than being used for navigation, it was used for another purpose, this time as an aid in astronomical observations. Astrolabes continued in use in the Greek-speaking world and later in the Roman Empire. They were further developed in the medieval Islamic world, where they were finally discovered to be of use as an aid to navigation and as a way of determining the direction of Mecca to pray.

Meanwhile, in China, the compass came into use as an instrument of navigation during the Song Dynasty of the eleventh century AD. These later compasses were made of iron needles, magnetised by striking them with a lodestone. Once the Chinese had sorted that, it didn't take too long for the technology to spread, helped along by the expansion of the Mongol Empire. Dry compasses (i.e. without the needle floating in a fluid, as is the case in most modern compasses) began to appear around 1300 in medieval Europe and the Islamic world.

So, while the astrolabe was used after 1300 in the West, it had been superseded by Iron Age Chinese technology. It's just that it would take our ancestors a little bit of time to realise that.

When the Romans Fought a Greek Phalanx

You know those 'ultimate' conversations? The ones where you talk about whether Rocky Marciano in his prime could beat Mike Tyson in his? These conversations are about comparing greatness, and occasionally history offers an actual answer.

So, when both sides had enough men to make it count, which was better: a Roman legion or a Greek phalanx? The answer comes in the Battle of Cynoscephalae in 197 BC. The battle was fought over Rome's increasingly confident place in Mediterranean politics. Rome had just come out of the Second Punic War, an era in which many Greek city-states had become vassals to but not ruled outright by Rome. During this war, neighbouring forces had attacked the Greek cities, and Rome didn't have the resources to protect them. However, after the war was won, it was payback time. It was a chance to warn the Greek states to remain loyal and an opportunity to prove to all that the Roman legions were the force of the age.

The two opposing leaders were Titus Flamininus, a highly capable Roman general, and King Philip V of Macedon. Both sides had around 25,000 men, but the Romans brought a few dozen war elephants, too. The notorious problem with an assault on a Macedonian phalanx was getting past the layers and layers of spears. A phalanx was virtually indestructible when engaged head-on, so an enemy general had to flank them … unless the Greeks had cavalry to protect the vulnerable flanks, which they did, again in their thousands.

This battle saw an unusual amount of manoeuvring on the battlefield; it was the closest a real-world battle has come to a game of chess (only with some war elephants for good measure). This was unsurprising. Philip knew that to get the best out of his army he had to fight the Romans head-on, and conversely, Titus Flamininus knew that allowing this to happen would lead to certain defeat.

The battle did not start well for the Romans as Titus Flaminius tried to break up the Greek formations with his cavalry, but Philip countered at every turn. Eventually, the Romans began to be pushed down the hilly terrain, and although Philip knew the rough ground would break up his tightly packed phalanxes, he sent a third of his army into the centre where the Roman forces began to buckle.

The key came from the flanks where the Romans managed to hold on, and Titus sent in his war elephants, which proved to be the tipping point on one of the flanks. Philip could see his front line losing cohesion. The vulnerability of the phalanx once the formation is lost is that it becomes just a bunch of individuals armed with overly long spears. Philip knew it was game over, time to surrender. So the phalanx raised their long spears as a sign of capitulation. Either the Romans didn't know what this meant or didn't care, because they kept attacking. The result of this particular action led to the heaviest Greek losses of the day. However, Philip was able to retreat with a large part of his force intact.

The battle was a turning point. After this, Rome conquered all of Greece/Macedon, and Philip became a vassal ruler, having to pay an indemnity and send his youngest son to the Romans as a hostage. Philip continued to play ball until his death, long enough for another son to become the new king; however, his heir would be the last king of Macedonia as the area was absorbed into the Roman Republic just a few years later.

The Battle of Cynoscephalae proved that the Greek phalanx, while unstoppable head-on, wasn't as flexible as a Roman legion. This is why it failed.

Snakes on a Ship

The year was 190 BC and Hannibal, after failing to take out Rome, took refuge with Prusias I of Bithynia on the northwest coast of Anatolia, where he was put in command of a fleet on behalf of Prusias, who was then at war with King Eumenes II of Pergamon (a neighbouring kingdom that was then most of western Anatolia). The fact that these were all independent kingdoms in areas we now consider to be the centre of the Roman Empire reminds us that Hannibal was fighting the Roman Republic before it had a chance to spread its dominance eastwards.

Hannibal, as always, was a shrewd tactician, and even though he was more often a general than an admiral, he could see that he was heavily outnumbered by both ships and men. So Hannibal had an idea and ordered his men to gather all the venomous snakes they could find and put them into pots. His next challenge was to locate the king's flagship, which was somewhere in the midst of the enemy fleet.

Hannibal sent a message to request a meeting with Eumenes II, but the message wasn't the expected offer to negotiate peace; rather, it contained a slew of insults, designed to enrage the king. Eumenes II disregarded the request for a meeting and, in his anger, set sail directly towards Hannibal's fleet, presumably intent on retaliation. The insults meant that battle was inevitable, but they also enabled Hannibal to identify which vessel was the flagship.

Hannibal's orders were for most of his smaller fleet to go on the defensive and hold themselves against enemy ships. Meanwhile, the remaining ships closed in on the king's flagship and began to launch their pots of snakes. At first the Pergamons found this amusing, thinking that a desperate Hannibal must be hurling pots at them in some kind of mad last-ditch effort. But it wasn't long before numerous angry snakes began to explode out of the pots and start attacking the men on board.

Laughter was soon replaced with shouts and screams, and in the ensuing chaos, Hannibal's men boarded the flagship. The soldiers of Pergamon stood no chance as they faced an onslaught from both the infantry and the venomous snakes. With the king captured and the flagship taken, the attack by the Pergamon fleet faltered and then crumbled. Hannibal had defeated Eumenes II and won the naval battle through sheer cunning.

As a postscript, it is worth noting that the use of poison as a weapon was reviled in the ancient world. It was seen as a loathsome way to win and was banned on numerous occasions. Everyone has heard of Hercules, but most people don't realise he was said to have been killed with poisoned clothes, which led to an agonising death. Almost every time poisoned weapons are mentioned in ancient texts, it is with a feeling of revulsion. So, in the eyes of his contemporaries, it was a win for Hannibal but not the noble win of his previous victories.

The Horologion of Andronikos Kyrrhestes Has a More Romantic Name

The Tower of the Winds in Athens is believed to have been built in the second century BC (although it could have been later). It is notable for its unique design as an eight-sided, free-standing tower and is one of the first purpose-built laboratories designed to observe certain natural events. The more romantic name is apt as the only major sculptures to adorn this octagonal tower are those of the Greek gods of the winds who appear in a frieze depicting the eight major points of the compass. In case you're a little rusty on your Greek wind gods, they are Boreas (N), Kaikias (NE), Eurus (E), Apeliotes (SE), Notus (S), Lips (SW), Zephyrus (W), and Skiron (NW).

The fact that the tower has eight sides allows it to have eight different sundials, so that it was possible to tell the time during any part of the day – as long as the sun was out. Inside, it had a clepsydra (water clock), and it is thought that it originally had a weathervane at the top. So, this was the first dedicated weather research facility using all the state-of-the-art equipment and measuring tools of its day. It was also the precursor to the church clock tower, which would often have a weathervane and sometimes a sundial as well as a clock.

When the Tower of the Winds fell into disuse, other cultures repurposed it. The early Orthodox Church changed it into a bell tower. This was unsurprising as many Christian sites overlaid pagan places of importance either as a case of 'if you can't beat 'em, join 'em' or as an attempt to eradicate a pagan past. Later, under the Ottomans, the tower became a centre for the famous whirling dervishes, an Islamic Sufi meditative order of Muslim holy men. It is likely that by this time the original purpose of the tower had been long forgotten.

Today, the tower has been renewed and still stands as a shining example of learning and science from the ancient world, a symbol of the waxing and waning of the different civilisations that have occupied the area over the last 2,000 years.

Gaius Cassius Longinus, the Forgotten Traitor

When Julius Caesar was killed at the Roman Senate in 44 BC, everyone associated this act with Brutus. While it is true that Brutus' betrayal was shocking, he wasn't the man leading the assassination. The exact details will remain forever opaque, but it seems that Cassius (which is how his name is traditionally shortened), if not the head of the plot, was certainly more of a key player than Brutus.

The man who will be forever known simply as Brutus lived his life under several names, all of which showed his familial and political allegiances at the time. He started life as Marcus Iunius Brutus Minor. His father was killed by one of Pompey's men when the young Brutus was just twelve, and he was adopted by his uncle, Quintus Servilius Caepio, who was an important politician. To show his loyalty to and respect for his adopted father, he became Quintus Servilius Caepio Brutus.

When civil war broke out, Brutus acted rather strangely. He allied himself with Pompey, the man who had ordered the murder of his father, and the nemesis of his greatest benefactor, Julius Caesar. He justified this allegiance by saying that whatever his previous wrongdoings, Pompey was protecting the republic, so he (Brutus) had no option but to follow the orders of Pompey against the dictator Julius Caesar.

When Brutus followed Pompey into the Battle of Pharsalus, 'Caesar also was concerned for his safety and ordered his officers not to kill Brutus in the battle, but to spare him and take him prisoner if he gave himself up voluntarily', according to Plutarch. After Caesar's decisive victory, Brutus wrote Caesar a letter of apology. Caesar not only forgave him but took him into his inner circle. He made him Governor of Cisalpine Gaul and, in 45 BC, nominated him to serve as an urban praetor. Brutus was the last man who should have turned on Caesar, a man who had shown him nothing but kindness and generosity, but no. After the murder of Caesar, Brutus changed his name once more, this time to Gaius Servilius Ahala, referencing a man who had killed an earlier tyrant of Rome and a man said to be related to Brutus.

Back to the lesser-known Cassius, who was a senator and the brother-in-law of Brutus and who, as such, had been involved in the civil war between Caesar and Pompey. Nominally, this had been a war between dictatorship and democracy, but nobody was fooled. Had he won, it was likely that Pompey would also have taken on dictatorial powers (Cicero was one of those most outspoken about this).

Once Caesar had won the war and installed himself as dictator for life, Cassius became friendly with Cicero, and it was Cassius who turned the cabal of senators against Caesar, convincing them that rather than trying to depose him, they should assassinate him. Brutus was their figurehead, and, with the ear of Caesar, the man who could fit all the pieces together. But, make no mistake, Cassius was the strategist behind it all.

Caesar was murdered on 15 March 44 BC, and for a moment it looked as if the plan had worked. However, Caesar was more beloved than the conspirators had thought, and Mark Antony moved rapidly to bring Rome to heel. It was Cassius and Brutus who were now the bad guys, and the pair fled to Syria where they raised an army (of which more later).

The interesting thing about the assassination of Julius Caesar is that while no one debates that Caesar was murdered, there are problems with contradictory historical records. No one knows exactly how the event unfolded, and who did what is a swirl of contrary views. Some historians have even pieced together enough circumstantial evidence to suggest that Caesar was not only aware that he was ailing and unable to continue to wow the people, but that he may have known about the plot and might even have gone along with it. It's an unprovable theory with the records that exist.

There are at least four accounts of Caesar's death, written by Cassius Dio, Plutarch, Suetonius and Virgil. Some, like Virgil, were contemporaries of Caesar; Cassius Dio, on the other hand, was writing centuries later although he may have had access to records that are no longer extant. Despite contradictions in the various accounts, what is clear is that after Caesar won the civil war, he had himself declared dictator for life. The Senate, however, was not disbanded and continued to make rulings even though it had to do things Caesar's way. The records agree that a group of disgruntled senators gathered together to plot Caesar's assassination when he arrived in the Senate on the Ides of March (15 March).

One of Caesar's loyal generals, Mark Antony, was approached by one of the conspirators, Servilius Casca, because he was terrified of retribution should the plot fail. Mark Antony went to warn Caesar on the morning of the 15th, but the senators had anticipated both that Servilius would crack under the pressure and that Mark Antony would want to warn Caesar, so Antony was deliberately delayed as he made his way to the Senate.

Caesar arrived at the Forum armed with nothing more than a toga, and the senators crowded round him on the pretence of wanting to present a petition. Exactly who took the first dagger lunge at him is contested, but what followed was a scrum of senators descending on the unarmed Caesar, cutting and thrusting in such frenzy that they ended up wounding each other in the heated attack.

And what were Caesar's last words? Well, not 'Et tu Brutae?' which is from Shakespeare (who never let facts get in the way of a good story). Again, the accounts are conflicting. Some say it was, 'You, too, my child?' a question aimed at Brutus; others report that he said nothing at all, which, after multiple stab wounds, is probably more likely. Caesar was then given the earliest recoded autopsy (not sure why; the cause of death was pretty obvious), which showed that he died of blood loss.

With Caesar dead, the assassins ran through the streets of Rome, shouting, 'People of Rome, we are once again free!' The Romans responded by locking themselves in their houses. They knew a fresh storm was coming. It was in 42 BC, at the Battle of Philippi (in modern-day Greece), that Mark Antony and Octavian (later Caesar Augustus) met Brutus and Cassius. The battle was relatively inconclusive, but Cassius believed a false report that Brutus had been defeated and committed suicide. After a second battle, Brutus realised that he was fighting a lost cause and he, too, committed suicide.

The assassination of Julius Caesar is about as famous as any historical event, but Cassius, the mastermind of it all, is surprisingly absent from the popular narrative.

Yoga's Hidden History

Yoga is old, really old. It is linked to various Hindu texts from the first millennium BC, and it seems to have been a standard practice of spiritual meditation by the middle of that era, but records are sketchy and dates are debatable. Hinduism predates Judaism and is about a millennium older than Christianity, so it's been around for a long time.

When someone says 'yoga', we start to think of all those poses, but – surprise – these are not ancient; the steam locomotive predates them. Yoga, as we know it today in the West, is a twentieth-century invention. What exactly yoga involves depends on which practice is under consideration. Bhakti yoga or Buddhist yoga? Or Laya yoga? There are about a dozen different kinds of practices with a myriad of local variations. However, what most of them have in common is meditation, training the mind to fix only on the present moment to achieve a mentally clear and emotionally calm and stable state. While meditation sometimes has a religious connotation, it is a useful practice for non-religious reasons as well. Prayer and meditation are sometimes interchangeable even if the word 'meditation' would be frowned on in the context of some religions.

Hatha yoga is the closest we come today to practising an ancient version of all the familiar yoga positions. The core founder of the tenets of yoga is Patanjali, a Hindu sage from the second century BC. He (it's debatable if he existed, a bit like Homer in ancient Greece) is believed to be the author of a number of ancient spiritual texts written in Sanskrit, including the *Yoga Sutras*, regarded as the foundation texts of yoga. Then there's the *Haṭhayogapradīpikā*, one of the most influential texts of Hatha yoga. It was compiled by Svātmārāma in the fifteenth century AD from earlier Hatha yoga texts, which, in the context of the tradition as a whole, means it is about 2,000 years old. Hatha does not encompass the more extreme modern positions; it's largely broken up into sitting, breathing and (unsurprisingly) standing positions.

Hatha yoga made a comeback through its Western followers in the late nineteenth and early twentieth centuries by taking the concept of different positions for meditation and expanding on it. The idea behind a position such as the 'downward dog' is that the move enhances thought in an example of body and mind working together for the well-being of the practitioner. People presume this is what Eastern monks were doing 2,000 years ago, but that's unlikely. It's far more likely that they were sitting under a tree (possibly in the lotus position), eyes closed and minds free, no mats and no movement, no downward dog.

The modern concept of yoga is that the mind and body are fused with the spirit, that they are essentially one, so the body should be getting a physical workout at the same time as the mind. This is not to denigrate contemporary Western forms of yoga. Many studies have shown that yoga, and meditation in particular, can reduce anxiety, improve mental health and lower blood pressure. It's just a little more modern than you might have thought.

Deadly Food

When it comes to deadly foods, most people have heard of *fugu*, the Japanese pufferfish delicacy which, if prepared incorrectly, delivers a lethal dose of a neurotoxin. *Fugu* bones have been found from the Jōmon period, dating back to about 300 BC. The Tokugawa Shogunate (1603–1868) banned it in the capital Edo (later Tokyo), but, interestingly, as their power waned, the dish crept back on the menus. During the Meiji era (1867–1912), *fugu* was again banned in many areas, but the Japanese seemed to love a gamble with fugu. One of the most famous recent deaths occurred in 1975 when a famous Kabuki actor ate five helpings ... and died. Even into the twenty-first century, there are cases of people being hospitalised as a result of *fugu* poisoning.

But *fugu* is not alone; other dishes from around the globe can be fatal. The ancient Egyptians were pretty smart and were unlikely to eat something lethal, right? Well, let's consider an Egyptian delicacy of sundried and salted mullet called *fesikh*. This is closely linked to the festival of Sham Ennessim, an ancient celebration (Plutarch wrote about it in the first century AD) in which the ancient Egyptians offered salted fish to the gods. Today, the festival marks the beginning of spring and falls on the day after the Eastern Christian Easter. Despite the Christian-related date, the holiday is celebrated by Egyptians of all religions and is considered to be a national festival.

So what's the problem? The drying and salting process is quite elaborate, but get it wrong and *Clostridium botulinum* bacteria develop and produce a powerful poison which can cause severe paralytic disease. On average, a couple of people every year die from eating *fesikh*. However, when the government put out a health warning in the early 2000s, consumption went up – and so did the mortality rate. A little like Japan, it seems that even when the risks are known, the locals just can't get enough of the stuff.

But before we are quick to condemn the Egyptians, it's important to point out that processed meat (such as sausages, salami, bacon and ham) are mildly carcinogenic and that regularly consuming them leads to an 8 per cent increase in the chance of developing bowel cancer. But that's probably not going to stop anyone from chomping down a BLT sandwich, is it?

Valeria Messalina, Roman Temptress or Victim of Gossip?

Valeria Messalina had an exalted but tainted bloodline. She was a cousin of Emperor Nero (you know, the mad one) and a second cousin of Emperor Caligula (you know, the other mad one). And she was the third wife of Emperor Claudius (another cousin, once removed, but not too mad).

Messalina was an obscure figure in Roman power playing until her marriage to Claudius, but after that, things got pretty crazy pretty quickly. In AD 41, Caligula was murdered by the Praetorian Guard, and Claudius was made emperor – less to do with his ability and more to do with him being the obvious heir after the recent rash of poor emperors suffering early demises. As such, the historical writers of the age (but writing a generation or so later) are not kind to Claudius and portrayed him as ineffectual and vacillating. Because of this it was thought that there had to be a puppet master, and Messalina, accurately or not, was believed to be the power behind the throne. This, according to the standards of Roman patriarchal society, made her husband look even weaker and more foolish.

Among the likes of Tacitus, Messalina had a reputation as someone ruthless, predatory and sexually insatiable. Her husband was represented as being easily led by her and oblivious to her many adulteries. Promiscuity was frowned upon in Roman society, so by making an issue of this, Tacitus (and others) were making the case, in a deliberate smear, that she was unfit in any role to govern. While there has been much debate about how mad Nero and Caligula were, there is no debate about the fact that they were poor rulers. It could be that Messalina was simply following in her family's footsteps – or that an aristocratic woman was an easy target for the chroniclers.

In AD 48, when Claudius returned from a trip away, he was informed that Messalina was not only having an affair with a senator but had also married him … despite, y'know, still being married to Claudius. While many would have ordered her death, the emperor offered her another chance. This was despite the rumours that an assassination attempt on the young Nero at around the same time was also likely to have been ordered and paid for by her.

Seeing all of this as weakness on the part of the emperor, one of Claudius's officers in the Praetorian Guard went behind the emperor's back and ordered Messalina's death (the imperial bodyguard spent a lot of time killing members of the imperial family, including emperors). When the time came, the officer gave her the chance to die with honour by committing suicide. She tried to go out in style but just couldn't do it and was cut down by one of the guards. On hearing the news, Claudius did not react and simply asked for another glass of wine.

The Roman Senate ordered a *damnatio memoriae* so that Messalina's name would be removed from all public and private places and all statues of her would be taken down. This meant that all that remains are the voices of her critics, and we have no opportunity to see the other side of the story, if there is one. To this day Messalina is portrayed as an erotic siren, alluring and dangerous. This may be true, or it may be propaganda; we'll never know.

The Most Romantic Period of Chinese History

If we Brits are nostalgic about any time in our history, which one is it? Life under the Tudors? The Victorians? The Raj in India? It's probably true that most countries have romanticised certain periods in their history, and the Chinese are no different.

The time from AD 169 to 280 saw the decline and collapse of the Han dynasty, leaving China with its very own Hundred Years War (only, this being China, it happened 1,000 years earlier and involved a lot more death). Ironically, around the time of the European Hundred Years War, the narrative from this era of Chinese history became hugely popular. It has remained so ever since, and was even turned into a Chinese opera.

One of the key characters in the romantic stories from this time is Lady Sun. It is notoriously hard to separate myth from truth when investigating her life as contemporary facts are thin on the ground. What we do know is that she was the daughter of the much-feared General Sun Jian, who also had four sons. When they grew up, they became the next generation of martial players during the civil war.

Lady Sun was married off to the warlord Liu Bei in what was likely a move that ratified a strategic alliance. Lady Sun, however, was not your usual aristocratic lady. For one thing, she had one hundred female servants who were all armed and trained in martial combat. It seems the apple didn't fall far from the tree when it came to the Sun siblings. Indeed, Liu Bei, a feared warlord, became scared of his wife. It was said that whenever he entered her room, he felt a chill in his heart. Unsurprisingly, the relationship faltered, and when Liu Bei went off on campaign (roughly around AD 211), Lady Sun seized the opportunity to escape and, with the help of her brothers, returned to her family.

What happened next? Infuriatingly, we know nothing, which reminds us again of the patriarchal bias of records from most parts of the world at this time. Of course, the legends are full of wild conjecture, but that makes for a good story and not historical fact. However, to even get a mention in Chinese annals means she must have been every bit as formidable as the legends around her suggest. Whatever the truth of the matter, the Chinese today cannot get enough of Lady Sun and her stories.

The Murderous Emperor

Caracalla was technically the Roman Emperor from AD 198 to 217. However, up until 211, he had to rule with his father, Septimius Severus. And the top of the heap was getting crowded because in 210–11, he also had to share the imperial title with his younger brother Geta. Caracalla's solution? Well, all he had to do was wait for his father to die (which he did, aged sixty-five in York, England). That left his younger brother, whom he had murdered. This was a naked, cold-hearted grab for power, but a plus for the empire as the act of fratricide prevented the outbreak of civil war (something that had become alarmingly regular during this period). On the minus side, it revealed Caracalla's ruthless side which turned out to be his only side.

Caracalla's real name was Marcus Aurelius Severus Antoninus Augustus, but Caracalla was a nickname from a type of hooded clothing he introduced (a lot of emperors are known by nicknames, Caligula being another name that comes from fashion and means, literally, 'little boots'). He was very much a soldier, fighting on two continents, but while he was certainly bellicose, he was not a great general. He seemed to know this as he tried to emulate lots of things about Alexander the Great, even going so far as to put some of his legions in the phalanx formation even though it was the Romans who had made it an obsolete formation centuries earlier. (For more on this, see the earlier article 'When the Romans Fought a Greek Phalanx'.)

Caracalla kept trying, but despite his energy, he was totally incompetent. For example, he made unsuccessful agreements with the neighbouring and warring Germanic tribes, and although he tried to improve the position of the currency, his efforts led to a steep rise in inflation. He was completely ineffectual, but any teacher would give him an 'A' for effort – as opposed to many other ruthless emperors who just sat in luxury in Rome watching everything crumble around them.

Unsurprisingly, it didn't end well for Caracalla. While on campaign in Anatolia, he was approached by a soldier, Justin Martialis, and stabbed to death. Martialis did not carry out the assassination for the greater good of the empire. Instead, rather pettily, he was furious over Caracalla's refusal to grant him the position of centurion. A lesson there about working with people, I think. Unfortunately, things did not get better for the Roman Empire as Caracalla was replaced by Macrinus, who reigned jointly with his son Diadumenianus for only about a year. They, in turn, were overthrown by Elagabalus, a fourteen-year-old who treated the empire like his personal plaything. But that's another story.

The Black Saint

There aren't many black saints, and there are even fewer who are well known in Europe. Of those that do exist, one of the most notable is St Maurice. The story goes (and evidence is hard to come by) that in the third century AD, Maurice was one of the commanders of the Theban legion, part of the Roman war machine. At the time, Egypt was experiencing an increase in civil disobedience among its Christian population, so Emperor Maximilian ordered a massacre of the Christians. Most of the stories of Christian martyrs are from the first and second centuries; by the third century, violence against Christians was starting to wane as there were simply too many to round up and kill. As if to prove the point, Maurice himself was a Christian as were his men, so they disobeyed their orders and were subsequently rounded up and executed themselves.

Many so-called histories of saints are no such thing; they are little more than hagiographies (tales invented to make the subject look good), and many of those concerning the early Roman saints follow a suspiciously standard pattern. From a historical point of view, we know that there was a Theban legion, and the fact that we don't know the names of all the leaders is not unusual. Maurice could well have been one of the officers, but the story is usually placed around AD 250, and Maximilian was not emperor until a generation later. Also, while there would have been Christian legionnaires even by Constantine's era (several generations later), no one legion was entirely Christian. The cult of the war gods and *Sol Invictus* (Unconquered Sun was the official sun god of the later Roman Empire and a patron of soldiers) were far more likely to have been the dominant religious points of reference at the time. Also, almost everything we know about this story comes from medieval Christian sources written roughly a thousand years later.

All of that said, it's rare for saints to be completely made up, so this could be a mangled account of a Roman Christian officer who refused to carry out orders on the grounds of his religion and was subsequently executed. Either way, as a Roman officer, St Maurice was a hugely influential warrior saint who was very popular among the martial classes of Europe in the Middle Ages. He was usually (but not always) portrayed as black, which would have made him even more exotic to the average French or English knight. Of course, medieval likenesses have him in the armour of the time, making him look more like a knight than a Roman soldier. This is a visual warning that just because a story is old and often told does not mean it's historically accurate or factual.

The Real Saint Valentine

While we are on the subject of the difference between mythical stories of martyrdom and proven historical records, let's look at the most famous saint in the world. Valentinus is a very standard Roman name, so we know he was a Roman rather than a subject of the empire. The first time the date of his martyrdom was established as 14 February was in the *Martyrologium Hieronymianum*, a sixth-century compilation of earlier sources, in which Pope Gelasius I includes Valentine among those 'whose names are justly reverenced among men, but whose acts are known only to God'.

And … that's it. That's all we know about him. We don't even know when or where he died. All we can say for sure is that he was a Roman and he was martyred for his faith. Exactly why he became connected to romance is unknown, but the link started in the Middle Ages and now, a thousand years later, his name is inextricably associated with romantic love. Not the worst thing in the world!

If Valentine is the world's most popular saint, Patrick is No. 2, thanks to the Irish communities in America. George is No. 3; he's another martial saint and is the patron saint of England, Russia and Portugal and the inspiration for the name of the country of Georgia. Valentine, however, not only gets to be remembered throughout countries that are or were predominantly Christian, but also gets a feast day which is celebrated in many non-Christian countries such as Japan.

Saint Valentine: we only know his name and his faith, but today he is a global multibillion-dollar enterprise.

Pumapunku, the Mysterious Site in Bolivia

According to the Incas (whose empire covered Peru, large areas of Chile and portions of Bolivia, Argentina and Colombia at its peak from 1400 to 1533), Pumapunku was the place where the world was created. However, the Incas arrived in the area centuries after the disappearance of the original civilisation that built it.

Pumapunku was built in the sixth century AD and is composed of a man-made earthen mound, a terrace and carved stone blocks. The largest of the stone blocks is 7.81 metres long, 5.17 metres wide and averages 1.07 metres thick; it is estimated to weigh about 131 tonnes. All of the blocks are made of sandstone from a quarry about 10 kilometres away. Even the smaller blocks weigh 50 tonnes or more. What is even more impressive is that the Pumapunku civilisation, like the later Incas, did not have iron or steel; there were no horses and they did not have the wheel. So, while built millennia later, the engineers of Pumapunku had only the same kinds of equipment to build this site as that available at the time of Stonehenge. And yet, the stones were sometimes five times the weight and far more carefully carved than anything at Stonehenge. Pumapunku is one of the greatest prehistoric building achievements in the world.

But the story of this amazing engineering feat becomes even more ridiculously impressive in the way the blocks were assembled: each stone was finely cut to interlock with its surrounding stones in a perfect fit, and they did this without the use of mortar and without leaving even the slightest of gaps. It is assumed that rollers or greased sledges were used to move the stones and that the precision stonework was almost certainly done by pulverising rock against rock. The enormity of the undertaking makes it seem an almost impossible achievement. It is a remarkable testament to this lost civilisation's skill in engineering that they were able to do this without any modern tools or apparatus (such as cranes).

How to account for this remarkable site? There are always those who will explain such a feat by declaring it the work of aliens. But no. Putting it simply, with some basic engineering concepts and enough time, manpower and tenacity, it can be done. It is remarkable what can be achieved when we aren't binge-watching Netflix.

Sixth-century Italy Was Very *Game of Thrones*

Theodoric was king of the Ostrogoths (475–526), ruler of Italy (493–526), regent of the Visigoths (511–526) and a *patricius* (nobleman) of the Roman Empire. So, he was one impressive guy, but his daughter Amalasuntha was just as impressive.

In 515, Amalasuntha married Eutharic, an Ostrogoth noble of the old Amali dynasty. It was important to Amalasuntha's father, Theodoric, that she marry into a legitimate royal family to stop her own family's legitimacy being questioned. When Amalasuntha's husband died, he left her with two children, Athalaric and Matasunth. On the death of her father in 526, her son Athalaric, then only ten years of age, succeeded him, but Amalasuntha held the power as regent. Her tremendous influence in this position can be seen in a royal diptych in which she appears alongside her son in 530. Deeply imbued with old Roman culture, she tried to bring these influences to her rule and ensured that her son's education had a more refined and literary emphasis than was thought to be appropriate by her Gothic subjects.

Conscious of her unpopularity, she banished and later had assassinated the three Gothic nobles whom she suspected of conspiring against her. At the same time, she opened negotiations with Byzantine Emperor Justinian I, intending to move herself and the entire Gothic treasury to Constantinople.

The Roman Empire in the West had collapsed, but the Eastern Roman Empire under Justinian was in rude good health. It was a worthy plan for Amalasuntha and her family, but her son's death changed everything.

After Athalaric died, Amalasuntha became queen, ruling independently only for a short while before making her cousin Theodahad a partner on her throne. Her intention was to strengthen her position as she believed this pairing would help make supporters of her harshest critics, and once again, she was the power behind the throne as she plotted to maintain power. Her decision to partner with Theodahad was a high-risk strategy as her cousin was a prominent leader of the Gothic military aristocracy, the very group that so opposed her pro-Roman stances. Ultimately, her plan failed. Theodahad fostered the disaffection of the Goths, and either by his orders or with his permission, Amalasuntha was imprisoned on the island of Martana in the Tuscan lake of Bolsena. In the spring of 534/535, she was murdered in her bath.

So, yes, all of this sounds as if it could come from the pages of George R. R. Martin, but unlike *Game of Thrones*, all of this happened.

Middle Ages

Buddhist Temples in the Sky

Buddhism is so ingrained in Chinese history and tradition that many assume it originated in China. It is Indian in origin but had reached China by the 200s BC, where it almost instantly became integrated into Chinese culture and imperial philosophy.

The Fanjingshan is a mountain in south-west China with a long and illustrious connection to Buddhism. According to tradition, the mountain will be the site of the awakening of a future Buddha. (Buddha is not the name of a person but a state of mind. The most apt translation is 'enlightened one'.) But Buddhists have been waiting for a while. The first recorded temples on the mountain date back to the AD 630s. This makes them old but hardly the first. Since then, while they have been damaged and restored, there have always been religious buildings on this mountain; they have survived everything from the Mongols to Mao's Cultural Revolution. Despite the site's importance as a centre of Buddhist learning and culture, it remains obscure outside of China.

Fanjingshan's location inspires the spirit. The temples seem to perch precariously at the top of breathtaking peaks, making the entire complex look as if it had been built by the supernatural. It wasn't – nor were aliens responsible. It was created by thousands of dedicated workers over centuries of construction, repair and restoration.

The Fanjingshan National Nature Reserve was established in 1978 and designated a UNESCO Biosphere Reserve in 1986. In 2018 it became a UNESCO World Heritage Site. Google some images. Regardless of any religious views, it's astonishingly beautiful.

Exorcism Is a Sinister Thing

Perhaps the most chilling line in the whole Bible occurs when Jesus asks the spirits inside a man's body what their names are and they reply, 'My name is Legion: for we are many' (Gospel of Mark, 5:9). Jesus cast out the spirits from the man into pigs, which then threw themselves in the river and drowned. According to the Bible, Jesus was not human but actually the Son of God and part of the Holy Trinity, so it is unsurprising that he could expel evil spirits. However, this passage has been interpreted as proof that the highly devout could do the same thing. The idea that priests could battle evil spirits has been around for a long time, but the specific phrase '*Vade retro Satana*' (Step back, Satan) as being key to an exorcism comes from 1415, whereas the official Catholic book on exorcism was not released until the early 1600s, which seems very late to the scene.

Casting out spirits is not unique to Christianity. The idea of possession occurs in most of the world's major religions (notably Catholicism), and some religious sects still conduct exorcisms. In Islam, exorcism is called *ruqya* and is used to repair the damage caused by black magic. Exorcisms today are part of a wider body of contemporary Islamic alternative medicine called al-Tibb al-Nabawi (Medicine of the Prophet).

Rabbi Yehuda Fetaya wrote *Minchat Yahuda*, a book which deals extensively with exorcisms and his experiences with possessed people. The Jewish exorcism ritual is performed by a rabbi who has mastered practical Kabbalah and is conducted in the presence of a *minyan* (a group of ten adult males), who gather in a circle around the possessed person. The group recites Psalm 91 three times, and the rabbi blows a *shofar* (ram's horn).

In Hinduism the idea of reincarnation and spirit transfer is prevalent, so reading the third, seventh and ninth chapters of the *Bhagavad Gita* and mentally offering the result to departed souls helps to release them from a kind of spiritual limbo. Here it's less about being possessed by an evil spirit and more about the person's own spirit becoming entangled with or tainted by other spirits. Exorcism, in this case, is seen as something a holy person can fix with the right words.

Buddhists make exorcism an annual event. The Tibetan religious ceremony of *gutor* (literally, offering) is held on the twenty-ninth day of the twelfth Tibetan month, with its focus on driving out all negativity, including evil spirits and misfortunes of the past year, and starting the new year in a peaceful and auspicious way.

Most of these forms of exorcism predate Christianity by centuries and seem to show that there is an almost universal belief that evil spirits interfere in human affairs. Of course, science doesn't recognise possession and points out that most of the symptoms of possession can be traced to mental or neurological illnesses such as epilepsy or Tourette's syndrome.

Exorcism is a fascinating example of living history. It was one way our ancestors dealt with strange behaviours and yet is still practised today.

The Mercian Queen

The reason why the early Anglo-Saxon era has been called the Dark Ages (a term now considered to be derogatory and inaccurate) is mainly due to the lack of written information about the period. So often we have snippets of what seem to be intriguing stories, but as the chronicler does not provide more information, the rest of the story is a complete mystery. Take, for example, Osthryth (Edith) of the Mercians. Anglo-Saxons didn't have the title 'queen' or see any such role in quite the way we would think of it today, but Osthryth was, in essence, the Queen of Mercia (the Midlands of modern-day England) in the late 600s. Unlike the other Anglo-Saxon kingdoms, Mercia had a few female rulers over the centuries, so it's easy to assume they treated these queens well. Whatever the case, they certainly didn't treat Osthryth well because, in 697, some Mercian nobles murdered her.

Why? Well, as the assassination was mentioned with no explanation, we'll never know. It's tempting to think of an innocent woman murdered by a manipulative and chauvinistic court, and that could be the case, or it could also be that she was a tyrant who needed to be removed. The circumstances remain a mystery.

We know that the Anglo-Saxon kingdoms eventually united to become England, so there is the temptation to assume that relations between them were friendly. They weren't. They fought vicious wars, and smaller kingdoms were often absorbed into bigger ones via conquest (e.g. Sussex was conquered by Wessex). Because of this, the assassination of a leader was not unheard of and probably had nothing to do with the fact that she was a woman; it's far more likely that she was simply on the losing side of a political power play.

Saying that, think of how you felt when you read the facts above. A woman was assassinated: what assumptions did you make and what biases influenced them? I don't know what you're thinking, but this particular fact is as good as any to reflect our own internal prejudices. We all have them, but good historians try to recognise and resist them.

The Roman Pornocracy ... Bet That Got Your Attention

In papal history, the sixty years spanning AD 904 to 964 have been referred to as the Roman Pornocracy (Roman Catholicism uses the Latin term *Saeculum Obscurum*, or Dark Age). The first person to suggest grouping the popes of this period together was not an atheist or a Protestant, but a Renaissance cardinal called Caesar Baronius. The popes of this time were weak (there was a pope by the name of Lando, but the only famous Lando is from Star Wars, not papal history) and were, invariably, the puppets of the rich, powerful and completely corrupt Theophylact family.

It's also important to point out that the Vatican wasn't then quite like the later medieval one. To understand its position, we have to go back to the early Roman Church. Matthew 16:18 famously quotes Jesus as saying, 'And I tell you that you are Peter, and on this rock I will build my church.' Because of this pronouncement, Saint Peter the Apostle (and one of the Twelve Disciples) is often seen as the first pope, but the reality is that the first few centuries of popes have more to do with legends than historical facts. Once Emperor Constantine made the Roman Empire Christian, it pretty quickly evolved into five centres of Christian power, each with a church leader known as a patriarch.

The five cities were Jerusalem (naturally), Alexandria, Antioch, Constantinople and Rome. At first Jerusalem had the advantage of being the site of the holiest places in Christendom, but in the seventh century, it fell with Alexandria to the new Muslim Empire and so their positions of religious importance waned. Antioch later followed suit, after which there was strong competition between Constantinople and Rome for supremacy in the Church. The Roman patriarch became known as the Father of the Church and was nicknamed Papa, which is where the word pope comes from. But the patriarchs of Constantinople and Rome would continue to be at each other's throats until a formal split of their churches in 1054.

With all of this in mind, the position of the Roman popes as the supreme authority in the Church in the 900s was not to be taken for granted, and while they craved that level of recognition, duplicitous nobles could play power politics as everyone jostled for position. And the popes of this era were bad. They were often implicated in less than holy endeavours and frequently had lovers (to put it politely). Pope John X was deposed, imprisoned and finally murdered. Pope Stephen VIII was imprisoned, tortured and maimed. There were about a dozen popes in this period, some lasting just months. The final one, Benedict V, was deposed after just one month in his office.

The person at the centre of this was Marozia, a woman who was born into the wealthy and influential Theophylact family and who became the mother of many of the key players. Her mother was Theodora, herself a master manipulator who used her power and riches to control the papacy for personal interests. Piety had nothing to do with any of it, and the popes of this time were, without exception, corrupt, short-lived and ineffectual. Of course, the concept of a hereditary pope is an oxymoron, a big no-no and a sign of how corrupt the Church had become by the 900s when Theodora paved the way for her fifteen-year-old daughter Marozia to become the mistress of Pope Sergius III.

A few years later, in order to counter the influence of Pope John X (who may have been another of Marozia's lovers), Marozia married his political opponent, Guy of Tuscany, who apparently loved power as much as she did. Together they attacked Rome, arrested Pope John X and incarcerated him in the Castel Sant'Angelo. The stakes increased when he died in 928, perhaps from neglect or ill-treatment – or possibly because Guy had him strangled. Marozia seized power in Rome in a coup d'état. The following popes, Leo VI and Stephen VII, were both puppets who didn't last long. In 931 she imposed her son as Pope John XI; he was only twenty-one at the time and had precisely no interest in carrying out the Lord's work.

This was a period of papal history which is best forgotten, but it was also a time when Italy was under serious pressure from Arab raiders and pirates, and while the papacy regularly called for assistance to stop the threat, nothing came of it because of their obvious poor leadership. As an example of the neglect and confusion that marked the papacy at this time, consider Popes Marinus and Martinus. Because of the similarity of their names, Popes Marinus I and Marinus II were, in some sources, mistakenly given the name Martinus (and were then listed respectively as Martinus II and Martinus III). It didn't help that Pope Marinus II (942–6) was such a non-event that nobody cared either way. Thus, in 1281, when the new pope took the name Martin, he became Pope Martin IV when in fact he should have been Martin II. Got that?

When her husband died in 929, Marozia negotiated a marriage with his half-brother, Hugh of Arles, who had been rather handily elected King of Italy. There was the little problem that Hugh already had a wife, but he had that marriage annulled so that he and Marozia could be married. It was an eventful wedding: Alberic II, another of Marozia's sons, was opposed to the rule of Marozia and Hugh, so he imprisoned his mother at the wedding and kept her confined until her death. Meanwhile, Hugh escaped and appears to have made no attempt to save his bride. Marozia remained in prison for five years and seems to have died of natural causes. It could have been neglect, but prison for an aristocrat was rarely a bare cell and chains.

So, the papacy at this time constituted just another everyday story of power, corruption and supposedly noble people acting in less than noble ways. It wasn't until 965 that things began to change, and Pope John XIII showed signs of independence and proved unwilling to blindly back the Theophylact family. The term 'pornocracy' arose because both Theodora and Marozia, mother and daughter, were the mistresses of two popes (at least) and the alleged mothers of a few more. So, it might not just have been sixth-century Italian nobles who inspired *Game of Thrones*. Who said church history is boring?

The Real Valkyries

There was no such thing as a 'Viking' civilisation. The word is old Scandinavian for a wanderer. So the people who left the area to trade or explore or pillage were called Vikings, but when they came home again, they reverted to their former names, probably something like Olaf the Fisherman. However, the term Viking is so widely accepted that I will use it, but you now have a bonus fact you can use to impress your friends.

In the late nineteenth century, the archaeologist Hjalmar Stolpe was excavating Viking gravesite Bj 581 in Birka, Sweden where he discovered the remains of a tenth-century Viking warrior, complete with armour, weapons and ... a board game. It was a fine example of a Viking burial but nothing special, or so it was thought for more than 100 years. It wasn't until 2017 that Charlotte Hedenstierna-Jonson from Uppsala University had a hunch that the buried warrior could be female. The shape of the pelvis and the thinness of the jaw are characteristics more commonly found in women than men, but the skeleton was tall for the time, about 5 feet 6 inches or 170 cm. There just wasn't enough physical evidence to prove her theory. So, a DNA test was conducted and found no evidence of a Y (male) chromosome; in other words, the body was female and this burial site was that of a Viking shieldmaiden, a semi-mythical woman described in Viking sagas.

While the idea of female Viking warriors had never been completely dismissed, this was the first physical evidence of one. Viking women had far more rights than most other women in the world at the time. They could own land and divorce their husbands – and the sagas comment on female fighters in a more matter-of-fact way than medieval chronicles would have done. (It should also be remembered that the Valkyries of Norse legend were female warrior spirits who carried dead male warriors off to Valhalla.) One example of a shieldmaiden as described in the sagas occurs in America when Leif Erikson's pregnant half-sister, Freydís Eiríksdóttir, fought bare-breasted against the *skrælings* (this term seems to be the Old Norse for what we would now call Native Americans).

The burial showed that the warrior had the finest weapons and armour of the age, so she was either a high-status female or had slain men who were better equipped. The supposed 'board game' may, on reflection, have been a battle map which she used to plan her military engagements. She died in her thirties, with no evidence of wounds. The cause could have been any one of the myriad diseases that would have left no clues on a skeleton – or, of course, that unique threat to a woman's health, childbirth. But the fact she was buried with full military honours shows that she was seen as a warrior first and foremost.

Rare Anglo-Saxons

Today we have about 4 million words in work written by Charles Dickens, including his final but unfinished novel *The Mystery of Edwin Drood*. That's an impressive number, but what puts it into sharp perspective is the fact that the total number of Old English (Anglo-Saxon) documents to have survived into the modern era amounts to about 3 million words. So, we know more about the language and grammar of one Victorian author than we do about the entirety of the

English language from AD 550 to 1150, which was when English as an official language was born.

Nothing of the Anglo-Saxon story of *Beowulf* survives from the period; our earliest copy of the manuscript is medieval, and that was nearly destroyed in a library fire during the Victorian era. Today we have the 'right to be forgotten' (an online facility that allows individuals to have information about themselves deleted from internet records), but more significantly, any and all information can be uploaded, stored, backed up and retrieved. Just thirty years ago, if that original film or that untranslated text was destroyed or lost, it was gone forever.

But I digress. The point I want to make is how different the Anglo-Saxon era was to the one that preceded it, the Roman era. The Romans were avid writers and documenters. The Anglo-Saxons, who were part of a wider pagan Germano-Scandinavian culture, were not. It is therefore tempting to think of them as ignorant and/or barbaric, but that's our inherent bias. In the West we tend to believe that anything emulating Greco-Roman values is 'good', but the Anglo-Saxons did things differently and, as a result, had their period in history labelled as the Dark Ages. It was no such thing. The Anglo-Saxons might not have been great record keepers, but they loved a good story.

Beowulf, the earliest story we have in Old English, would not have been read out; it would have been performed by a travelling minstrel. It's a long story so the minstrel would probably spend several evenings telling the tale to an enraptured audience in a great hall, rather like binge-watching a box set. But *Beowulf* more closely resembles a play; it's more a performance piece than a work of literature. And it would have been sung, so more like an opera or, at the very least, something like a stage version of *Les Misérables*.

This is the opening line of the text and this is what English looked like nearly 1,500 years ago:

Hwæt! We Gardena in geardagum, þeod-cyninga þrym gefrunon,
hu ða æþelingas ellen fremedon.

Need a translation?

Ho! We have heard tales sung of the Spear-Danes, the glory of their war-kings in days gone by, how princely nobles performed heroes' deeds.

It's the opening *Hwæt* that has been long debated amongst academics. Some say it's a command to listen; others say it's an instruction to scream to get the attention of everyone in the hall before the story begins. As an opening line, it's certainly gripping. Who doesn't want to hear a story about war-kings and heroes?

The tale of *Beowulf* truly is an epic, spanning years and telling of monsters, with a brave (pagan) warrior hero at the centre of it all. It is clearly from the same tradition of storytelling as the Viking sagas and is most definitely not a tale the average Roman would have been familiar with. The sagas are dripping with blood, and martial prowess is the ultimate noble undertaking. Step aside, you philosophers and artists, it's time to send in the brave warriors.

But for all their love of an exciting adventure yarn, the Anglo-Saxons weren't mindless barbarians. Just as they are in later morality plays, attributes like greed, cruelty and arrogance are invariably punished, and the brave warrior is recognised as a hero. It's just that here there is far more imagery of crows pecking at the corpses of the slain than in, say, Dickens.

But why should we care about a story that's 1,500 years old and needs translation into modern English to be understood? Because that's the starting point of English, the mongrel language that smashes together Latin, German, French and Scandinavian and ends up as the most widely spoken language in the world today.

Bluetooth Technology's Namesake

For a long-dead civilisation, the Vikings do keep cropping up. (Okay, I know I said there is no such thing as a Viking civilisation in the fact on 'The Real Valkyries', but work with me.) Yes, there is a popular TV series, and yes, Thor is doing a great trade in the superhero department, but there's more. The scanning and recognition protocol found in our smartphones, known as Bluetooth technology, is named after a Danish king.

Harald 'Bluetooth' Gormsson was a tenth-century Scandinavian king who, according to the legend, brought Christianity to Denmark. The story involves Harald being baptised by a monk called Poppa, but none of this can be verified, and if Harald did convert, tenth-century Denmark didn't drop all its pagan iconography overnight.

Harald wasn't the violent raider that comes to mind when we talk about Vikings. In fact, Harald is associated with many prestigious building projects, including Scandinavia's first bridge, a series of ringforts and the restoration of the Jelling runic stones, a project which marks the transition from pagan

Nordic culture to Christianity. While Denmark was largely peaceful under his rule, he did go to war with Norway (which he conquered) and Germany (which beat him and forced him to relinquish Norway). It was, however, his success in unifying Denmark's warring families that connects our smartphones to his legacy in Scandinavia.

The first documented appearance of Harald's Bluetooth nickname is in the *Chronicon Roskildense*, written 200 years after he died. The traditional explanation is that Harald must have had a conspicuously bad tooth that appeared to be blue. This is contentious, but the worst explanation – that his teeth were blue as a result of his love of blueberries – is too ridiculous to contemplate.

The Bluetooth wireless specification design was named after him, and the Bluetooth logo consists of the Viking runes for his initials, H (✱) and B (ᛒ). His name was chosen to be a modern brand because it was said in the *Chronicon Roskildense* that he wanted all his conquests to communicate with one another in the same language. This rather obscure edict is, of course, what the technology allows phones on different operating systems to do. Yes, it's a tortuous connection, but I didn't name the technology. It is, however, wonderful that a largely forgotten tenth-century Scandinavian ruler gets name-checked in the era of mobile communication.

The Green Hermit

Saint Romuald started life as the rather spoilt son of an Italian aristocrat. His life changed forever around AD 970 when he acted as the second for his father in a duel over family land. Romuald was devastated when his father killed a relative in the dispute, and he fled to a nearby monastery, where he renounced his affluent life and became a Benedictine monk.

As a brother in the monastery, he led a very simple and disciplined life. As well as the vows of poverty, chastity and obedience, he was obliged to pray at designated hours eight times a day, including once in the middle of the night and again at dawn. Food was never plentiful but there were regular meals. Work might involve copying out scriptures or working in the gardens. It wasn't back-breaking work, but it was hard and meant to provide periods of solitary reflection. And there was the coarse material of his clothing – everything was stripped back and made as basic as possible. It wasn't the life for everyone and, eventually, it wasn't the life for Romuald either.

The problem was that Romuald didn't think it was severe enough. So, he decided to become a hermit, and in doing so, he established one of a number of doctrines around a hermetic holy life. He is an example of the zealous but heartfelt spiritual movement that existed in the Middle Ages, one which many of us find hard to fathom today. While hermits were a feature of life in medieval Europe, Romuald took things to a whole new level. He decided to live in (not by, *in*) a swamp. He was so regularly immersed in its fetid waters that his hair fell out and his skin became not only puffy but 'as green as a newt'. This was a sign of how seriously he took his penances, which could have killed him. He became known as the green hermit for obvious reasons, and his life of hardship and self-sacrifice brought regular visitors to ask him for spiritual guidance. Visitors are, of course, the last thing a hermit wants, so he felt forced to give up on the whole living-in-a-swamp thing.

The rest of his life was a little more mainstream. He was the founder of the Camaldolese monastic order, an independent offshoot of the Benedictines founded in the early eleventh century at Camaldoli, Italy, as part of the monastic reform movement of the eleventh and twelfth centuries. The order combined the solitary life of the hermit with an austere form of the common life of the monk. He spent years in libraries and then spent more years founding new monasteries and hermitages or reforming existing ones to promote his belief in asceticism. He died in the mid-1020s. As a result of his life of hardship, piety and devotion, he was canonised by Pope Gregory XIII in 1582.

It seems appropriate that we should include some words from Saint Romuald to consider: 'Empty yourself completely and sit waiting. Sit in your cell as in paradise. Put the whole world behind you and forget it.' But perhaps don't sit in a swamp until your hair falls out and you go green.

Edmund Ironside: Cool Name, Forgotten Ruler

Edmund became King of England in 1016. This was after the Viking invasion of England in 1014 which had forced Aethelred the Unready to flee the country. Edmund was the third son of Aethelred and wasn't expected to become king, but after his elder brothers died, Edmund II had the unenviable task of fighting Cnut the Great to claim the throne of England. Somewhat unexpectedly, he took to the task with vigour; it was his martial prowess that got him the nickname Ironside, possibly because he always wore a sword or just because he was consistently brave.

It was Edmund who mounted a last-ditch effort to revive the defence of England and save it from the invaders. When the Danes laid siege to London, Edmund headed for Wessex, where the people rallied around him and he gathered an army. He fought inconclusive battles against the Danes and their English supporters at Penselwood in Somerset and Sherston in Wiltshire. Undaunted, he raised the siege of London and defeated the Danes near Brentford, showing considerable martial skill (this is the only interesting thing about Brentford; I know, I grew up near there).

The Vikings renewed the siege while Edmund went to Wessex to raise further troops, returning to relieve London once more, defeat the Danes at Otford (that's not a typo) and pursue Cnut into Kent. At this point, one of the great noblemen of the age, Eadric Streona, switched allegiances to join Edmund. He had switched sides a couple of times and was regarded as a necessary evil. On 18 October 1016, Eadric and his men once again proved to be less than reliable and fled the battlefield, allowing Cnut to defeat Edmund at the decisive Battle of Assandun. There may have been one further battle in the Forest of Dean, after which the two kings negotiated peace and divided the country between them. Edmund received Wessex while Cnut took Mercia and probably Northumbria. In the space of one year, Edmund had confronted Cnut about half a dozen times. He hadn't won every time, but he was an energetic and competent warrior king who was a serious thorn in the side of the mighty Cnut and his Viking warriors.

So why isn't this amazing man more famous? Well, it's because of how he died. On 30 November 1016, a Dane lurked in a slit trench used as a toilet when Edmund answered a call of nature. The unpleasant truth is that Edmund suffered multiple stab wounds to his posterior whilst doing what we all do but don't like to talk about ... and died as a result. This just doesn't make for a satisfying end to a heroic tale.

On a practical point, Edmund's death sealed Cnut's conquest of England. As Edmund had no heir apparent, the treaty that had separated the country between the Anglo-Saxons and the Vikings was abandoned. For the first time ever, the whole of England was now ruled by a Scandinavian dynasty.

The Mesoamerican Torture God

Are you surprised to find a story about the Aztecs in the section on the Middle Ages? Many people think that they were contemporary with the Romans in the West. Not true. While Mesoamerican culture does go back that far, the Aztecs only began forming their empire from a coalition of city-states in the 1300s. The empire was not even 200 years old when Cortes arrived.

A big problem with understanding much of anything about the empire is the lack of sources, an issue for many eras and cultures. But the Aztecs are particularly frustrating because about a hundred years before the Spanish arrived, the emperor ordered the destruction of the old scrolls and chronicles in order to create a new, Aztec Empire-friendly history. Any genuine, factual history was further undermined when Cortes arrived and carried out a combination of deliberate and accidental social annihilation.

Most of what we know about this era was written by Christian priests who travelled to the New World and gave first-hand accounts. How honest were they? How much did they remember? Were there instances of miscommunication and/or mistranslation? The answer is that we will never know, therefore all the 'facts' from this era and culture need to be treated with a certain amount of caution.

This article is about an Aztec god. Right away the subject becomes contentious because even experts in the study of the Aztecs cannot agree on how many gods there were. Some gods had other forms, so is that two gods or one? Some gods seem to have had overlapping authority, so again, is that a lesser or a greater god; is one an avatar of the other? It all gets pretty messy.

It is not unusual for another culture's religions and mythologies to seem odd and hard to understand. In this context it's worth saying that all faiths have elements that appear to defy logic and can be difficult to explain to the uninitiated. Saying that, the Aztec culture is *very* alien to almost everyone else. So, in keeping with the themes of controversy and confusion, the god described below does have two different forms. Here's his story.

Allow me to introduce Xipe Totec, the Aztec god of agriculture, war and … torture. The name literally means 'Our Lord the Flayed One'. He has some other wonderfully vivid names too, such as Tezcatlipoca, 'Red Smoking Mirror', and my favourite, Youalahuan, 'the Night Drinker'. He was said to cause rashes, pimples, inflammations and eye infections … among other things.

Xipe Totec is portrayed wearing flayed human skin. Torture and flaying are linked to the sacrifices that must be made for a successful harvest, and this flaying and renewal emulates the changing of the seasons. Sometimes he is seen with his skin on and sometimes with his skin removed, so he practised what he preached. Given his name and his representations, it's unsurprising that there was a darker side to his already dark side.

At least pimples and rashes are better than being flayed, which didn't happen ... except during his festival. The annual festival of Xipe Totec was celebrated on the spring equinox, before the onset of the rainy season. It was known as Tlacaxipehualiztli, or 'the flaying of men' festival, and this is where it gets darker. Forty days before the festival, prisoners captured in war were dressed to represent the living Xipe Totec. This occurred in every ward of the city, so multiple slaves were being selected for sacrifice during the great gladiatorial combats that opened and closed the festival's central rituals. On the second day, the 'game of canes' took place between two opposing teams. The first team was comprised of brave and fearless soldiers who took the part of Xipe Totec, dressed in the skins of the prisoners of war who had been killed the previous day ... so the blood was fresh and still flowing. The opposing team was composed of prisoners who lost to the representations of the great god. At the conclusion of this game of fierce combat, the winners (those who wore the human skins) went around the town, entering houses unhindered and demanding that they be given gifts for the love of Xipe Totec. Kind of like carol singing meets ... er... *Hellraiser*?

Xipe Totec is still making news. In January 2019, Mexican archaeologists confirmed their discovery of the first known surviving temple (dating from around AD 1000–1200) dedicated to Xipe Totec. Dark as he was, his importance in the Aztec pantheon of gods has been confirmed.

The Twice-widowed Queen

Ealdgyth (another Anglo-Saxon name translated as Edith in the modern English tongue) is not a big name in history, but her story should be better known. Ealdgyth's year of birth is uncertain, but she came of age in the late 1050s. Her father was Ælfgar, an Anglo-Saxon aristocrat who lived in a dangerous time of power-playing when external forces were hungrily eyeing the prize that was England. Ælfgar was on the losing side and was forced into exile in Ireland where he took up his cause with Gruffydd ap Llywelyn.

Briefly (so as to not get too distracted from our heroine), Gruffydd ap Llywelyn is the only man who has ever claimed to be King of Wales. It's technically not accurate as he never had a coronation and he was never anointed. A more apt comparison would be with Braetwalder in England, a local prince who beat up the other princes and ruled them all as their overlord until his death – which is exactly what Gruffydd ap Llywelyn did.

To seal his alliance with Llywelyn, Ælfgar arranged a marriage with his daughter Ealdgyth. The couple had a daughter and life was good. Contemporary sources speak frequently of Ealdgyth's beauty, and her nickname, Swan-neck. Like a swan, she had a long, graceful neck (minus the feathers), so her very nickname attests to her grace and beauty. However, when it came to power, she was no more than a political pawn in her father's games.

Alas, everything began to fall apart in 1063, when Harold Godwinson, on behalf of King Edward the Confessor, invaded Wales with his brother Tostig and carried out an ambitious and highly successful pincer movement across Wales. Llywelyn rode out to meet the English menace but died in the fighting. Now Ealdgyth was alone and vulnerable, but it was at this point that she showed particular cunning, using her beguiling beauty and turning her attention to the conqueror of her adopted country. Putting aside the fact that Harold had just killed her husband, she became his mistress and, around 1066, became the wife and queen consort of her late husband's nemesis.

Of course, she could not foresee the fact that William, Duke of Normandy would invade England in 1066, or that she would lose a second husband in battle. At the news of Harold's death, Ealdgyth's brothers went to London to fetch her and immediately sent her to Chester for shelter. Although a popular legend states that she went to Hastings to identify Harold's body, there is no evidence of this, but it makes a great story. Although her daughter married into the Anglo-Norman aristocracy, Ealdgyth herself disappeared from history after this.

The Real Lady Macbeth

Macbeth is an odd play. It tends to be lumped together with Shakespeare's tragedies, but unlike *Hamlet* or *King Lear*, Macbeth was a real person. Mac Bethad, to give him his medieval Gaelic name, is part of the history of Scotland. While Shakespeare's histories may show bias or get some information wrong, they generally follow the trend of history (for example, *Richard III* may be a hatchet job on that monarch's reputation, but at least he dies at the Battle of Bosworth). *Macbeth*, however, is fiction. Why the great playwright chose to use the name of a real King of Scotland for a fantastical tale, we will never know.

The real Macbeth ruled Alba from 1040 to 1057. He was roughly contemporary with Edward the Confessor, which means all the stuff about castles is also made up as they came after the Norman Conquest. But Macbeth did, indeed, have a wife and her name was Gruoch ingen Boite.

If the play is libellous regarding Macbeth, it's probably even more so with regard to Gruoch. There is no evidence that she was a manipulative tyrant, hell-bent on murder. In fact, little is known about her at all. What we can state as fact is that she was associated with the endowment of the Culdee monastery at Loch Leven, a pious and noble connection. We also know that after the real Macbeth was killed in battle, her son Lulach became king until he was murdered by Malcolm, who took over the throne ... so, virtually the opposite of what Shakespeare wrote.

If you agree that people should know the truth about the real Lady Macbeth, then please share this fact. At least we can undo a little of the bad PR around Gruoch – plus you get the chance to be a know-it-all.

Leif Erikson Knew He Wasn't the First Viking to Reach America

The Viking sagas are a tricky bit of history. They are purportedly written versions of oral history; however, by the time they were written, Scandinavia was Christian, so questions arise: Are the blood-soaked sagas exaggerated to show how barbaric their pagan past was? Are they a true reflection of the Viking-era culture? All the sagas have heroic and/or fantastical moments, a little like Homer's *Iliad*, so exactly how much is history and how much is ... well, just story, is very hard to say.

Putting all of this to one side, even Leif's own story talks about a merchant called Bjarni Herjólfsson who claimed to have sighted land to the west of Greenland when he was blown off course. That would have made Bjarni the first European to discover the Americas, but that's it for Bjarni. There are no other references to him in the written records.

It's interesting that Leif himself claims only to have arrived on the shores of North America when he, too, was blown off course. What can't be disputed is that archaeological evidence dating from around AD 1000 (when Leif was in his prime) shows that there was a small Viking settlement in Newfoundland. We even have existing Viking names from this moment of history. They named the area they settled Helluland, and the local Native Americans they called *skrælings*. All of this reminds us how thoroughly overrated Christopher Columbus is because:

He wasn't trying to find the Americas;

He thought he had found part of Asia (so he was off by thousands of miles);

His so-called discovery was no such thing. He'd been beaten by the Vikings by around 500 years.

Trial by Combat

The early medieval world was a harsh one in Europe. Centralised power was minimal and lawlessness was common, and it was in this context that a superstitious form of criminal trials, called 'trial by ordeal', took place. An example would be for the accused to hold a red-hot metal bar for ten paces, then his hand would be bound and left for, say, a week, to see if he had been blessed by God. If all the wounds had healed, it meant he had been telling the truth and was, therefore, innocent of the charges. This was, of course, an unreliable way of determining innocence or guilt.

The same idea was behind 'trial by combat', when two men would fight it out to determine who should win a court case. Those involved were allowed to use 'champions', who would fight on their behalf because even our early medieval ancestors recognised that big guys would beat skinny blokes every time. Again, the logic was that God was on the side of justice and guided the innocent to victory.

These ridiculously defective processes were used because there was an absence of anything better, and they are often claimed to have still been in use as late as the time of the Hundred Years War (1337–1453). Similarly, it was the same thinking that led to a fashion for reliquaries in the tenth and eleventh centuries, when portions of dead saints were believed to imbue people with magical healing powers and to bless the surrounding area. There were even different potencies of relics: the more famous the saint, the greater the aura of healing. Even the dust that gathered on the reliquaries was thought to be imbued, so it was collected and distributed (for a fee). The dust wasn't as potent as touching the actual remains of the saint, but it was believed that it would have absorbed some of the healing element.

The weird religious and legal quirks of our ancestors are a source of fascination and crop up in movies about the Middle Ages or even in more fantastical films like *Black Panther*. However, such practices waned as central authority strengthened, grew more sophisticated and became able to impose law and order according to more informed standards. So the idea that such backward methods were still widely practised during the Hundred Years War is wrong; they would have been seen as archaic by someone like Edward III.

What Do You Get If You Mix Alcohol and Anti-Semitism with a Terrible Ruler?

The depressing answer is the 1066 Granada Massacre. Islam and Judaism have a complex history, but overall (until the twentieth century), it could be said that Jews had a better life in Muslim territories than in Christian ones. Think of Muslim Iberia and, later, the Ottoman Empire. However, since the first-century diaspora of the Jewish people, they have always been vulnerable, no matter where they lived. In the eleventh century, Spain was still largely under Muslim rule. The Muslim princes of Spain were hugely powerful and, compared to their more northerly counterparts, exceptionally well educated, with access to luxuries from across the Middle East.

The spark in Granada in 1066 was provided by the grand vizier (prime minister) Joseph ibn Naghrela, a Jew in the court of King Badis of Granada, who had a reputation for being a drunk with an unhealthy streak of paranoia. Joseph wasn't worried and believed his position to be safe since he was running the show effectively despite, rather than under the orders of, King Badis. However, anyone in such a position is likely to attract jealousy, and Joseph himself, while wise and patient, could have shown a little more humility in his dealings with Muslim aristocrats. If nothing else, his power and his arrogance would have antagonised some of the other courtiers. While it was technically true that Joseph outranked them (he was second only to Badis in terms of authority), he was neither ethnically nor religiously part of the ruling elite.

Muslim courtiers seized their opportunity to falsely accuse Joseph of several acts of violence, which enraged the Berbers, the Muslim ruling majority at Granada. The most bitter of his many enemies was Abu Ishak of Elvira, who hoped to obtain an office at court and wrote a hateful poem (surely the classiest form of slander) maligning not only Joseph but also his fellow Jews. The poem made little impression on the king, who trusted Joseph implicitly, but it created a sensation among the Berbers. A rumour spread to the effect that Joseph intended to kill Badis, deliver the realm into the hands of Al-Mutasim of Almería, with whom the king was at war, and then kill Al-Mutasim and seize the throne for himself. None of this was true and there is no evidence to support it, but it played into the anti-Semitic cliché of the scheming Jew.

On 30 December 1066, Muslim mobs stormed the royal palace where Joseph had sought refuge. They crucified him and a massacre of the Jewish community followed. According to later testimony, 'more than 1,500 householders' were killed. Of course, once the sectarian violence had ended, a productive and industrious element of the local population had been wiped out, and a poor king had lost his only useful courtier, leaving him even more vulnerable than before. Badis clung to power for another seven years before dying in 1073, when his grandson succeeded him.

The 1066 Granada Massacre benefitted no one and achieved nothing but mindless bloodshed.

Was Matilda of Scotland the First Scottish Ruler of England?

This title is deliberately provocative. Matilda (born Edith ... yes, another one) was the daughter of the Anglo-Saxon princess Margaret of Wessex and the Scottish king Malcolm III. She spent only a few years in Scotland, and most of her youth was lived in her mother's country of England.

Matilda was destined to remain a minor noble until King William II of England died in a 'hunting accident' (that's a whole other story) in 1100, and his brother Henry grabbed the throne to become Henry I. The new king needed a queen and fast, and he chose Matilda. Then, to secure his position, Henry's next job was to confront his other brother Robert on his way back from the First Crusade. This meant going to what was then the English-held territory of Normandy, so Henry needed a regent to run England in his absence. Matilda got the job.

Henry was away for quite some time, but as things turned out, the situation worked surprisingly well for the couple. Matilda did a fine job as regent and the militarily inexperienced Henry met the grizzled veteran Robert on the field of battle – and won an unlikely and emphatic victory at the Battle of Tinchebray in 1106. Robert was put under house arrest until he died of old age, and Henry's position as both King of England and Duke of Normandy was sealed ... which was great, except that now he had to spend time hopping back and forth across the English Channel to deal with one thing or another. As Matilda had been so successful the first time around, whenever her husband was away she ruled in all but name and left many surviving charters with her signature.

Matilda led a literary and musical court that enabled the arts and showed a level of sophistication not always associated with queens. She was also pious and embarked on significant building projects for the Church. Her interests paint one of the earliest portraits of a powerful woman in a male-dominated time. She courted little controversy, but

her daughter (also called Matilda), Henry's official heir to
the throne, would cause anger and division. The aristocracy
in general and the barons in particular couldn't stand the
idea of a female heir, to the point where young Matilda was
forced to give way to her cousin Stephen, which resulted in a
twenty-year civil war.

The original Matilda undeniably ruled England, but she
did so as regent. When she died in 1118, Henry seemed to
be genuinely bereaved because he showed no inclination to
remarry – not until the death of his son in 1120, after which
he had no male heir, only Matilda. Under the circumstances,
he felt obliged to marry again, and in an attempt to deliver
the male heir required by the barons, he married Adeliza of
Louvain in 1121, but they were to have no children.

Henry died in 1135 in an ignominious fashion. He loved
eating lamprey eels even though he knew that they made him
constipated. He regularly ignored the advice of his doctors
and after one particularly large meal of his favourite dish
became, ahem, constipated. The doctors gave him a powerful
laxative and … well, there's no pleasant way to put this … he
defecated to death.

Bread Is Important

Bread has been around for thousands of years. In fact, the first
evidence of bread dates back to the end of the Palaeolithic
Age, approximately 30,000 years ago. The first bread had
no yeast, so it was unleavened, like flatbread or pitta. It does
sometimes contain naturally occurring yeast spores, which is
why it fluffs up a little, regardless of whether yeast is added.

It wasn't until around 300 BC that yeast was introduced to produce deliberately leavened bread that would rise to resemble the loaves we know today.

Bread has been a food staple across the globe for millennia and has always played an important part in culinary cultures. Bakers caught selling deliberately small loaves could be severely punished, and the Romans used it as a distraction from politics. The slogan 'bread and circuses' summarised their use of food and entertainment to divert attention from the harsh realities of everyday life. There is also the term 'breadwinner', meaning the person in the family group who earns enough to meet the material needs of the family.

Henry III isn't that well remembered, and yet he was the king who ratified Magna Carta after his father, King John, died, and he went on to rule for around fifty years. During his reign, there was the somewhat forgettable Assize of Bread and Ale of 1266, which set the price of ale and the weight for a farthing loaf of bread. The price of a loaf never changed but its weight fluctuated with the price of wheat. Later, the law established the only acceptable weights for the sale of bread in England. 'So what?' I hear you ask. What relevance has that to the breads on sale today? When was this medieval law repealed? The answer is not until 2008! Yes, that's right, 2008. Up until then, bakers could sell loaves only in the specified weights established in medieval law. Once this nearly 750-year-old law was repealed, they were free to make their loaves in any weight.

The importance of bread and the regulations around it can be seen in this one simple English law – a law, by the way, which lasted longer than the much more famous Magna Carta.

The Crusades Were an Era of Innovation

The crusades between Christians and Muslims in the Middle East were a time of extreme violence on both sides. The massacres of the multi-ethnic populations of Jerusalem by the First Crusade in 1099 were mirrored in 1268 when Baibars massacred the population of the great city of Antioch. The violence is undeniable, but it was not the only interaction that happened between these two major spheres of influence, and the closer we look at the day-to-day, the harder it is to see a genuine 'clash of civilisations'.

There is a proviso: there was definitely more information and innovation travelling from east to west than the other way around. However, there are some fascinating grey areas. Take for example classic philosophy: even though the likes of Socrates and Plato had been dead for about 1,500 years, they are part of this story.

By the crusading era, innovative thought from ancient Greece had long since spread throughout the known world, and many of the texts of the great philosophers had been translated into multiple languages over the centuries. The Muslims in particular devoured their teachings. Epicentres of learning in Cairo and Baghdad had huge libraries which included translated works by these great thinkers.

The source of these texts was, of course, Western, but after the collapse of the Roman Empire in the West, some of these texts were lost or forgotten. It wasn't that the new countries evolving in the early medieval world were barbaric, it's just that they had their own cultures and did things differently. As such, it was the Arabic editions of these ancient Greek ideas that enabled the great works to be translated back into Greek and Latin by a new generation of Western scholars.

The concepts original to classical philosophy were now widely accepted even by the Church, a point that can be illustrated by two examples from Renaissance Italy. First up is Dante's *Divine Comedy* and its nine circles of hell as described in the first part, the *Inferno*. The outermost circle is the least cruel and is reserved for the nobles as well as the souls of unbaptised infants and virtuous non-Christians. Among the virtuous pagans were the ancient Greek philosophers. Because they were born before Jesus, they couldn't be in heaven, but it was clear that men like Ptolemy or Aristotle were in no way evil.

It was Ptolemy who stated that the earth is in the centre of the solar system and all other planets (and the sun) go around it. Copernicus and Galileo, two Western Christians who had come to their conclusions through observation rather than received wisdom, faced the wrath of the Church because it backed Ptolemy, a pagan. This highlights the continued influence these translated sources, which had been preserved in the Middle East, had and continued to have on Western thinking and science – for better or worse.

It does, however, get stranger, particularly in the realm of mathematics. While our alphabet and much of our Western languages are based on Latin, our numbering system is not. For example, the Roman numeral for four is IV, literally meaning 'one before five'. Similarly, thirteen is XIII, which literally means 'ten and one and one and one'. This is an inefficient way to deal with mathematics. Instead, our numbers today are based on the much more sensible and efficient Arabic system. With the introduction of Arabic numerals into Europe, it became possible for mathematicians to do far more complex calculations, and numbers were much easier to express. For example, 1,973 rather than MCMLXXIII.

But we are not quite there yet when it comes to numbers. What's the Roman numeral for zero? The answer is they didn't have one. The zero was invented in India and came to Europe via Arab scholars during the Middle Ages. It is called *zephyr* in Arabic, which is where we get the words zero and cypher.

To this day we have a weird relationship with the humble 0. The Church did not embrace this new number because it was nothing … a void. And what lives in the void? The devil! Yes, zero was considered to be evil by the Church, and there was an attempt to suppress its use. How does this manifest itself in your life right now? 0 comes *after* 9 on the keyboard and not before 1, which is where it should be. It's a big button at the bottom of a calculator/phone pad. Further, it has many names: three is just three, that's it. But zero can be called (depending on context) nought, oh, nothing, nil and love, to name just a few.

There is one final implication: the number before 1 is 0 and the number before 0 is -1. Why is that important? Because what year was Jesus born? You can't have the Son of God born in the evil year of 0 (besides which, 0 was unknown in the West when the calendar was first created); consequently, he's born in the year AD 1. The year before that is 1 BC, so the year 0 is missing. The result is that whatever year you are reading this, that year is in error and one year should be deducted for accuracy.

A number of scientific concepts are also Arabic and made their way to the West during this era. Most scientific words that start with 'al' are of Arabic origin, so alkaline and algebra, and, slightly surprisingly, alcohol. These are echoes of medieval Islamic names and are a permanent reminder of the transfer of ideas that went on in the background even as Christians and Muslims clashed over territory.

A more ephemeral sharing of culture is food. Chronicles from crusaders arriving in the Middle East marvelled at the diversity of fruits and spices readily available in the Outremer, which led to many of these travelling west. Two fruits that were especially popular among European aristocracy were lemons and pomegranates. Indeed, it's from this point onwards that images of the Virgin Mary show her holding a pomegranate, a fruit with many seeds, a sign of fertility. The association of Mary with this fruit didn't exist before the crusading era.

Then there was sugar. Before the slave plantations of sugar cane in the Caribbean, sugar was both rare and expensive. From the eleventh century to the end of the thirteenth century, virtually all sugar in Europe came from the East. However, once the great trading power of Acre fell in 1291, the consumption of sugar also fell. Genoa and Venice still had trading connections, but as people were now less exposed to Middle Eastern tastes, it seems demand also waned.

But one spice did linger on in the collective culinary memory and that was pepper. It spread originally throughout the Roman Empire, but after its collapse in the West, we seem to have lost our taste for it. However, the spice was a staple in the Middle East and was reintroduced to Europe as a Middle Eastern culinary innovation during the era of the Crusades and continued to be popular in Europe on into the fourteenth and fifteenth centuries – and beyond. Once it returned it seems that the populations of Europe never wanted to let go.

Given the nature of the crusading era, perhaps the most obvious innovation was in the conduct of war. One thing the West was able to teach the East was the art of siege warfare. The giant wooden siege tower was key to the crusaders winning back cities like Acre in 1191. These towers had existed previously during the Roman era but were not a weapon of war the Muslim powers knew about. However, the East would become siege masters thanks to the fact that, as some have argued, the story of the Crusades in the Middle East is fundamentally a story of siege warfare.

The Europeans happily took innovations from the East and applied them in the West. An example is the Tower of London. Its three lines of defence are separated by roughly 100 years (with later alterations and additions). The central White Tower was built just before William the Conqueror died and is, in effect, a fossilised wooden motte-and-bailey design. In other words, it is a classic stone keep. It was cutting edge for the 1080s but simply not fit for purpose 100 years later. So, the next curtain wall was built in the 1180s/90s, under the instructions of Richard I, the English king most often linked to the Crusades. This is a much more complex form of defence, with an octagonal tower and a curtain wall to give depth in protection. By now it was understood that the most vulnerable shape of a tower was a square or rectangle because undermining or barraging just one corner could bring down the whole tower.

So, within the Tower of London, we see the evolution of defensive towers: the central White Tower is rectangular, but the new octagonal tower, with more walls, makes the tower harder to destroy. Not only that, but the actual construction of the walls is different, with greater use of medieval concrete and stone-capped walls rather than the more basic use of simple stone blocks. These are building innovations that came from the Middle East.

Finally, the outer curtain wall of the Tower of London was built in the 1280s by Edward I, who went on Crusade and was nearly killed by an assassin. His more recent design is something far more concentric, with semicircular towers protruding from a wall that is lower than Richard's to allow a clear field of fire for anyone foolish enough to try a frontal attack. Edward is the one whose name is synonymous with cutting-edge castles in Wales, all of which were the greatest castles of their time and used techniques that had been refined in the Middle East. It can be argued that Edward's crowning achievement was Caernarfon Castle in north-west Wales. It has many tricks up its sleeves, but what it doesn't have is a single rectangular tower because those were now obsolete. Many of its walls have bands of different-coloured stones, similar to the patterned walls of Constantinople, which at that time had withstood all onslaughts for about 800 years and which Edward would have seen on his journey east.

What many consider to be the ultimate medieval castle is Crac des Chevaliers (rock of the knights) in modern-day Syria. This castle in the Middle East was a bastion of Christian strength and one of the key fortifications of the Hospitallers military order. Some of its walls are 70 feet thick and, unusually for a castle (rather than a town), it could house a garrison of 2,000. Muslim powers tried several times to take it, but it was so well defended that too many resources were needed to take it on. That all changed under the bloody rule of the Mameluke ruler Baibars, who in 1271 brought a vast army to the castle.

Rather than being able to breach the inner walls to capture the castle, it took a two-month siege and a surrender of the garrison before Baibars could claim victory. While this brutal ruler massacred the population of Acre in 1268, he allowed the defenders of Crac des Chevaliers to leave in peace. It had been a hard fight.

Crac des Chevaliers is such a formidable fortification that even as it turned into a ruin it was used by Arab rebels during the First World War (Lawrence of Arabia wrote about it during that time). More recently, it has been used by several sides during the Syrian war in the twenty-first century – a testament to the strength of its walls and its strategic placement.

All of this shows that when East and West work together greatness can be achieved. Unfortunately, some of the greatest innovations of the crusading era were those of war, but there were certainly more peaceful and productive interactions too. There is, however, one final innovation that headed west, one that goes much unheralded but to any gardener or manual labourer is greatly appreciated: the wheelbarrow. Yes, it may sound strange, but the wheelbarrow had to come from somewhere and, while it looks quite at home in an allotment in Surrey, its ancestry is from another continent. This simple yet strangely elegant tool has helped in the construction of all major building projects in the West from the twelfth century right up to the modern age. There are, as we have seen, worse legacies.

The Greatest Knight

William Marshall did not come from a great aristocratic house. His family was only just noble enough to allow William to have the right to learn the martial skills to become a knight. As a young knight Marshall first served King Henry II. Little did anyone know that he would be around to serve the king's grandson and defend a total of four English kings, one of whom he had fought and beaten earlier in his career.

Every country has its amazing warriors. What's unusual about England is that it fails to remember almost any of them, instead opting for the legends of Robin Hood and King Arthur. William Marshall's story is the kind that not only matches these legends but beats them into bloody submission – and his story is true.

As the younger of two sons in the family, William could not expect to inherit his father's lands, so he opted to learn martial skills and was knighted in 1166. Within two years he had become the scourge of tournaments both in England and France. These were little more than staged battles in which dozens of knights competed for the amusement of the crowds. It was excellent training in the art of war, and it was a thrilling spectator event, but there was another reason to take part: if you could defeat and capture a rich noble in the course of the tournament, you could demand a sizeable ransom. That's exactly what Marshall did – over and over again, until he became rich. This warrior did not become wealthy through inheritance or conquest, but through kidnapping (albeit, an acceptable version as set out in tournament rules). How good was he? On his deathbed, he recalled besting 500 knights during his career.

Eventually, in the mid-1180s, Marshall caught the eye of Henry II and received 'royal favour', which meant he had the support and backing of the king. A few years later and Marshall was fighting for Henry against his son, Richard the Lionheart. Richard is perhaps the most famous real warrior in English history. He was a lousy king but his reputation as a fearsome warrior was well deserved. It is, therefore, telling that when William and Richard met in a skirmish when Richard was in his prime, William Marshall is the only man to have unhorsed the most famous warrior king in English history. That's how tough and skilled William was.

It may sound odd but when Henry II died, William had no problem switching his allegiance to Richard; his loyalty was always to the Crown, not the man. When Richard rode off on the Third Crusade, he left Marshall in England to defend his authority.

When Richard died in 1199, William continued to be a key player to the monarchy, this time in the service of King John. When John died at a feast, everyone saw William Marshall as a safe pair of hands to protect the new nine-year-old King Henry III. By now the role was largely a symbolic one, but it still indicates the esteem in which this decades-long loyal servant was held.

On his deathbed, William Marshall had one last wish: to be invested as a Knight Templar. His many years of service to the English Crown meant that he had failed to achieve one knightly duty – to go on crusade. His wish was granted and he is buried in the Temple Church in London. The church survived the Reformation and the Dissolution of the Monasteries, and the tomb was only slightly damaged during the Blitz in 1940. It remains today, a little battle-scarred but a fitting place of rest for an unsung hero.

The Legendary (but Real) Female Samurai

Samurai is a male-only title, so technically, this is the story of an *onna-bugeisha*, Japanese for 'female warrior'. The woman's name is Tomoe Gozen, and apart from her amazing martial record, not much is known about her. She first appears as an already established warrior of the Minamoto clan in the late 1100s in feudal Japan.

At this time the Minamoto clan was tearing itself to pieces in its own vicious civil war, and it is in this context that she is recorded as having beheaded her opponents in two separate combats, showing lethal skill in swordsmanship. Female warriors weren't unheard of but they were usually archers or fought with a specific type of spear. To be so up close and personal with a male samurai within arm's length was truly unusual.

Tomoe Gozen was there when her master Minamoto no Yoshinaka made his last stand. As the enemy began to surround them, he told her to flee because he wanted to die with his foster brother, adding that he would be ashamed to die with a woman. As an obedient servant of the clan, she followed his order, but this was no sign of cowardice. While everyone rated her martial abilities, there was just no breaking down the patriarchal culture of the time.

Gozen evaded capture at the battle, but she was chased by Hatakeyama Shigetada, another feared warrior who was allegedly blessed by a goddess. Despite his supernatural blessings, Tomoe slipped from his grasp. All this did was enhance Tomoe's already fierce reputation. As well as her proven prowess with a sword, it seems Gozen was even more deadly with a bow. There's a description of her in a roughly contemporary account: Tomoe was especially beautiful, with white skin, long hair, and charming features.

The above account goes on to describe Gozen as being so fearless she would have happily fought and beaten demons.

Nobody knows her fate. Did she die in another battle? Did she settle down and start a family? The unknowable only adds to the mystique around her, so it's unsurprising that a cottage industry of fictional stories has grown up around her. However, beyond the shores of Japan, she is almost completely unknown.

What Is an Exchequer?

Residents of Britain are familiar with the title Chancellor of the Exchequer; it's, y'know, the person in charge of all the money. But the term 'exchequer' pre-dates Parliament and even British democracy. The original exchequer was a Norman invention. We get all the early information from a twelfth-century manuscript called the *Dialogus de Scaccario*, which was a treatise on the practice of the English Exchequer. The original exchequer wasn't a group of men or a collection of laws; it was an actual physical thing. A table, to be precise.

Present-day use of the term came from a table used to calculate taxes in the medieval period. The table was large, 10 feet by 5 feet, with a raised edge about four fingers high on all sides to ensure that nothing fell off when the counters were used to represent various values. The term exchequer referred to the resemblance of the table to a chess board (called an *échiquier* in French, which was widely spoken at the time) as it was covered by a black cloth bearing green stripes about the width of a human hand, in a chequered pattern. The spaces represented pounds, shillings and pence. It was, in essence, the Anglo-Norman equivalent of an abacus or calculator.

The term exchequer later referred to the twice-yearly meetings held at Easter and Michaelmas during which government financial business was transacted and an audit held of sheriffs' returns. Taking away all the jargon, this was the time to add up the tax revenues and determine whether the projections matched what was in the treasury. Any shortfall might be an indication of 'misappropriation' by a crooked local representative ... in which case, time to dig out the thumbscrews and sharpen the executioner's axe.

Because the term had become so closely associated with reviewing government finances, it continued in use through the Age of Enlightenment and on into the Industrial Age. And it's still here nearly 1,000 years later. I find that reassuring.

The Story of Countess Isabella de Fortibus

To the extent that history records anything about women, it's certainly true the records show that women did not have an easy time of things. In the thirteenth century, a woman was little more than the property of her husband, so it's unsurprising that the aristocratic Isabella (born in 1237), daughter of the Earl of Devon, was married off at the ripe old age of eleven or twelve to seal an alliance between two families. Over the next dozen or so years she had six children with her husband, William de Fortibus, Earl of Aumale. So far so normal for feudal Europe, and to be fair, the age at which she married was not unusual for the time. At least she had married well. William was extremely wealthy, with many estates throughout England. However, he died when Isabella was just twenty-three, so now, at this tender age, she was a widow with six children.

As the head of a household with no husband or owner of all these lands, it was expected that Isabella would remarry (although it was not legally necessary). She was wooed by many other aristocrats of the age, including Simon de Montfort, the man who would rise up and lead a rebellion against Henry III. Later still, Henry III tried to get his son Edmund married to her; instead, Isabella got Edmund to marry her daughter, who was ten years old at the time.

However, it was Henry's eldest son who was to become Isabella's biggest threat. Edward I was not known for his patience, and he showed the same force of will when it came to the extensive de Fortibus lands. The new King of England used his considerable resources in the English courts to try and create a legal argument as to why he should have her properties.

Let's pause for a moment. The reputation of medieval kings is that they did what they wanted to do, that they were above the law, but any close inspection of contemporary events shows that the masses always had an issue with a leader who flagrantly disregarded the law. Compared to modern legal systems, the law courts then were still evolving, particularly when it came to the rich and powerful. But the elites didn't always win in court, and if rulers were seen to be too biased or arbitrary in the dispensation of justice, they knew that rebellion or civil war could erupt. Saying all that, a widow versus the king was a huge mountain to climb in terms of contemporary cultural expectations.

While the de Fortibus estates in the north of England were awarded to the Crown, lands in the south (including Carisbrooke Castle on the Isle of Wight) remained in Isabella's hands until she died at the age of fifty-six in 1293. So while this was not exactly a case of a poor widow versus the king, it was a widow who faced one of the most feared rulers in medieval history and prevented him from bullying her into submission.

The Temple of Kukulkan

El Castillo ('the castle') is the Spanish name for the world-famous Mayan pyramid (except it's not a pyramid) referred to as Chichen Itza ... except that's the name of the city it's in, not the stepped temple itself. So, let's call it by its most accurate name: the Temple of Kukulkan. Built between the ninth and twelfth centuries AD, the temple is one of the most famous monuments in the Americas and is about 1,000 years old. It is part of the urban complex of Chichen Itza, which at its peak was about 1.9 square miles in size, with a population rivalling or exceeding London's in the Middle Ages.

The Temple of Kukulkan is not only a temple but a giant three-dimensional calendar as well. Each slope has ninety-one steps, with a final step up to the flat site at the top – that's 365 steps, one for each day of the year. Furthermore, the north-east and south-west corners are together aligned to the rising and setting of the sun on each of the two days of the two solar solstices, so marking the passage of the solar year.

The structure is in no way a fortification, so while the castle name is inappropriate, it reflects the fact that the conquistadors had nothing in their vocabulary and no point of reference for such a building, alien as it was to what they understood to be places of worship. To those who theorise that the temple (and others in the region that are similar) is a pyramid built by the Egyptians (or the lost civilisation of Atlantis – or aliens), well, there are too many inexplicable differences between the pyramids in Mexico and those in Egypt. First of all, the

Mexican temple is not a true pyramid; it has a square base, with smaller and smaller platforms added as it rises from the ground. The great pyramids of Giza were built about 3,000 years earlier; all had smooth sides and were built on a much grander scale. While there are stepped pyramids nearby, these are even earlier, so the evolution of the pyramid design shows that Egyptian architects gave up on this type of building in favour of smooth sides. Had they built the Mexican temples, they would not have used a design that had been abandoned millennia earlier.

Further, their purposes are completely different. In Egypt, pyramids are mausoleums, tombs for the dead. In Mexico, they are temples for the living, places where people congregate to worship; their use was similar to that of a church rather than a mausoleum. So, no aliens or lost civilisations are necessary to explain their construction.

Many visitors do not realise that the Kukulkan temple is built on top of another temple, with a gap between the two sets of stonework. I've been lucky enough to crawl into the cramped area between the two and ascend the 45 per cent slope up to the top where there is still a red jaguar statue with seventy-four jade inlays for its spots, jade crescents for its eyes and white flint for teeth and fangs. When it was originally discovered, the remains of human sacrifices were still lying around it.

Another interesting feature of this unique place of worship is that the angles of the Kukulkan temple's build and its decorative carvings produce a strange sound. In the right position, the echo from a handclap sounds not like a clap, but like the twang of a guitar string. No one today knows if this was deliberate. Also, at certain times of the year, shadows on the stonework look like the undulating coils of a snake. This would seem to be yet more artistry linked to the passing of the seasons, but it also connects the building to its dedicated deity. Kukulkan means 'feathered serpent' and is closely associated with the deity Quetzalcoatl of Aztec mythology. This is the most important god in terms of the development of the Yucatan peninsula because it was the first to be widely worshipped and helped to bind together territories with different languages and/or identities. The worship of a universally revered god (there were many more) provided a common cultural reference.

Finally, the epic photographs of the temple do not convey that it has been only partially rebuilt. Photos are always taken on the reconstructed sides so that we get an impression of the temple in all its glory. It is, deservedly, a UNESCO World Heritage Site.

Forgotten Emotions

Our human emotional history is fascinating but difficult to research; while the ancient chroniclers record what happened in our past, they rarely report how people were feeling. However, we know that emotions are both universal and timeless; they do not disappear. Fear is fear and we've been getting scared since we were hominids. Humans today experience the same huge range of emotions that would have been familiar to our ancestors no matter how far back we go. What's different is that some of the things we felt in the past are no longer identified in the same way. As our understanding has grown, old labels have disappeared, making it seem as if those emotions have been forgotten. They haven't; they've just found new labels.

Melancholy is an example of a term that is rarely used today. The feeling is now better understood and is called depression. Similarly, there's the term 'shell-shock', an emotive reaction that was only recognised in First World War. There can be no doubt that people have always experienced this, but the idea that terrifying and/or traumatic events can cause anxiety and mental impairment after the events are over has been updated to become PTSD, post-traumatic stress disorder.

And then there are the very recently invented terms to describe more transitory feelings such as 'hangry' (angry because you're hungry). Feeling hangry is a real thing because 80 per cent of the body's serotonin (one of the happiness chemicals) is made in the gut, so lack of food means lack of serotonin means lack of patience, which can result in anger ... or, at least, irritability. So, although the term is new, people in the past certainly suffered from it. I'm looking at you, Henry VIII.

But then we come to 'acedia'. What's that? According to the Christian Church, it's a state of restlessness and the inability to work or pray. Acedia was the feeling of lethargy about religious duties and the resulting feeling of guilt this created. Some saw it as the precursor to sloth, one of the seven deadly sins, and it was a genuine cause of concern for monks and nuns in the Middle Ages. Contrary to popular belief not everybody in this era was fervently religious, but a lack of desire to carry out the Lord's work created genuine anxiety in the religious orders, where, let's be frank, devotion was pretty central to the job description.

It would be a fair generalisation to say that people who join the clergy and/or religious orders today do so because of deeply held beliefs. But five hundred years ago it was one of the few options open to a nobleman's third son, who was surplus to requirements when it came to inheritance. Absence of opportunity was probably not the best motivation for doing the Lord's work. Although acedia as a term has passed out of usage, lack of motivation to tackle a job is still around – but it's probably best not to use it as an excuse when you call in sick.

The Italian Joan of Arc

Joan of Arc is often portrayed as unique in medieval Europe. While it is true that others were not burnt at the stake, a number of very religious women claimed to have had religious visions and conversations with God/Jesus/Mary. Catherine of Siena is an example and one that is more famous in Italy than Joan.

Catherine was born in 1347 (in Siena … obviously), one of twins; the other twin died shortly after birth. Catherine was apparently a happy young girl, but around the age of six, she had a vision of Christ, seated in glory with the Apostles Peter, Paul and John. So, at age seven, Catherine vowed to give her whole life to God. If a six-year-old made a similar declaration today, the whole thing would probably be dismissed. At a time when people had a palpable sense of the divine intermingling with our earthly world, however, such visions and interactions were taken seriously.

As a sign of her devotion, Catherine put herself through many trials and fasted when, as a teenager, she disagreed with family decisions. She especially disappointed her mother by cutting off her beautiful long hair as a protest against being encouraged to improve her appearance to attract a husband.

When she wanted to join a convent, her family refused, so, at significant cost and without anyone's permission, she gave away clothing and food, while always refusing anything for herself. (Some might see her behaviours as those typical of rebellious teenagers today ... in which case, they could be in line for sainthood. Just a thought.)

Her family approved of her faith but despaired at the extremes of her actions and beliefs. By staying with her family, she could live out her rejection of them more vividly. She did not want their food and referred instead to the table laid for her in Heaven with her 'real' family. Like Joan, we see a very young woman whose faith was absolute, someone who believed she had been born for a higher purpose. Both women frustrated the establishment, and while Joan ultimately took up arms, which Catherine did not, both had a similar zeal and believed that they were on a holy mission.

Things turned very weird when she was twenty-one, and she described in her letters a 'mystical marriage' with Jesus. Her wedding ring was made from ... er ... his foreskin (which would have been the only physical remains He could have left on earth). The ring was invisible and only true believers could see it (the emperor's new clothes, anyone?). Less weirdly, she began helping the sick and the poor and took care of them in hospitals or homes. Her early pious activities in Siena attracted a group of followers, both women and men, who gathered around her in pious belief.

Her fame led to her involvement in the heady brew of politics and religion so prevalent in medieval Europe. She swayed some anti-papal groups to join with Rome and even preached a new crusade against the infidel, showing that her religious views were very much a reflection of the age.

While she was widely adored across the political spectrum, she regularly picked sides consistent with the teachings of the Church. Her work was believed to be blessed by God, and she received the stigmata, wounds on her hands matching those of Jesus on the cross. These were visible, at Catherine's request, only to herself.

She founded a monastery and survived an assassination attempt carried out not by unbelievers but by groups who felt her preaching was dangerous to their power bases – a reminder that politics and religion, particularly in Italian history, are closely intertwined. She continued to put herself through the physical trials of fasting, which undermined her health and took a toll on her body. In Rome in April of 1380, Catherine suffered a severe stroke which paralyzed her from the waist down. Eight days later, she died. She was thirty-three – the age at which many believed Jesus to have been crucified. Her last words were, 'Father, into Your Hands I commend my soul and my spirit.'

Catherine of Siena was canonized in 1461.

An Ottoman Legend

According to legend, Ottoman sultan Mehmed II asked the Byzantine emperor for some land to build a castle. Like most legends, no date is associated with this story, nor is the name of the emperor ever mentioned.

The emperor responded by throwing the sultan an animal hide and said, 'You can have as much land as this covers.' The Byzantine courtiers had a good laugh at Mehmed II's expense. But the sultan thanked him for such a generous gift and left. When he arrived at the site he had in mind, he ordered the hide to be cut into fine leather string and, using this, he marked out the boundaries of the space needed for his new fort.

This never happened. Mehmed II did not seek permission from the terminally ill and terminally shrinking Byzantine Empire for anything. The Ottoman Empire was on the rise and by the time of Mehmed II, the so-called Byzantine Empire was little more than the greatly reduced city of Constantinople, much of which had fallen into disrepair, with fields of crops being grown inside the city walls. Mehmed built his fort precisely where he planned and nobody had the power to stop him. Byzantine Emperor Constantine XI knew exactly what Mehmed intended and the threat this posed to his city, but all he could do was lodge his protests, which fell on deaf ears.

While the story of the cowhide is not true, Mehmed's fort is real. Rumeli Hisar (Rumeli Castle) was built on the European side of the Bosphorus, directly across from Anadoluhisar (Anatolia Castle, built earlier by Sultan Bayezid I) on the Asian side at the strait's narrowest point. It seems that on some level, the Ottomans had long understood that Constantinople could not be defeated unless they had control of the waterways, particularly the Bosphorus.

But Mehmed's fort had the second, more sinister name of Boğazkesen, which is a pun in Turkish. The fort was built on the shores of the Bosphorus strait, known as the *boğaz* or 'throat' in Turkish. *Kesen* means 'cutter' ... so the castle was called the 'throat cutter' because it could fire its cannons across the Bosphorus, in effect 'cutting' the strait. It's a pun because the term also indicated what the fort was going to do to Byzantine trade when the Ottomans controlled the Bosphorus with a fort on each side. Venetian traders who refused to side with the Ottomans were the first to feel its wrath when their ships were sunk by cannon fire from the Boğazkesen fort. The reality was that Constantinople was a trading hub whose trade was now controlled from outside its walls by the Ottomans.

It is unsurprising that it was Mehmed II who, in 1453, successfully besieged and captured the city.

A Really Bad Year for Genoa

If you know anything about the Battle of Crecy in 1346, you know it was a decisive victory for Edward III, King of England, against the French. However, the first casualties of the battle were Italian. To summarise, Crecy was one of the first medieval battles in western Europe in which one side was highly effective at killing from a distance. While it was not the first battle to see the use of the longbow, it was the first on the continent to see it used *en masse*. If that was not enough, Edward also brought the first cannons to be used in battle in western Europe, although they were bell-shaped and fired really big arrows rather than cannonballs.

The longbow's main drawback was that it took years to develop the strength and skill required to draw it to its full penetrating power – as well as to aim it, of course. Apart from that, it was, in every way, better than the crossbow. Its range was longer and, most critically, a proficient archer could loose about twenty arrows in a minute, whereas a crossbowman could manage two at best, not to mention that he was also more vulnerable. As they cranked the crossbow's string back, crossbowmen were forced to stoop over, so they wore protective shields strapped to their backs.

Genoa was famous for its mercenaries, so King Philip VI of France hired thousands of Genoese crossbowmen to serve with him in his battle against Edward, specifically at Crecy. Philip was aware that Edward had longbowmen (but not the cannons; they would come as a nasty surprise later in the battle) and sought to neutralise them with the finest crossbowmen in all of Europe.

However, the Genoese crossbowmen were rushed to the front of the army without their pavises, the special shields strapped to their backs to protect them as they reloaded. To send them into battle without them guaranteed a massacre and meant that the Genoese mercenaries were effectively dead men as soon as they loosed their first volley. It took only a few minutes of slaughter before the Genoese broke and ran back towards the main French army, desperate as they were to escape the rain of death being launched, volley after volley, by the English (and Welsh) longbowmen. The French knights, disgusted by the perceived 'cowardice' of the Genoese, began charging through the retreating men, killing even more.

Of course, those French knights were to face exactly the same problem, and while Philip had the better-equipped and larger army, Edward had created a kill zone with his archers. And the rest, as they say, is history.

But this wasn't the only terrible thing that happened to Genoa in 1346. While the city-state was well known for its mercenary forces, they were a secondary revenue earner compared to Genoa's importance as a trading hub. The military forces grew out of the need to protect the flow of goods that had made it a major trading power by the 1300s. By then it had fought multiple wars against Venice to secure trade routes to the East. A giant leap across the continent of Europe to the Crimean

Peninsula brings us the location of Genoa's jealously guarded trading post at Caffa. This was Genoa's link to the Silk Road and the Mongol Empire. In 1346, Caffa was besieged by the Mongol leader of the Golden Horde, Jani Beg. This was bad enough, but things got a lot worse. Jani Beg's men started dying from a strange and virulent illness. The mortality rate was so high that he knew he would have to break the siege. Apparently in his frustration over this, he ordered some of the corpses of the infected men to be fired from catapults into the city of Caffa.

Imagine for a moment what that must have been like as the wet sound of splattering corpses landed on the tiled roofs and cobbled streets, the bodies rupturing and spraying the nearby area with blood and entrails, all of them containing lethal and highly contagious pathogens.

Jani Beg failed to capture the city, but that was not enough to stop some of the population from leaving, partly because it was included in the Genoese trade hub but, perhaps more pressingly, because of the fear of infection. So, if Caffa didn't fall to the Mongols, why was the city a second reason for 1346 being a bad year for Genoa? The answer is that the name of the disease that was wiping out Jani Beg's army was the Black Death. And it was the Genoese merchants fleeing Caffa who brought this pestilence into Europe, where it swept through the continent over the next few years, killing between a third and half of Europe's population.

Humans are skilled and resourceful when it comes to attacking fellow humans, but the Black Death and related plagues prove that nature can kill humans far more effectively. That the Genoese were responsible for introducing it to Europe makes 1346 the worst year in Genoese history.

The Real Braveheart

If there's one name that symbolises effective Scottish resistance against the English, it has to be Andrew Moray. You've never heard of him? Then read on.

William Wallace (aka 'Braveheart') is a classic example of the danger of mixing history and legend. What happened and what has been enhanced to make an even better story are two different things. Almost everything we know about William Wallace, a real man, comes from the extremely reputable-sounding source known as Blind Harry, a minstrel who lived nearly 200 years after the events he describes.

Contemporary sources about Wallace are sparse, to say the least. In his twenties, he may have been a soldier in the army of Edward I, and he seems to have been reprimanded for theft when he went off carousing with an English soldier. Hard evidence is thin on the ground. The reality is that Wallace seems to have been the junior partner to the resistance leader Andrew Moray, who had already been fighting against the English before the Battle of Sterling and had won considerable parts of southern Scotland for King John Balliol.

In the 1290s, Scotland was just as feudal as England or France, and as Moray was higher up the hierarchy of families and titles than Wallace, it would have been very odd for Wallace to have been the leader of the resistance. So why is Moray forgotten and Wallace gets a monument, a film and a cottage industry around his legend? The reason is simple: Moray died at the Battle of Stirling Bridge in 1297, the scene of, ahem, Wallace's greatest victory. It was a battle of tactical genius. The English were heading to Stirling Castle and would have to cross the very narrow Stirling Bridge. The English army was far larger than the Scottish, so a head-on fight would have meant certain defeat. Moray's strategy allowed a portion of the English army to cross the bridge while the majority were waiting for their turn, so the army was out of formation when the Scots ambushed it on the bridge. The smaller English force fled the slaughter right into the river where hundreds drowned. Because of the narrowness of the bridge, reinforcements could not move forward, so in this situation, the Scots had the superior force and the English were easily beaten. It was exactly the right ambush in the perfect location and was an emphatic victory for Scotland.

The losses on the Scottish side were light compared to the heavy damage inflicted on the English. Moray's death indicates he was in the vanguard of the Scottish attack – a brave move and the sign of a true warrior. However, with his death, somebody had to claim the victory, and it seems all eyes fell on Wallace.

While there were more variables at play in this story, it's important to say that the next battle between Wallace's army and the English led to a crushing defeat for the Scots. Could it be because the Scots missed their real, now dead, leader? The last bit is conjecture, but Scots who refer to glorious victories against the 'auld enemy' fail to give credit to the Scot who was more likely to be the bane of the English, falling for the stories of Blind Harry.

Arrows Were the Swiss Army Knives of the Middle Ages

An arrow is a pointy stick designed to be loosed from a bow. A Swiss army knife is a pocket knife on steroids. (Free fact:

the term 'Swiss army knife' was coined by American soldiers after the Second World War due to the difficulty they had in pronouncing *Offiziersmesser*, the German name.) A Swiss army knife would be no one's first choice as a weapon of war any more than someone would set off on a camping trip with an arrow in their pocket. So what do they have in common? Answer: versatility. Just as the knife is multi-functional, depending on which blade is used, the arrow is equally so, depending on the arrowhead.

It would be easy to underestimate the importance of arrows in medieval battles, but skilled archers could and did make all the difference to a battle's outcome. Of equal importance was the variety of arrowheads they used. When we see the term 'arrowhead' we tend to think of triangular-shaped arrow tips, but arrows were far more diverse in shape than that, particularly in medieval Europe.

For starters, that classic triangular arrowhead could be used in a battle against unarmoured enemies and became the main arrowhead for hunting animals. The wide end would have helped with accuracy and the sharp point would, of course, ensure penetration. It was designed to slide into the body like a dagger, so perfect for hunting boar or hitting poor, unarmoured peasants in battle. But the key word is 'unarmoured', and if there's one thing people know about battles in the Middle Ages it's that a lot of men were clad in some form of armour.

So, we come to the famous battles of Crecy and Agincourt, where archers were key and where the usual image of their arrows shows that triangular arrowhead. But the fact is that the arrowheads from these battles would have looked like long steel nails – no flanges, no detail, just a really long steel spike that could puncture the plate armour and the thick padding underneath to inflict a serious wound on a knight inside his many layers of protection.

But there are even more exotic examples. A very rare one is a relatively classical-looking arrowhead, but behind it is what looks something like a whisk with fingers of metal and a hollow centre. It stumped me when I first saw one until it was explained that the gap behind the head is where the archer would put a cloth drenched in oil and – voilà – you have one flaming arrow. Filmmakers love to use flaming arrows, but they were a rarity. It was much easier to take down a target with the penetrating power of a standard arrow than to attempt to burn people to death. It looks great in the cinema but serves very little purpose on the battlefield.

The way these fire arrows are depicted by filmmakers is that the archer wraps a cloth around the arrow and sets it alight. Two problems with this: one, it altered the arrow shaft, so the archer was far more likely to miss the intended target. Secondly, the cloth could fall off. But our ever-resourceful ancestors thought of all this and came up with an arrowhead that had a compartment for an oil-soaked cloth, which resolved the earlier problems.

There are also crescent-shaped arrowheads. It seems an odd shape for an arrow until you realise that arrows spin in flight, and one with a crescent shape would cause even more damage as it tore into the target. It's an unnecessary amount of trauma for a human but perfect for a horse, making it the perfect anti-cavalry weapon. While these rarely killed, they were guaranteed to maim, and if the horse became lame, it was likely to throw off the rider, who was usually an armoured knight. Discovery of a number of these when excavating a battlefield would mean that archers had been used to break up a cavalry formation.

With all of this in mind, an archer in a medieval battle would probably have had several kinds of arrows and would reach for the one appropriate to the situation. Edward III is on record as having ordered several million goose feathers for the arrows to be used in just one campaign. That's how important they were.

An Evil Knight

Joan of Arc was the epitome of saintliness and nobility, with God on her side, right? And we're all well aware of how that ended. However, despite her goodness and virtue, Joan kept some questionable company.

Step forward Gilles Baron de Rais, a lord and a knight of Brittany, Anjou and Poitou, a leader in the French army and, perhaps most interestingly, a companion-in-arms to young Joan, who was initially treated with suspicion. While she was later accepted by the dauphin, she did not earn everyone's approval. For Gilles to have been an early ally and to have remained loyal to her shows him to have been a surprisingly open-minded man for the fifteenth century. However, when he wasn't backing the Maid of Orleans and fighting to oust the English from his country, he was developing a reputation as someone not to be trusted around children. He was later convicted as a serial killer of children, crimes to which he confessed.

Long before he came to the attention of the authorities, it was rumoured that Gilles was into the occult and that he tried to summon demons. When he was finally arrested in 1440, he admitted to this under torture, but this was the era when they burnt Joan of Arc, a teenage girl, for the crime of dressing like a man and saying she could talk to God. So, how much of this so-called confession was valid is up for debate.

During his trial, Gilles confessed that he had begun killing children as part of black magic rituals which involved other forms of physical abuse, but let's not go into detail. The fact is that in 1437, the remains of forty naked bodies of children were discovered in Machecoul, a tiny village on the west coast of France that Gilles was known to visit. Instead of hard evidence, circumstantial evidence suggested that he was the guilty party even though it was not clear if he had killed all of them.

Gilles' murders came to light only because he was initially investigated on another charge. In May 1440, Gilles kidnapped a cleric during a dispute, and it was this act that prompted an investigation. It was then that local parents testified that it was Gilles who had also kidnapped their children. It was not unusual in this era for powerful men get away with all sorts of crimes, so if the law was intent on prosecution, his crimes were likely to have been so extreme that even the courts couldn't turn a blind eye to the evidence, and even by the dubious standards of medieval courts it seemed Gilles was guilty.

He and two accomplices were executed by hanging and burning on 26 October 1440. The best evidence of his guilt was that the abduction and killing of children stopped after this.

The Siege of Malaga in 1487 Is Not a Well-remembered Event

The siege of Malaga took place in Spain between the Christian north and the Muslim south of the Iberian Peninsula at the tail end of a centuries-long clash. This has incorrectly been remembered as the 'Reconquista', but let's be clear, it was no such thing. Barely a century after the collapse of the Western Roman Empire, Muslim powers swept into the Iberian Peninsula and settled there. So, by 1487, Malaga had been under Islamic rule for about 750 years. Christians from the north had never previously ruled this area.

Malaga was the second city in the Emirate of Granada. This rump of lands stretching across the southern coast of modern-day Spain was then all that remained of the Muslim territories on the peninsula. When Queen Isabella and King Ferdinand captured the city, their success confirmed the inexorable collapse of Islamic power in the region. Granada, the last Muslim city on the peninsula, would fall just five years later.

The siege of Malaga was a big deal at the time, but it was quickly forgotten by everyone apart from a few historians. However, this three-month siege left a memorable legacy: the first recorded use of something we would recognise as an ambulance service, when supply carts and wagons were used to transport wounded men away from the front lines. However, this was done only during lulls in battle, so men could lie bleeding for hours, if not days, before being moved. Also, and perhaps most importantly, the service missed one vital factor: medical aid. All the transport did was take men from the field of battle to the rear of the army ... where no medical care or doctors were available. Interestingly, it was the Muslim civilisations of this era and earlier that were often ahead of their Western counterparts, but on this occasion, it was the Christians who recognised a need to remove the wounded from further danger. While it can be argued that this was a rather unhelpful, half-baked idea, it laid the foundation for what was to come.

This seedling innovation was occasionally used again after 1487, but it would take more than 300 years for this initial foray into battlefield medicine to become something more comprehensive and practical. It wasn't until the Napoleonic era, when Dominique-Jean Larrey developed a medical assistance system for wounded French soldiers, that the rest of the concept took on a more recognisable form. Larrey was inspired by the speed at which the artillery could distribute teams of horses over the battlefield. He reinvented the carts and wagons used to transport the wounded and created swifter, more responsive vehicles. He also set up mobile hospitals at the rear and staffed them with doctors ready to tend to the wounded (as best they could in the eighteenth century).

Larrey's innovations were tested at the Battle of Metz in 1793, where he successfully demonstrated the value of field ambulances. A national competition to design the best type of vehicle followed. Napoleon always had a reputation for caring for his troops, and Larrey reinforced that reputation by establishing guidelines for the care and treatment of war casualties. These were revolutionary in prioritising patients by the seriousness of their wounds over their rank or other factors. As a true man of medicine, he was also the first to enshrine the treatment of captured enemy soldiers as standard practice.

It's with this French officer that the story of battlefield medicine really begins, but we shouldn't forget its humble start in medieval Malaga.

The Forgotten but Fabulously Wealthy Jakob Fugger

Jakob Fugger was a German Renaissance-era entrepreneur and banker whose name you are unlikely to know. What's that you say? Banking is boring? Okay, how about this: Fugger is probably the most obscure rich man in history. To give you an idea of his wealth, the richest person in the world as of writing is Elon Musk, the founder of Tesla. He's worth around $185 billion. Converting old revenues into modern equivalents is notoriously hard to do, but Jakob Fugger is estimated to have been worth (in modern money) about $277 billion. Musk has a lot of catching up to do!

As well as Elon, others in the top ten on the world's rich list include Bill Gates and Mark Zuckerberg, both innovators in new technology. Along with Musk, both Gates and Zuckerberg created new products and revenue streams. There is no medieval equivalent to Microsoft or Facebook, so just how innovative was it possible to be in the fifteenth century?

Jakob Fugger was born into a prominent merchant and banking family in Augsburg, Bavaria, in 1459. The family was wealthy but hardly the dominant economic force on the continent ... yet. Jakob was the third of seven sons and while he could expect to be looked after, the usual career for a third male heir was in the Church. Fugger received his formal education in Venice as a teenager, but plans for the priesthood had to be abandoned when their father died unexpectedly, and later, one of the two older sons also died. Everything changed for Jakob and the fortunes of the Fugger family when the young man who was expected to become a priest showed an unusual flair for making money.

When he completed his education at the age of fourteen, Jakob served a brief apprenticeship before being put in charge of the family business in Innsbruck, Austria. This is a mountainous region rich in mineral deposits that were only then being discovered. Most of the mines belonged to the ruling Hapsburg dynasty who used them as collateral to secure huge loans provided by Fugger. The Hapsburgs were wealthy but profligate and frequently failed to repay what they had borrowed, and it was in this way that Fugger acquired extensive mining interests in the Tirol.

Meanwhile, the family banking business grew, and the original trade in raw cotton expanded to include silks, herbs, rare foods, and even gemstones; the Fuggers also controlled much of Europe's pepper market for decades. Jakob was an astute manager and the large profits from his interests in the Tirolean mines encouraged further investments in mining operations in Silesia (Poland today) and, later, in copper mining in Hungary; however, it was the expansion into mining that took the Fugger business to a whole new level. Banking was good business, but minerals were a valuable resource. The acquisitions eventually comprised the greatest mining centre at the time, giving Fugger a virtual monopoly on European copper, a metal vital in trade and warfare. In other words, whoever he backed was likely to win a trade deal or an actual war.

Even though Fugger refused to support Maximilian I's bid for the papacy, he supported the Holy Roman Emperor financially and, for better or worse, became closely identified with his policies. However, when it came to manipulating events, Fugger's greatest achievement was financing the election of Charles V, Maximilian's successor, as emperor. As well as being Holy Roman Emperor, Charles was also the King of Spain, a country then awash with precious metals coming in from the New World, so Jakob knew the emperor/king would be good for the eye-wateringly large sums of money he borrowed. In 1516 Fugger also made an ally of King Henry VIII of England by granting him various loans. It never hurts to have a ruler or two in your pocket and in your debt ... while earning you interest as well.

In 1503, Fugger intensified his contacts with the Vatican in Rome. For the new Pope, Julius II, Fugger financed the establishment of the Swiss Guard, the pope's bodyguard, which still exists today. He also helped in the collection of payments for papal indulgences, so it wasn't just the Fuggers making money. The Vatican then had a virtual industry profiting from the sale of these indulgences, and the concept was theologically brilliant. The rich generally became and/or remained rich through acts that were often contrary to Church teachings (stealing, killing, etc.), but they still wanted to go to heaven. So, why not use their wealth to ensure a place in the afterlife? For a fee, the Church would wipe the slate clean of any sins. Papal indulgences were the means to this end, and the money flowed like a torrent into the Vatican. However, somebody needed to collect and count the money, and it was Jakob Fugger who was willing to help ... for a fee. It was the sale of these same indulgences that provoked Martin Luther and led eventually to the Protestant Reformation. Luther even mentioned Fugger in a letter:

'Fugger and similar people really need to be kept in check.' (So, not a fan.)

Fugger died at the age of sixty-six in 1525, having conquered Europe through trade and enterprise while allowing national leaders to pursue their wars and battles even as he counted the profits. At the time of his death, he was the lord of dozens of towns and had collected a long list of titles but was always more interested in creating a business empire that stretched across Europe.

Jakob Fugger was the pre-eminent star of a family that dominated European business in the fifteenth and sixteenth centuries and influenced continental politics for decades to come. In terms of innovation, Fugger cast off the traditional economics of the Middle Ages and was key to the development of capitalism as an economic concept. In fact, the Fugger family can be considered a prototype of an early capitalist trading company.

Fugger's marriage was a childless and unhappy one, and as his health failed he passed the business on to his nephew, Anton Fugger, who expanded the family's interests to Buenos Aires, Mexico and the West Indies. Jakob and Anton made little use of their titles (and seemed to have limited interest in all the things money can buy), but the three surviving branches of the family, who have shown little talent for business, have been able to fund extravagant lifestyles thanks to the lands acquired by Jakob and Anton.

The concept of the 'super-rich' or '1 per cent' is not something new. Fugger was far richer than the current richest person in the world – and he was wheeling and dealing 500 years ago.

Early Modern

An Ancient Calendar

It may seem odd to start the Early Modern section with the Aztecs, but compared to other civilisations, they were late on the scene. The empire was barely a hundred years old when the conquistadors arrived in Mexico, but by then the Aztecs were only the latest in a series of Mesoamerican civilisations.

The Aztecs had several different calendars to organise and manage time. For instance, their famous Long Count calendar finished in 2012 and was due for renewal. It was never meant for matters on earth but was, instead, an astronomical calendar with cycles 2,880,000 days long (about 7,885 years). Contrary to popular belief, it was not used to mark an apocalyptic event but rather to denote the completion of one universal cycle. To put it another way, it was thought that all those days, all that time, added up to one year in the universe. So, rather than signalling that it was time to hide under the bed and wait for the end of days, the completion of an astronomical year meant only that another one was starting. It was believed that to have this cycle end in any human's lifetime would be a great honour, but since an astronomical year never ended during the time of the Aztec Empire, we'll never know if this event was meant to be marked by wild partying.

Unsurprisingly, there was a much more useful calendar that had a fifty-two-year cycle, the completion of which was celebrated with a festival called Xiuhmolpilli, the Binding of the Years, and a five-day ceremony where it was 'out with the old and in with the new'. Items that were worn out were destroyed, and symbolically, all fires were extinguished. It was a tense time of change and unrest as the Aztecs believed that the end of the cycle could mean Armageddon, a time when a goddess might descend on the world and destroy it.

In what was known as the New Fire Ceremony, the festival's finale took place at Huixachtlan on the eastern bank of Lake Texcoco (now dried out; it is in Mexico City today), on the site of an extinct volcano that could be seen for miles. The Aztecs believed that the ceremony ensured the sun's renewal, and like many Mesoamerican peoples, they also believed that it was important to appease the gods with human sacrifice. In this ceremony the victim had his chest cavity hollowed out and fire placed inside. This new flame would then be shared out and light returned to all areas of the empire. Ceremonies completed, the new fifty-two-year cycle could begin.

The Affable King

Charles VIII of France (born 1470, ruled 1483–98) seems to have been an effective if forgotten ruler of France. Some kings get poor monikers (I'm thinking of you, Aethelred the Unready) while others get great ones, like ... er ... Alexander the Great. Charles, however, was neither the best nor the worst; he was known as 'the affable', a middling sort of title.

By all accounts, Charles VIII was a well-mannered man who spent much of his reign as a minor, with his mother acting as regent. Once of age, he tried his best but was a terrible general who embroiled France in a number of financially ruinous wars. Some he won, some he lost, and some were inconclusive. Charles VIII's Italian War is a case in point. Very few people today have even heard of it, and yet it sucked in many of the European powers, with France and Milan on one side, and everybody else, including Venice, England, Spain and the Papal States, on the other. The battles were neither epic nor noteworthy, and in the end, Charles lost. Worse still, his soldiers returned to France with a new illness after an outbreak of syphilis occurred among the French troops in what was the first widely documented outbreak of the disease. So, he may have been a pleasant man but he was certainly a poor leader.

It is, however, the way he died that seals his reputation as a lacklustre monarch. Charles died as the result of an accident in 1498, two and a half years after he retreated from Italy. While on his way to watch a game of real tennis (the original form of tennis) in the town of Amboise, he struck his head on the lintel of a door. You read that right: he failed to get through a doorway without injuring himself. It wasn't until he was returning from the match that he suddenly fell into a coma and died nine hours later, most likely of a subdural haematoma. Yes, one of the most powerful kings in Europe died on the way to *spectate* at a sporting event. There is nothing in the story of his life and reign to indicate the nickname 'affable' was anything but apt, and it was as good a moniker as he was ever going to get.

Snatching Defeat from Victory

The Stuart line of Scottish monarchs had an almost unnerving amount of bad luck. James I was assassinated, and his son James II died at the age of twenty-nine while standing next to a cannon that exploded. His son, the imaginatively named James III, died aged thirty-six in battle. Another example of Stuart bad luck was the Battle of Solway Moss in 1542.

The Scottish King James V (another Stuart) had refused to break from the Roman Catholic Church as urged by his uncle, King Henry VIII, who subsequently launched a major raid into Scotland. By now the Scottish and English royal families were well and truly intertwined, so it was not uncommon for close relatives to fight each other. James responded by assigning Robert, Lord Maxwell the task of raising an army to invade England.

When an army of 15,000–18,000 Scots advanced into England, it was, for the times, an unusually large and well-provisioned Scottish force. James had done his homework and had left nothing to chance. Just south of the border, this mighty army was met by a rather meagre English army of about 3,000. The problem was that while Lord Maxwell had been tasked with raising the army, James had neglected to tell anyone who the overall commander-in-chief would be.

Oliver Sinclair, James V's favourite general, stepped up and declared himself to be James's chosen commander. However, the other commanders refused to accept him in the role, and the command structure disintegrated right when the English attacked with their small contingent of cavalry. This lack of cohesion goes against the common Scottish narrative that the Scots were united in their animosity towards England. There are countless examples of Scottish nobles doing what was best for them at the expense of doing what was best for Scotland against the 'auld enemy'. These show that fairly standard squabbles among aristocrats were blown out of proportion as they looked only for easy victories and the honour of winning. The Scottish foot soldiers and archers at Solway Moss were waiting for leadership, but this was still the age of feudal society, and an army with no orders wouldn't do anything.

However, Thomas Wharton, 1st Baron Wharton, in the English ranks had no such reticence. He had been a lord in the Scottish border areas for twenty years, and he was a competent leader. On this occasion he did exactly the right thing: he took decisive action and attacked with all his might, despite being badly outnumbered.

So the Scots, despite outnumbering the enemy by about five to one, bickered among themselves over who should give the orders and soon found themselves pinned between a river and the Moss (a peat bog). The fighting was intense, but the battle was over quickly, and several hundred Scots drowned in the marshes and river in the panicked rout that followed. What should have been an easy win for the Scots turned into a humiliating and emphatic defeat when they surrendered themselves and their ten field guns to the English cavalry. Many of the squabbling Scottish nobles were taken prisoner or killed. By contrast, the English forces suffered seven deaths, making it one of the greatest shock victories in military history.

James, who was ill with fever in Scotland, died two weeks later at the age of thirty. He could not know that the Stuart curse would only get worse, with the most famous tragedies yet to come, notably the executions of Mary, Queen of Scots and Charles I.

La Malinche, the Most Controversial Woman in Mexico

When Cortes arrived in Mexico in 1519, he had a tiny number of men against the vast Aztec Empire. He may have had the advantage of gunpowder and steel armour, and he accidentally had an advantage when his men spread European illnesses to the local population, but none of this is enough to explain how a boatload of men could defeat an empire in its prime. To fully understand how it happened, we have to turn to La Malinche, first a native slave and then the lover of Cortes. La Malinche (roughly, 'the captain's woman'), also known as Marina, was the chief guide and translator for the Spaniards. She was obviously smart as she was able to pick up a completely alien language in a short space of time, but it's her part in the downfall of the Aztec Empire that makes her controversial.

Despite common perception, the Aztecs were not a unified nation. As stated earlier, the empire was only about a century old when the Spaniards arrived; however, this empire, like all empires, was created by conquest. Add to this the ceremonial sacrifices in which locals were forced to fight in ritual combat (think the Hunger Games, only real), and there was bound to be a heady mix of anger and resentment bubbling below the surface of the conquered people. Like a lot of Aztec history, there is much we don't know and much that is controversial because the sources are contested, but the concept behind the 'flower war' fights was not about conquest but about acquiring prisoners for sacrifice to the gods. It was all highly ritualised and warriors fought with clubs embedded with jade shards. The idea was to cut the legs until the opponent couldn't stand up, after which they would be taken away for sacrifice and offered up to the Aztec gods. This was the scenario when the Spanish arrived. So, Cortes and La Malinche were able to leverage the underlying bitterness to create an army of locals eager to bolster the tiny Spanish force.

Cortes was guilty of many imperial crimes, but most of them would have been impossible (or much harder) without local help. La Malinche is a symbol of that help, but from her point of view, she was simply swapping an evil overlord for a more benevolent one. The result of all this was the Battle of Tenochtitlan, the Aztec capital, where Cortes led a coalition of Spanish troops and indigenous people to defeat the Aztec Empire. La Malinche may not have been in the thick of the fight, but we know she was present as the city was besieged and thousands died. She witnessed first-hand the consequences of her actions.

Following the fall of Tenochtitlan in August 1521, La Malinche retired to live in the house Cortes had built for her and gave birth to a son, Martin Cortes, in 1522. The fall of the capital of the Aztecs is often seen as the end of the story of the conquest of Mexico, but of course, there are always areas that refuse to capitulate and become a source of rebellion. This was the case when Cortes took La Malinche to help quell a rebellion in Honduras in 1524–26, and she was seen serving, once again, as an interpreter (and as this was an entirely different region, it shows, yet again, that she was quick to pick up local languages). While in central Mexico, she seems to have married another conquistador, Spanish nobleman Juan Jaramillo. After that, she disappears from the historical record.

It was her overt and emphatic backing of Cortes that makes La Malinche the most controversial woman in Mexican history. As various political power groups come and go in that country today, she is sometimes portrayed as the pawn of a cruel regime, sometimes as the noble native working for the greater good, sometimes as an evil temptress who seduced multiple conquistadors for personal gain and, finally, as someone who betrayed her people. What's interesting is that each reading is, in part, true. She was all of those things. Like most humans, she was a multifaceted individual and, in this case, one whose personal story is undocumented.

Like all folk heroes, legends have grown up around La Malinche, but it's the historical facts that make her one of the most divisive people in Mexican history and one of the most controversial 'traitors' anywhere.

Henry VIII Didn't Like Catholics ... Right?

Well, all of that is in hindsight, but falling out with the Roman Catholic Church was never the plan. Let's start with the fact that Henry was never meant to be king; he was the 'spare' to the actual heir. Henry was the younger brother of Arthur, who, had he not died of the 'sweating sickness', would have become King of England. Arthur's wife was Catherine of Aragon, who also caught the illness, but unlike her husband she survived and would later become Henry's first wife. How different history would have been if the wife had died and Arthur had lived.

Henry was not anti-Catholic. In fact, when the Protestant Reformation exploded out of the Holy Roman Empire in the early 1500s, Henry felt compelled to write a philosophical response attacking the 'heresy' of Protestantism and defending the 'true' Catholic faith. His treatise, called the 'Defence of the Seven Sacraments' (*Assertio septem sacramentorum*), was published in 1521. This 30,000-word text became a surprise bestseller and can still be purchased today.

It is worth pointing out that this was the first book to be written and published by an English king. This, alongside his love of poetry and music, shows a more sensitive side to a man who is often portrayed as a fat, misogynistic brute and warmonger. That image was very much the later Henry, after he had picked up a few illnesses that made him short-tempered and bellicose. The young Henry was a very fit man. The only two kings who are recorded to have been able to do an armoured vault onto a mount (that's when, in full plate armour, they would run up to the rear of the horse, place their hands on its rump and vault into the saddle) were Henry V and Henry VIII.

To thank Henry for his royal intervention in the widening dispute against the rise of Protestantism, Pope Leo X named him Defender of the Faith. Henry was thrilled to be so recognised by the pontiff, and this launched a series of diplomatic favours between the two, showing that Henry was very much an ardent Catholic early in his reign. This title, however, was to provide irony when Henry finally broke from the Church.

England's separation from the Roman Catholic Church, contrary to popular belief, was not a sudden decision. The first rumblings began in 1527 and stemmed from Henry's desire for a divorce from the same Catherine of Aragon. Leo died in 1521 and the reluctance of the new Pope, Clement VII, to grant the king his wish was not religious but political, and there were ample occasions to patch things up. Papal affairs at this time were notoriously complex and span the politics of the entire continent of Europe, so let's summarise by saying that Clement's backers didn't want the divorce to take place. In 1534, Henry raised the stakes by declaring that the monarch was the supreme religious leader in England, but the declaration was not ratified until 1537, a full ten years and three popes since the initial discord. This shows patience and a keen legal mind rather than looking like the work of a bull in a china shop.

Ironically, Henry liked the title Defender of the Faith so much that he kept it after the split from the Roman Catholic Church. In a strange way, it made even more sense when the monarch became head of the Church of England. Indeed, the title has stayed with the British royal family ever since – it is one of Queen Elizabeth II's official titles today.

Catherine Parr after Henry VIII

Continuing with the Tudor theme, of all his wives, Henry VIII's last (and the only one to survive him), Catherine Parr, is the one that is least discussed. But that does not mean there aren't some fascinating things to know about her.

Firstly, Henry was not her first husband. When she was seventeen, she married Sir Edward Burgh who died just four years into their marriage; they had no surviving children. Henry wasn't her second husband, either; that was John Neville, 3rd Baron Latimer. They were married in 1534 when

Catherine was twenty-two. This time, she was married for nine years before he was dead too. Both men died of natural causes, which shows that Henry VIII was not necessarily the most lethal thing to happen to marriage in the 1500s.

At the age of thirty-one, Catherine was twice a widow. Her choice of husband had shown a steady increase in political clout, but to snag the king? That would be quite a catch ... well, sort of. The welfare and longevity of Henry's wives had a patchy record, and Henry's fifth wife, Catherine Howard, had only recently been executed for adultery. Henry was, by then, fifty-four and ravaged with all kinds of ailments. At this point in life, he seemed to want a nurse more than a wife. The pair were married in 1543. When Henry went off on his final campaign against France the following year, he left Catherine as regent, showing a respect for her that he had not always shown his other wives.

Catherine was a capable regent. Due to all the dynastic marriages over the centuries, Henry and Catherine were distantly related, and she was known in the court. Thanks to her connections, she had allies in the regency council which enabled her to perform her duties with little opposition and a great deal of support. She was also a woman of sincere faith and in 1544 wrote *Prayers or Meditations*, the first book to be published by an English queen in her own name. She published a second book, *The Lamentation of a Sinner*, a few years later.

During Henry's final years, Catherine did an excellent job of sorting out his messy family life. As a stepmother several times over, she ingratiated herself with all of Henry's children from other marriages (she and Henry did not have any of their own). She successfully reconciled Henry with his daughters

Mary and Elizabeth and seemed to get on well with Edward. She even installed the stepchildren from her second marriage into various posts at court.

Henry died on 28 January 1547, aged just fifty-five. His last words were, 'Monks, monks, monks.' We don't know if he found them annoying or if he was, in his last moments, regretting the Dissolution of the Monasteries, but his death left Catherine in a weak position. She may have been the last queen standing, but the sixth wife of a dead king didn't carry much clout. So she made the only move a woman in the Tudor era could make: just six months after Henry's death, she married Thomas Seymour, 1st Baron Seymour of Sudeley, as a fourth and final husband.

The problem with this practical choice was that she was meant to be in mourning for her husband. Under normal circumstances such a move would result in disapproving gossip, but with her late husband having been the King of England and her stepson the new king, there was quite the scandal at court. It was a tense time for Catherine, but the ruffled feathers subsided, in part because time heals all wounds, but also because England's political landscape was starting to change. Under the circumstances, everyone had better things to worry about – not least of which was the health of the new king, Edward VI. Meanwhile, Catherine invited Henry's daughter Lady Elizabeth and her cousin Lady Jane Grey to stay in her new home at Sudeley Castle in Gloucestershire, where the dowager queen promised to provide education for both.

It was with Thomas that Catherine was to have her one and only child, Mary Seymour, but she died of complications from the birth shortly after. A year or so later, Thomas was executed for treason, while Mary is believed to have died at about the age of two. Catherine's story is that of many noblewomen across Europe in this era. Society had no place for a single woman; the only way to get ahead was through marriage, and childbirth could be fatal.

The Three Francises of Elizabeth I

Queen Elizabeth I is rightly credited with many abilities, but one that rarely gets a mention is her knack for delegation. This may seem simplistic, but the reality was that in the 1500s, it was hard to be a woman in a man's world even if you were a queen. The social norms were such that society just wouldn't allow Elizabeth to be seen to be doing certain things. Putting that to one side, nobody can rule a country on their own. Successful rulers are always backed up by an effective support network. Administrators, generals, tax collectors, effective judicial procedures – it can get a bit dull, but managing the complex affairs of a country, if done effectively, shouldn't be exciting, it should be more like tending a garden. Bad leaders aren't always mad or stupid, but they almost always do a poor job of delegating important jobs to the right people rather than to the sycophants and corrupt nobles who usually hover in anticipation. That was not the case with Elizabeth I, which can be seen in the unnerving effectiveness of the three men in her life called Francis.

First, there was Sir Francis Walsingham, who was, in all but name, her spymaster, although his official title was Principal Secretary. Elizabeth lived in an unusually tumultuous period of history even for Europe. Protestants clashed with Catholics, France clashed with everyone, and Spain was power-mad with the resources that were pouring in from the Americas. England, by comparison, was poor and, even worse, led by a woman. At the time, England – and therefore Elizabeth – had many enemies, both religious and political.

There are two famous examples of Walsingham's effectiveness. One involved the Vatican's *Regnans in Excelsis*, a document stating that anyone who killed the heretic Queen Elizabeth would be absolved of all sins, the same deal that centuries earlier had been associated with going on crusade. It was the ultimate encouragement for all good Catholics to murder the English queen. There were regular attempts on her life as well as plots to overthrow her, but she survived to rule for decades thanks to Walsingham's spy network and deciphering team which ensured that all potential threats were neutralised.

The second instance of Walsingham's shrewdness involved Mary, Queen of Scots, a potential threat to Elizabeth. But was she plotting against her cousin? It was thanks to Walsingham's tireless efforts that a cryptographer was found who could break Mary's coded letters and provide the evidence Elizabeth needed to have her executed. (For more on this see the later article 'The Queen's Code'.) It was a controversial moment in history and entire books have been written about the pros and cons, but for the purposes of this article, Walsingham did his job. He outmanoeuvred every hostile Catholic power in Europe.

The second man who so effectively served his queen was the explorer Sir Francis Drake, the second man to circumnavigate the globe but the first captain to make it back alive. Drake was also a privateer, which meant he was a pirate who did his plundering for a specific country. In this case, Drake pirated for England, and he went after the biggest, juiciest targets he could: Spain and her colonies in the Americas. Drake fought a successful hit-and-run war against the richest empire of the age. He was particularly productive when attacking Spanish shipping off the coasts of modern-day Peru and Chile. One ship had (in modern terms) £7 million worth of pesos. Another contained 80 lbs of gold and 26 tons of silver plus jewels. Drake was a serious thorn in the side of Spain's mighty empire, and it was through him that England waged an effective economic war on Spain. Spain protested, but as Drake was a privateer, Elizabeth could claim ignorance.

In 1587, things became much more serious. Drake sailed into the Spanish port of Cadiz and burned a Spanish fleet. A year later the fleet had been rebuilt (showing the vast wealth of Spain), and this new Spanish Armada sailed into the English Channel intent on invasion. Drake was second in command of the English forces and helped to ensure one of the greatest victories in British naval history – and that's saying something. When he died in 1596, off the coast of South America, he was buried at sea in full armour and a lead-lined coffin.

Finally, there was Sir Francis Bacon, and, quite frankly, what didn't he do? A true polymath, he was a politician, philosopher, scientist and expert in law. Bacon stated that he had three goals: to uncover the truth, to serve his country and to serve his Church. He achieved all three. He is the father of the scientific method – that is, coming to conclusions through observation and measurement rather than received knowledge. For a time this was known as the Baconian Method. He was a key advisor to Elizabeth in all areas of government (except that of war and espionage as the other Francises had that covered).

Elizabeth couldn't have known it was Bacon who would ensure a peaceful transition of power to a Stuart monarchy after her death. The Virgin Queen famously had no heirs, so when she died in 1603 and a new monarch was needed, it was decided to ask the Stuart King of Scotland, James VI, son of Mary, Queen of Scots, to become the new King of England as James I. It was Bacon who led the committee to negotiate this unenviably awkward process. Accomplishing this peaceful transition without a drop of blood being shed was probably his greatest achievement.

The three Francises are clear examples of wisdom that recognises when help is needed and then gets the right person to do the job. Elizabeth I was exemplary at both.

The Pirates Who Enslaved Whole Towns

The problem with pirates is that people tend to think of only one type. The age of sail, muskets, cannons, tricorn hats and barrels of rum – these are the hallmarks of the stereotypical pirate from the so-called 'golden age of piracy' in the Caribbean of the early 1700s. The reality was that they were neither the longest-running nor the most successful pirates in history. Just a cursory look at pirate history reveals that they were around at the time of the ancient Greeks. Julius Caesar was kidnapped by pirates (while being held captive he told them he would crucify them, and on being released he raised a fleet, chased them down and did just that). In the nineteenth century, the Royal Navy battled them off the coast of China, and today, East Africa is littered with pirate bands. Piracy is robbery on water and it's not unique to a specific time and place.

One group that underlines this observation spanned the sixteenth and nineteenth centuries and was known as the Barbary Pirates. These Muslim war bands (no rum for them) were based on the north coast of Africa and raided along the coasts of southern Europe (and beyond) for centuries, not decades. They are personified by four brothers: Ishak, Oruç, Hızır and Ilyas, men who were born in the Ottoman Empire of Albanian/Greek stock. The brothers (minus Ishak, who stayed at home) started as privateers in 1500, plundering specifically for the Hospitallers (Christian fighters against the Ottoman Empire). Success encouraged them to strike out on their own, and they became independent raiders. So now they were definitely pirates who specialised in plundering North Africa and Italy. Sometime later they were attacked by their previous employers, the Hospitallers. Ilyas was killed in the engagement and Oruç was captured. He was held on Rhodes for three years before Hızır located him, crept into the Hospitaller fortress and set him free.

From here, Oruç went from strength to strength. At first, he was in charge of eighteen galleys, then twenty-four, when he participated in the Ottoman naval expedition to Apulia in the Kingdom of Naples, where he bombarded several coastal forts and captured two ships. On his way back to Lesbos, he captured three galleons and another ship. By now, like every good pirate, he had a new name: Barbarossa, meaning red beard, a nod to his less-than-Turkic heritage. After this, he approached the Mamelukes and met their sultan, who gave him another ship to raid the coasts of Italy and the islands of the Mediterranean. In 1503, Barbarossa managed to seize three more ships as well as the island of Djerba off the coast of Tunisia. This location became his new base of operations, allowing him to conduct raids in the Western Mediterranean. It was at this point that Hızır joined Barbarossa again.

The local sultan of Tunisia (the third Muslim power they had worked for) allowed them to use the port of La Goulette on the condition that one-third of their booty went to him. From here, they terrorised Christian Mediterranean shipping, plundering papal galleys and capturing a huge Sicilian warship with over 400 warriors on board. When not enriching themselves on the lucrative shipping routes, they raided the coasts of Calabria and Liguria. All of this was taking its toll on the European powers.

By this time, things were so good that Ishak finally joined in. In 1510, the three brothers raided Sicily and repulsed Spanish attacks on three different North African cities. By now they were not so much pirates as admirals of their own formidable fleet. In August 1512, however, during a battle in North Africa against the Spanish, Barbarossa lost his left arm. He had it replaced with a silver one and took up the even cooler name Gümüş Kol, 'silver arm' (take that, Goldfinger).

For the next four years they attacked everywhere in the Christian Mediterranean. The European powers were always one step behind the brothers, and dozens of ships were captured or sunk. Then, in 1516, they captured Algiers, and when Barbarossa proclaimed himself sultan, nobody dared to object. But it soon became clear that the role of sultan brought different challenges to that of pirate captain, and Barbarossa was shrewd enough to realise that he had overstretched himself. So in 1517, he offered Algiers to the Ottoman sultan. Suddenly, with no military effort or expenditure, the Ottoman Empire had expanded across vast tracts of the North African coast, and overnight Algiers became an Ottoman province.

Naturally Barbarossa became the Bey (Governor) of Algiers and was also made Beylerbey (Chief Governor) of the Western Mediterranean. The challenge now for the Ottomans was to hold the territory and protect it from the Spanish, who were flush with riches pouring in from the New World. So the Ottoman janissaries (the sultan's personal infantry), along with equipment that a pirate just couldn't afford, were brought in to stabilise the situation and resist any Spanish attack. A year later, the Spanish King Charles V arrived in North Africa to rid himself of the Barbarossa scourge. After a twenty-day siege at Tlemcen, both Barbarossa and Ishak were killed, but the Barbarossa name lived on as Hızır took on the title and continued the fight.

The first thing Hızır did was to recapture Tlemcen, and from there he went on and on. Not to be outdone by his brother, he, too, picked up a nickname: Hayreddin Pasha ('best of the faith'). He ruled Algiers for a time and became the most feared naval commander in the first half of the sixteenth century. He was so good that the French offered him anything he wanted to switch sides and lead their fleet. He declined, and, in 1545, he retired. With a long list of victories under his belt, he had plenty to write about, and as unlikely as it seems for someone who had been a pirate, he began work on his five-volume autobiography, which became essential reading for any naval officer in Europe at the time. His book is aptly named *Gazavat-ı Hayreddin Paşa* (*Conquests of Hayreddin Pasha*).

In conclusion, Ottoman expansion in North Africa happened by accident. No sultan ever planned to expand the empire with Muslim pirates who were so good at what they did that they were co-opted by the establishment. The pirates throughout this era were so effective in carting away entire villages of locals that some coastal towns in Spain and Italy were simply abandoned as nobody dared live in a place where a pirate attack was virtually guaranteed.

The number of people estimated to have been captured and enslaved is 1.5 million, a staggering number by any standard. And what fate awaited them? Some of the men became galley slaves, a miserable existence guaranteed to shorten their brutal lives; others were castrated and, as eunuchs, became high-ranking administrators in various realms in the Muslim world. (There is more than one documented story of an English eunuch who, when rescued, refused to return home; he had a better life in North Africa than he ever had in Europe.) Most of the women and girls were sold into harems and/or domestic slavery. While these are instances of Muslims enslaving Christians, the latter part of this era coincided with Christian Europe enslaving far more African natives. In the end, Christian expansion into North Africa eliminated the pirates' safe harbours, and by the 1830s, after 300 years of plundering, they were gone.

The Tale of ... Deep Breath ... Ana de Mendoza de la Cerda y de Silva Cifuentes, Princess of Eboli, Duchess of Pastrana

But everyone called her Ana de Mendoza because we all have lives to lead.

If Ana de Mendoza were better known she would probably be a feminist icon. She lived in sixteenth-century Spain at a time when she would have been expected to be a compliant little girl who would grow up to become a compliant lady.

Not unusually for the time, she was married off at the age of thirteen. By the age of fourteen, she was portrayed with an eye patch. It's not clear how she lost the eye, but it seems to have been in a fencing accident, so we conclude that this teenage girl was learning martial combat and taking it to such extremes that she lost an eye. While this is conjecture, it is unlikely that she lost it doing needlework.

Ana's husband was a chief councillor in the court of King Philip II, and her marriage put her in a position of immense power and influence, especially as she became a close friend of the queen. She had ten children, and when her husband died in 1573, she retired to a convent. While this was unusual, it was not unheard of as some aristocratic women who had lost their husbands but had a large number of children felt it was a sign that they should devote themselves to God.

But Ana, more rebellious than the average Spanish woman of her time and position, had a change of heart. She returned to the court and formed an alliance with the king's undersecretary of state, Antonio Pérez. Things started well, but when they were accused of betraying state secrets, she was arrested and imprisoned in 1579. But this time around, she no longer had any influential friends, and she remained in prison where she died thirteen years later in February of 1592.

So, Ana de Mendoza: wife, mother, courtier, schemer, fighter and nun ... that's a pretty comprehensive list and an equally impressive life.

In 2017 Martin Scorsese Released *Silence*

Silence is an intense and impressive film featuring neither America nor gangsters, which is what many associate with

Martin Scorsese. This beautifully shot film is a fictionalised account of the persecution of Catholics in Japan in the early seventeenth century. This may sound counterintuitive, but the historical context is absolutely true.

In the 1500s, Catholic missionaries brought Christianity to Japan where it was initially embraced. A number of high-ranking lords converted, and it was seen as the religion of the elite, rather like a special club where members might be given secret information. Of course, this enviable cachet meant that lower-ranking officials became intrigued and wanted to know more about the alien faith. At a time when so many European countries had become Protestant, the Catholic Church was delighted to find a new land to convert. It's thought that Japan had about 300,000 Christians at its peak, but then everything changed under the new Tokugawa Shogunate.

Ieyasu Tokugawa brought an end to the constant civil wars that had plagued Japan for centuries. In 1600, at the Battle of Sekigahara, he won an emphatic victory that began the era of the shoguns (rather than emperors). This was to last until the 1800s, and with it came a moratorium on international ideas, trade and interactions of any kind. Japan sealed itself off and anything that was considered non-Japanese was banned. Converts to Christianity often took Christian/Western names, which were then seen as an insidious influence that challenged the old, traditional ways. The result of this was taken to an extreme and led to the brutal persecution of Christians, who were hunted down and forced to apostatise (renounce their beliefs). There were even official inquisitors, not of the Christian variety but of the Christian-hunting type.

Perhaps the most infamous incident occurred in Nagasaki in 1597 (during Tokugawa's wars), when twenty-six Christians were executed for their beliefs. It was so difficult to quash the Christians that in 1632, fifty-five of them (all Japanese) were executed in the same city of Nagasaki. This atrocity became known as the Great Genna Martyrdom. Today there is a shrine in the city to remember and honour the dozens of Christians who were tortured and murdered for their beliefs.

Christianity would make a modest return to Japan once it opened up again in the latter part of the nineteenth century, but for centuries the faith was eradicated from the Japanese islands. *Silence* tells this story and shows the little-known role of Christianity in Japanese history. While the specifics are fiction, the events portrayed are, sadly, all too real.

Thomas Morley, a Name That Should Be up There with Robert Plant, Alice Cooper and Freddie Mercury … But Isn't

One of the reasons Thomas Morley's name is not associated with rock stardom is that he died about 400 years ago, so we don't know what he looked like or how he sounded, but in his day, he was not only hugely popular but controversial as well. He was one of England's foremost composers and musicians, living at the same time as Shakespeare. Indeed, Morley lived for a time in the same parish as Shakespeare. The two men's lives are intertwined enough to make it possible that in this era, Morley could be seen on one night and Shakespeare the next. Another connection between the two masters was that Morley borrowed 'It was a lover and his lass' from *As You*

Like It and put it to music. It has never been established as having been used in a performance of Shakespeare's play, although the possibility that it was is obvious.

Morley became England's foremost composer of secular music. His madrigals are light, quick-moving and easy to sing, like his well-known ballad (at the time and for generations after) 'Now Is the Month of Maying'. As we have seen, he was not afraid to borrow and took aspects of Italian style that suited his purpose and anglicised them. Morley also wrote instrumental music, notably for the harpsichord but also for the broken consort (an ensemble of instruments from different families).

But Morley courted controversy, mainly because he was a Roman Catholic, a serious crime in Elizabeth's Protestant England. He was able to avoid prosecution as a recusant by repenting and even went on to become the organist for St Paul's Cathedral as well as Westminster Cathedral, both epicentres of Protestant Anglicanism. Morley was also a shrewd businessman and had a monopoly in printing music, which he used to acquire wealth not available by artistic means. Around 1600, he married a woman named Susan with whom he had three children, which was a little less rock god but normal for the times.

According to the musical historians Philip Brett and Tessa Murray, Morley was 'chiefly responsible for grafting the Italian shoot onto the native stock and initiating the curiously brief but brilliant flowering of the madrigal that constitutes one of the most colourful episodes in the history of English music'. Putting all of this into a succinct, modern context, he could fill a venue, the establishment didn't like him, he was musically innovative and he had arty friends. Doesn't this sound like a rock god to you?

Real Witch Trials

If there is one topic that is synonymous with travesties of justice it has to be witch trials. Contrary to popular belief, these were not something from the early medieval era, nor were they especially prevalent in colonial America. It is also important to say that while the majority of people executed for witchcraft were women, men were accused and convicted too. To put these trials into context, over a period of about 300 years, fewer than 500 people were executed for witchcraft in Britain. This is, of course, 500 too many, but it means that witch trials were, in reality, relatively rare, and to have as many as twelve people accused at the same time (as in the case that follows) was almost unheard of.

Among the most famous British trials are the so-called Pendle witch trials which took place in Lancashire in 1612, when twelve people were accused of ten murders involving witchcraft. Ten of the accused were women and two were men, but one of the women died in prison, so nine women from two families, the Southerns and the Devices, stood trial. Almost everything that is known comes from a report of the proceedings written by Thomas Potts, the clerk of the Lancaster Assizes. Although written as an apparently accurate account, 'The Wonderfull Discoverie of Witches in the Countie of Lancaster' (their spelling, not mine) is not a record of what was said at the trials but is, instead, a reflection on what happened. In other words, an op-ed. The title suggests this was hardly a dispassionate report of what took place.

The concern about witches at that time had less to do with spells and potions and more to do with devil worship, the logic being that if their potent power didn't come from the Church, it must come from Satan himself. None of this was true; nevertheless, all of the women and one man were convicted and executed (the other man was found 'not guilty'). These were such unusual trials that it might be that the women had been working as healers and using spells as a means of earning a living. That doesn't mean that they were devil-worshipping murderers.

There were, at the time, rumours that the whole thing was invented to cover up a more serious Catholic plot to overthrow King James, who was James I of England and James VI of Scotland. He was fascinated by witches and even wrote a book about witchcraft. The whole subject had feverish followers and was something of a fashion of the times as reflected in Shakespeare's Scottish play *Macbeth*, with its Scottish connections to James I/VI and his obsession with witches. As a result, James feared threats from the supernatural as well as more real-world threats from the Catholic powers of Europe.

While the evidence that these women communed with Satan was thin, to say the least, linking them to a Catholic plot was even more of a reach. However, in the centre of all this conjecture is the fact that innocent people were executed for no good reason.

We All Have to Die of Something

Today in the West, the three most common causes of death are heart disease, cancer and dementia-related illness. Obviously, everybody that has ever lived had to die of something, but more than 99 per cent have died from causes such as famine, cholera or malaria (which holds the record for being the single greatest killer of humans). The simple fact is that we tend to remember the ones who died in dramatic ways. While history records the deaths of famous people, not all of them had what could be described as a 'fitting' death. Here are just a few:

AD 453 Attila the Hun, scourge of the Roman Empire and ruler of the Hunnic Empire, died of a nosebleed on his wedding night (insert joke here).

1135 Henry I of England loved lamprey eels. However, they made him constipated, and his doctors warned him about the consequences. During a feast, he really went for the eels, which resulted in severe constipation. When his doctors realised the dangerous situation, they gave him a powerful laxative, and he died from excessive secretions.

1190 Holy Roman Emperor Frederick Barbarossa fell off his horse into a small river in Anatolia and drowned. This was a key moment in the Third Crusade as the emperor had the largest army, but following his death, almost all of it went home before even getting to the Middle East.

1216 King John of England died when feasting on 'a surfeit of peaches'. It's unclear if this brought on a stroke or more 'excessive secretions', but the peaches brought an end to an ongoing civil war and the potential invasion of England by France. Could be a warning about taking the whole 'five a day' thing too far.

1286 Alexander III of Scotland, against the advice of his courtiers, left in a storm to spend the night with his new wife and rode his horse off a cliff in the darkness. This led to civil war which, in turn, led Edward I of England to interfere in the politics of his northern neighbour.

1574 Selim II (also known as Selim the Sot – i.e. the drunk), sultan of the Ottoman Empire, drank to excess and slipped on a wet marble floor in Topkapi Palace in Istanbul. The blow to the head killed him.

So, the rich and powerful are no more immune from ignoble deaths than anyone else. Final thought: the Office of National Statistics revealed that, on average, two Brits a year die putting on their trousers.

The Queen's Code

In 1567, at the age of twenty-four, Mary, Queen of Scots was incarcerated. Little did she realise she would remain under house arrest for nearly twenty years before she was murdered on the orders of her cousin, Queen Elizabeth I.

Mary has become something of a political figure. Scots use her as an example of English interference in their affairs, and while they have a point, she wasn't exactly a haggis-eating, tartan-wearing innocent. Her mother was French and her grandmother was Margaret Tudor ... of those Tudors south of the border. She was a Catholic and the focus of plots to dethrone the Protestant Queen Elizabeth of England and install her on the throne. How much Mary was an active player in all of this is where it becomes political. If she was the pawn of the real power players such as Spain or France, then Elizabeth looks like the bloodthirsty murderer of her cousin. If, however, Mary played an active part, then she is guilty of conspiring and getting caught. If you're plotting against the person who has you confined, then you can expect only one outcome as per the rules of dynastic clashes in the Renaissance era.

Mary was always a threat to Elizabeth, but there was a problem: the queen could not execute her cousin on a whim. Hard evidence was needed, otherwise it would set a very dangerous precedent about executing queens. There was a chance, though. Foreign powers were communicating with Mary, and, while defenders say she was a pawn in bigger games, her response to the letters wasn't exactly, 'Stop it, I'm loyal to Elizabeth and have no interest in your plots.'

Intercepting the messages was hard, and cracking the code they were written in was even harder. In the end, Elizabeth's spymaster Francis Walsingham (see 'The Three Francises of Elizabeth I') had to use every connection at his disposal to find a cryptographer who could do it. The queen's life hung in the balance as the Dutchman Philip van Marnix worked on the fiendishly difficult code before he finally cracked it and reported that the letter revealed Mary was prepared to support a Catholic invasion of England. The letter signed her death warrant. When the evidence was presented to Elizabeth, she vacillated. Whether this was due to misgivings about the execution of a blood relative or whether she was genuinely worried that the execution could backfire, we can't know. What we do know is that Elizabeth waited for about a week before confirming the death sentence that was possible only because of Walsingham's resolve and van Marnix's determination to crack the code.

Mary was executed on 7 February 1587. The first blow missed her neck and struck the back of her head. The second blow killed her. A third blow severed a remaining bit of sinew.

The Singing Floor

Ninja warriors are legendary – and real – and they were a genuine problem for the rich and powerful in feudal Japan.

First, a couple of quick facts. Ninjas were assassins and didn't walk around dressed like ninjas. It was important that they kept a low profile, so they often dressed as beggars or tradesmen. Nobody paid any attention to beggars, so they could sit and observe the security patrols of target buildings (usually castles or palaces) while hiding in plain sight. Equally, dressed as tradesmen, they could walk up to the gates to observe the security and, if asked their business, start selling their services to the guards. When they wore dark garb for assassinations, it was dark blue; black is too strong and dark blue works much better to blend into the night.

Once an assassin made it into the castle he was almost impossible to detect. What to do? The answer was the ingenious 'nightingale floor' found in many castles from the Tokugawa period. These are floors designed to 'sing' when metal nails scrape against a metal underfloor hidden beneath the visible upper floor. Any pressure on the floor results in a singing or chirruping sound which would alert the guards. Ninjas could scale the castle walls but would quickly be discovered as they approached the master's bedchamber via the singing floor.

For the guards who had to walk on the floors, an agreed tempo was set so that if the singing began and it didn't sound right, it could be investigated. So, a simple but ingenious trap stopped pesky ninjas from doing all their ninjaing (that's a verb I've just invented).

Candomblé or Satan's Temple

The Portuguese Empire tried to convert its black slaves and assumed that every one of them got the message and became a good Catholic overnight. However, some of the slaves detected a parallel between the Catholic veneration of saints and their own indigenous faiths. Add to this the native religions of the New World, and Candomblé is the result, a melting pot found alive and well to this day in some regions of Brazil, surviving as a fascinating example of African slave culture evolving in the New World.

Catholicism was the state religion in Brazil in the mid-1800s, a time when any other religious practice was regarded as a threat to the secular authority. Candomblé was, unsurprisingly, condemned by Rome, which sent an inquisition to root out the heretics and idolaters. This happened in the 1850s when it might be expected that the Inquisition had been consigned to the history books, but the Catholic Church linked the religion to devil worship. Temples were destroyed, and followers were violently persecuted by government-led public campaigns and police action. The persecution only stopped in the 1970s with the repeal of a law requiring police permission to hold public religious ceremonies.

Since then, the religion has surged in popularity, with as many as 2 million people professing to follow Candomblé .

It is particularly popular in Salvador and Bahia, in the north-east region of Brazil, which is relatively isolated from other influences and had a high percentage of enslaved Africans back in the seventeenth century.

The Three False Dimitris

In Russian history, the era from 1598 to 1613 is called the Time of Troubles. It was a disastrous period in the expanding country as the triple threats presented by a lack of central authority, famine and invasion by the Polish–Lithuanian Commonwealth led to a near-collapse of the Russian state. Millions died of starvation and violence, but there was such a bizarre grab for power that it makes the politics of the age look like a farce.

Tsar Feodor was a weak ruler, possibly mentally disabled, and had no heir. He was the son of Ivan IV (forever known as Ivan the Terrible), who created the concept of a Tsar (from the Russian word for Caesar) when he named himself Tsar of Russia in 1547. So, when Feodor died without an heir in 1598, his death triggered a dynastic catastrophe. The concept of a Tsar was barely fifty years old, and now the country was being invaded by aggressive foreign powers.

Which brings us to the first false Dimitri. This Dimitri claimed he was the youngest son of Ivan the Terrible, which would make him the brother of Feodor and the rightful heir to the throne – if he was genuine. Even though everyone thought the real Dimitri was dead (he was), this man gained the support of the Polish–Lithuanian Commonwealth, formed a small army and advanced into Russia in 1605. As he marched, his forces grew although he did have to fight a few battles along the way. Fortunately for him, they were minor affairs. It seems that he was considered the natural heir to the throne and had bolstered his credentials by showing the strength to lead an army.

This Dimitri arrived in Moscow in the summer of 1605, where he was crowned Tsar by a new Muscovite patriarch of his choosing. He married Marina Mniszech in May 1606, but for various reasons she did not convert to Russian Orthodox Christianity, which helped spread rumours that he was a secret Catholic who had made a pact with the Pope to reunite the churches. None of this was true, but it didn't stop an angry mob from attacking the Kremlin. Tsar Dimitri tried to flee by jumping out of a window but fractured his leg in the fall. When he tried to hide in a nearby bathhouse, he was recognised, dragged through the streets and apparently beaten to death (there are conflicting reports, but he was definitely killed). His body was put on display and then cremated, with the ashes allegedly shot from a cannon towards Poland (the direction whence he had come with the foreign army). This was followed by the massacre of his supporters. So far, interesting but not very weird … until Dimitri 2 arrived.

The second false Dimitri turned up about a year later, again at the head of a Polish–Lithuanian Commonwealth army, claiming to be the same Dimitri who had been beaten to death, burnt and shot out of a cannon. This was quite a claim, made all the harder to justify when he was taken to his widow. On seeing this new Dimitri, Marina Mniszech claimed it was a holy miracle that he had survived and that he was undeniably the same man who had died the previous year. This Dimitri did a bit better than the first one, and lasted until December 1610 when, in a drunken stupor, he was shot and beheaded by a Tatar prince who had been nursing a grudge having been flogged on Dimitri 2's orders.

Another man took his chances in March the following year (1611). This was the third (and final) false Dimitri, who again was no such thing and seems to have been a disgruntled deacon of the Church. This Dimitri did not seek the support of the Polish–Lithuanian Commonwealth but, instead, threw in his lot with the Cossacks who had been the backbone of the Tsar's paramilitary power. It was a shrewd move. They went on to plunder the surrounding areas of Moscow, and Dimitri 3 was formally recognised as the legitimate heir a year later in March of 1612. However, just a few months later, everything went wrong for him when he was deserted by his allies, captured by political enemies and executed without ceremony.

It was Michael I who finally put an end to all the chaos and confusion when he came to power in 1613. He was the first Romanov Tsar, the founder of a dynasty that would last for over 300 years.

Nur Jahan Was the Twentieth and Final Wife of the Indian Mughal Emperor Jahangir

Nur Jahan had originally been married to one of Emperor Jahangir's enemies, but the emperor became so enamoured of her that he ordered the execution of her first husband so that he could make her his wife and lucky number twenty. His beloved made him wait four years, during which time both she and her daughter acted as ladies-in-waiting to Jahangir's stepmother. When they finally wed, she used her newfound position to nurture her power, proving to be an even more decisive and aggressive leader than her new husband, who had already proven himself to be quite the conqueror. To give you an idea, she was the only Mughal empress to have coinage struck in her name. She was also often present when the emperor held court and even held court independently when Jahangir was unwell.

Their unusually balanced relationship has given rise to many legends, but these tend to be colourful stories rather than verifiable facts. Nur Jahan died in 1645 at the age of sixty-eight, and it is the Tomb of I'timad-ud-Daulah that cements her story of power and intelligence in a physical form. The tomb was a family burial site, and as such, she ensured that her relatives were enshrined in supreme opulence too. Built between 1622 and 1628, it is seen by many as a prototype of the Taj Mahal and is sometimes called the Baby Taj.

In accordance with Islamic tradition, there are no human images in the interior decoration, but rather an amazing collection of minerals inlaid in beautiful geometric patterns that show precise skill in both the arrangement of the stones and the mathematics required to determine the patterns. The walls are made of white marble from Rajasthan and are encrusted with semi-precious stone decorations. Cornelian, jasper, lapis lazuli (from Afghanistan, the ancestral home of the Mughals), onyx and topaz have been arranged into images of cypress trees and wine bottles (a little cheeky, seeing that the Mughals were teetotal Muslims, not Hindus) and even more elaborate decorations showing vases containing bouquets. Looking at these dazzling displays, it is easy to see why the tomb is referred to as the Jewel Box.

Nur Jahan's stunning tomb is near that of her husband Emperor Jahangir, both now in the country of Pakistan.

The Site of a Sea Battle That Is Now on Land

The Dutch Revolt (1568–1648), also known as the Eighty Years War, was the successful revolt of the northern, largely Protestant Seven Provinces of the Low Countries against the rule of the Roman Catholic King Philip II of Spain, who was the hereditary ruler of the provinces. This war was about 80 per cent as complicated as the Hundred Years War (okay, a poor joke), but created the independent state of what would eventually be called the Netherlands. The Battle of Haarlemmermeer is a largely forgotten moment from this conflict. The battle was a naval engagement fought on 26 May 1573, during the early stages of the war. It took place on the waters of the Haarlemmermeer, a large lake which, at the time, was a prominent feature of northern Holland.

A Spanish fleet and a fleet belonging to the city of Amsterdam (at the time, still loyal to Spain), commanded by the Count of Bossu, fought a fleet of rebellious Dutch Geuzen, commanded by Marinus Brandt, who was trying to break the Siege of Haarlem. After several hours of fighting, the rebels and Geuzen were forced to retreat. It's not exactly one of the greatest moments in either that war or, indeed, in naval history, but thanks to Dutch drainage initiatives and a desire to reclaim areas of land, the site of this naval battle has a new name … Schiphol Airport.

The waters around Haarlemmermeer have disappeared to give way to the major international hub of air traffic that it is today. In this context, it's worth remembering that about 17 per cent of the Netherlands is reclaimed land and was once marshland or under the North Sea.

King Philip's War – the One That Had Nothing to Do with France or Spain

The strange thing about this particular King Philip is that he was not European. He was, in fact, a Wampanoag Native American. His real name was Metacomet, but he changed it to King Philip as a sign of friendship with the English settlers, the original Pilgrim founders from the *Mayflower*. At first, all went well, and Metacomet was so happy to accommodate his new friends that he changed his name. But then everything changed, and the encroachment of settlers on native lands became the trigger for war.

In 1675, officials in the English colony of Plymouth hanged three Wampanoag men for the murder of a Christianised Native American. This was the final straw for an already enraged Metacomet/King Philip. First, the settlers took over his territory, then they spread their religion, and now they were applying their laws to his people. These executions gave King Philip and his allies from other tribes the excuse they needed to launch surprise attacks on colonial towns throughout New England. In the space of little more than a year, twelve of the region's towns were destroyed and many more suffered substantial damage. The area's economy was ruined and its population was decimated.

But then Metacomet's alliance began to unravel. By the end of the conflict, the Wampanoags and their Narragansett allies were almost completely destroyed. Metacomet anticipated the defeat and returned to his ancestral home at Mount Hope, where he was killed fleeing an ambush laid by the colonists.

This is one of those situations where war ravaged both sides and, in this instance, is seen as the single greatest calamity to occur in seventeenth-century colonial America. Some historians consider it to be the deadliest war in the history of European settlement in North America in proportion to the size of the population. So, nobody won King Philip's War.

The Cheeky Thief

'Colonel' Thomas Blood (he was never actually given the rank, he just called himself that) was born in Ireland but travelled to England in 1642 to fight for the Royalists at the outbreak of the English Civil War (1642–51). I use the term 'English' Civil War because it is the one most commonly used and is known to most people. Many historians, however, do not like the name as it fails to take into account that the conflict spread to Ireland and Scotland, so the more appropriate name in use today tends to be the Wars of the Three Kingdoms.

But back to Colonel Blood, who ended up changing sides (not as unusual as you might think), and who eventually received a grant of land under Cromwell's new Commonwealth. Everything fell to pieces for Blood when the Stuart monarchs of Britain, specifically Charles II, made a comeback in 1660, and the Colonel fled back to Ireland. Blood remained there for a few years, stirring up republican trouble, until he came back to England with an audacious plan to steal the Crown Jewels from the Tower of London. The idea of breaking into one of the most heavily guarded forts in Europe with a small band of men was so ridiculous that it might just have worked.

By all accounts, Blood was a charming man. Dressed as a parson, he befriended the Master of the Jewel House. His familiar presence meant that in May 1671, he and a few accomplices, hiding mallets beneath their cloaks, were able to enter the Tower grounds unopposed. They knocked out the Master of the Jewel House, tied up his family and used the mallets to batter the Crown Jewels flat enough to be hidden under their cloaks (the plan lacked subtlety). They almost got away with it ... until the Master's son removed his gag and shouted, 'Treason! Murder! The crown is stolen!'

Despite trying to escape on horseback while tossing jewels in every direction to divert the guards, Blood and his gang were caught red-handed. In desperation, they drew pistols and fired at the guards, but they were subdued. The robbers now faced the brutal realities of seventeenth-century justice. With that said, Blood's interrogation by the king didn't end the way anyone would have anticipated.

Charles II asked, 'What if I should give you your life?'

Blood replied, 'I would endeavour to deserve it, Sire!'

Charles II loved Blood's cheekiness and sheer audacity. While we cannot call them friends, they certainly got on well, probably because Charles ('the merry monarch') found Blood to be amusing. Contrary to all expectations, Blood was not only pardoned for a crime he most definitely committed but was also given land in Ireland that generated an income of £500 a year (a considerable sum in this era). He became a regular at court and died in Westminster in 1680.

The Black Samurai

If you type 'black samurai' into Google images, you will be faced with pictures of '70s dudes with afros and *katanas* (samurai swords). While this may have been considered the height of period cool, it was also highly unrealistic. Japan is considered by geneticists to be the most homogeneous country in the world. Centuries of rigid feudalism followed by centuries of isolation mean that Japanese blood is relatively 'untainted' by foreign blood, and the only racial minority in the islands of Japan is the Ainu people. So the concept of a samurai of African origin sounds ridiculous, but there was one apparently genuine black samurai.

Before the 1600s, the Portuguese were one of several European trading powers that went to Japan, and it is most likely that the black samurai came from Portuguese Mozambique. According to Japanese sources, he was called Yasuke, and he lived during the time before the Tokugawa Shogunate shut off Japan from the rest of the world in the late 1500s.

There are at least three different chronicles, European and Japanese, that mention Yasuke, but none are immediately contemporary, which means that the stories could be exaggerated. What they do generally agree on is that he was foreign, he learned Japanese, and he fought for the Nobunaga clan. He was also said to be a little over 6 feet tall (nearly 2 metres), so about 6 inches (15 cm) taller than the average Japanese male at the time. His height and skin colour would have made him a striking sight on a Japanese battlefield. Sources agree that he fought at the 1582 Battle of Tenmokuzan and was on the winning side.

Shortly after the battle, Nobunaga's power base in Kyoto was attacked by the samurai general Akechi Mitsuhide, who put an end to Nobunaga's attempts to consolidate power in Japan under his authority. Yasuke was reported to have been in the thick of battle on Nobunaga's side, doing what any good samurai would do to protect his lord. The defeated Nobunaga was forced to commit ritual suicide, after which

Yasuke fought alongside the heir to the clan but eventually surrendered. The victorious Mitsuhide didn't know what to do with Yasuke and sent him to 'the temple of the southern barbarians'. This was a place we would call a church, run by Jesuit Christian missionaries, some of whom were likely to be Portuguese. After that, Yasuke fades from the historical record. We just don't know how he lived out his days after this. What we know for sure is that if Yasuke was a real samurai, and if he headed back to his native Africa, he would have gone home with some unique tales to tell.

Name a Famous Queen of England

I'm guessing you said at least one of these or maybe all three:

    Queen Elizabeth I
    Queen Victoria
    Queen Elizabeth II

The reality is that for such a male-dominated society, we've had quite a few queens running the show in England/Britain, and they often ruled for quite a long time. There were two Marys; Matilda fought what amounted to a twenty-year civil war against Stephen; and then there was Queen Anne.

Until the 2018 Oscar-winning film *The Favourite* came out, Queen Anne had been strangely forgotten, but she's well worth remembering because of the number of key events that happened during her reign. Most importantly, she ruled when England and Scotland joined together under the Act of Union in 1707 to become the United Kingdom. This was the fulfilment of a long-held dream that went back to Athelstan in the tenth century AD, and seemed to require enormous bloodshed over the ensuing 800 years before it could become a reality.

A second achievement reflected the politics of Anne's age and the further development of a two-party system as a stumbling and imperfect democracy began to gain momentum. In general, the Tories were supportive of the Anglican Church and favoured the 'landed interests' of the country's gentry, while the Whigs were aligned with commercial interests and Protestant dissenters (the Labour Party wouldn't be established for another 150 years). While the politics of this age were appallingly sexist and racist, Britain had one of the most liberal systems in the world at this time.

And there was good news from the War of the Spanish Succession. It's a long story, but an alliance including Britain managed to hold in check the ever-expanding power of France. Some of the greatest French defeats at the hands of a British coalition were won under Queen Anne's rule.

This queen also partly paid for two of the most impressive structures ever raised in Britain, Blenheim Palace (as a thank-you to John Churchill, who became the 1st Duke of Marlborough, for his success in the previously mentioned war) and Saint Paul's Cathedral, finally finished after forty years of construction (it was started in 1669 under the reign of Charles II). The cathedral was a symbol of the rising power of the British Empire, which was spreading its influence in both Asia and North America.

Unfortunately, Anne's many successes as a monarch did not extend to her private life, which was particularly sad. Painfully aware that a monarch must have an heir, she had seventeen pregnancies, but only one produced a child that lived for any amount of time. This son, Prince William, died at the age of eleven. Despite her best efforts, the Stuart line of monarchs that had started in Scotland centuries earlier died with her in 1714. On her death, she was succeeded by her German second cousin George, who started the Hanoverian dynasty.

The French Lesbian Opera-Singing Duellist

Julie d'Aubigny was a lesbian. Some regarded her as bisexual, and while she did have a number of male lovers, they all seem to have been liaisons with ulterior motives: the men were rich, had connections or could teach her something of value. For example, when she was romantically linked with a fencing instructor, it was seen as an affair of the heart, but he was quickly dropped after he had taught her the requisite skills with a sword. By contrast, her relationships with women gave her no more wealth, no better standing in society nor any way of improving her education, so these relationships seem to have been more about true love than anything else. Such behaviour was regarded as scandalous for a woman in France in the late 1600s.

Sometime around 1687, when Julie was in her late teens, she had what seems to have been her first relationship with a woman. When the other woman's parents found out, they sent their daughter to a convent. Undeterred, Julie entered the convent posing as a postulant. In order to run away with her lover, she stole the body of a dead nun, placed it in her girlfriend's bed and set it on fire to cover their escape. This was remarkably lucid thinking for a young woman who had no criminal past. The affair lasted for about three months before the young woman returned to her family, and Julie d'Aubigny was charged (in absentia) with kidnapping, bodysnatching, arson, and failing to appear before the tribunal. Had she been caught, she would have been burned to death.

Julie met her first male lover under unusual circumstances when she was insulted by a young nobleman, Louis-Joseph d'Albert de Luynes, son of the rich and well-connected Duke of Luynes, and a duel was arranged. Julie won the duel by stabbing the man through his shoulder. The next day, when she asked about his health, one of his companions came to offer d'Albert's apologies. She went to see him, and they soon became lovers. After this, they remained lifelong friends. Most duels do not end this way.

Julie continued to duel even after she became a respected opera singer and had achieved fame as Mademoiselle de Maupin. Her love of women caused another scandal in 1695 when she kissed a young woman at a society ball. This was so shocking that she was challenged to duels by three different noblemen. She accepted all three challenges and beat them all in turn. However, due to the royal decree that banned duelling in Paris, she was forced to put her career on hold while she fled to Brussels, where she briefly became the mistress of a general and prince-elector of the Holy Roman Empire.

Julie returned to the opera in Paris a year or so later and had several more female companions until she retired to a convent after the death of her last lover in 1705. She is believed to have died of unknown causes in 1707 at the age of thirty-three.

Julie's is a fascinating story of a surprisingly modern woman in the 1700s. But it could all be another example of the danger of reading accounts that are not contemporary to events. Most of the information in this article comes from Theophile Gautier, writing in the 1830s. There is evidence from other sources that Julie d'Aubigny existed, but exactly how many of the events and romances are true is much harder to say. Just because it sounds good doesn't make it fact, and although 1830 sounds old, it's not the same as being an eyewitness to events 150 years earlier.

Elizabeth Wilkinson, the Cockney Bareknuckle Boxer

Women in the early 1700s were technically the property of their husbands. They had few rights and were meant to be placid little housewives and produce hordes of children. This prescriptive life was *not* for Elizabeth Wilkinson.

There are few undisputed facts about Elizabeth Wilkinson (later Stokes), right down to whether Elizabeth Wilkinson was her real name or a stage name. Whatever the truth, she was a sensation during her boxing career in the 1720s. At first, she fought other women, but when she married the boxer James Stokes, the two of them fought mixed pairs of boxers. Perhaps those who fist fight together stay together? Her career lasted for about six years at a time when it was clearly unusual for her sex to fight in the ring. Even so, she was seen in a positive light by the contemporary press.

But it's not as if she didn't face discrimination and exploitation. Advertising for one of her events stated, 'They fight in cloth Jackets, short Petticoats, coming just below the Knee, Holland Drawers, white Stockings, and pumps.' Why the list of clothing? Because prostitutes of the age would sometimes put on mock fights, bare-chested, to attract customers. The fact that Elizabeth and her opponents were fully clothed meant they were genuine fighters and nothing else! And Georgian boxing was tough; no rules were changed or concessions made if the fighters were women. There were an unlimited number of rounds, and both kept going until one conceded or couldn't stand up in the so-called scratch square at the start of the next round (hence the term 'not up to scratch').

As well as her boxing skills, Elizabeth had a reputation for brilliantly barbed put-downs. Apparently her mouth was as vicious as her right hook, and this tactic of 'trash talking' during the fight made her the 1700s answer to Muhammad Ali.

History does not record what happened to Elizabeth Wilkinson once she retired from the ring. As with so many people of non-noble birth, there was no interest in her as a three-dimensional person, just a fixation on what made her unusual. There can be no doubt that this remarkable woman was ahead of her time, so it would be nice to think that she retired to a good life.

The Controversial Trial of Admiral Byng

John Byng was never going to go down in history as one of the major players in maritime history. He served for decades in the Royal Navy in the mid-1700s, establishing a solid reputation as the ultimate safe pair of hands even though he never did anything of note. Following his career in the navy, Byng went on to become an MP in 1751, showing that he could serve his country in more than one way.

However, when the Seven Years War broke out in 1754 (and it did actually last seven years), things went horribly wrong for Byng. The war itself was truly on a global scale and boiled down to which country would have the pre-eminent empire in the world, France or Britain. These two superpowers of the age and their allies fought in North America, in the Atlantic, across mainland Europe and even in India. Admiral Byng's area of operation was the Mediterranean. The Spanish island of Minorca had been a British possession since 1708, and in 1756, France invaded. Byng was sent with a small fleet and some soldiers to recapture the British possession.

When Byng arrived, he was intercepted by a small French fleet and the Battle of Minorca ensued. It was one of those inconclusive affairs that everyone except the very crustiest of historians has forgotten about, and for good reason. Byng hung around the island for four days looking for his chance to land, but the conditions never seemed to be quite right. When he brought his officers together to discuss next steps, they decided *as a group* to return to the naval base in Gibraltar to refit the damaged ships, get reinforcements and come back for another go.

Except before that could happen, Byng was relieved of his command and found himself in court on a charge of cowardice. Although the court acquitted Byng of personal cowardice, it determined that he 'had not done his utmost', a key term used to describe the behaviours that should be demonstrated by a senior officer. Byng had failed to engage or destroy the enemy, thereby breaching the 12th Article of War. This was a serious charge, and the sentence sent shock waves throughout polite society in Britain: Byng was to be put to death by firing squad. Many people were scandalised that a senior British officer would be executed for failing to engage in and/or win a battle, and it is certainly rare in British history for any such failures to result in a death sentence.

On 14 March 1757, Byng was taken to the quarterdeck of HMS *Monarch*, where he knelt on a cushion and signified his readiness by dropping his handkerchief. At the signal, a squad of Royal Marines shot him dead.

Voltaire, the French satirist of the age, summarised these events in his work *Candide*: 'In this country, it is good to kill an admiral from time to time, in order to encourage the others.' To be fair to Voltaire, the British would go on to win the Seven Years War, a result that would transform the empire from an imperial power to *the* imperial power of the age. So, was Byng's a just punishment or not? You decide.

Was the Guillotine a Device of Mercy?

The guillotine was not the first mechanical device to carry out an execution, but it was used for the longest period and is the most infamous. The reality of executions is that most were not meant to torture but were meant to get things over quickly. When they didn't, it caused disquiet. For example, it took three blows from the executioner to completely behead Mary, Queen of Scots, which was regarded as disgraceful, especially for a royal. While axemen were the preferred option in England, France had specially trained swordsmen, but they were only for the executions of the highest-status nobles.

The guillotine was designed to ensure that it decapitated the victim first time, every time. It could, in theory, be operated by anyone with a bare minimum of training, and yet the result would always be a consistent and quick demise. The guillotine was invented in the 1700s by Antoine Louis, a physician, and Tobias Schmidt, a German engineer. It was Louis and Schmidt who suggested the angled blade to ensure a clean cut. So, why isn't the guillotine called something like 'the Louis-Schmidt'? That's because of Doctor Joseph-Ignace Guillotin, who was a member of the French National Assembly in the summer of 1789. Without getting into the ridiculous complications of the French Revolution, he was a republican but not an extreme radical. Rather ironically, Dr Guillotin was against the death penalty but suggested that if it had to be done, it should be done as quickly, efficiently and painlessly as possible, and it was he who suggested the use of the recent invention. It was an idea steeped in pragmatism, and the guillotine became synonymous with the mass executions of the French Revolution, when thousands lost their heads to the device during the Reign of Terror. And so it was a mild-mannered doctor, looking for a humane means of execution, who became forever linked with this mechanical death device.

The guillotine caught on because it had none of the shortcomings displayed by other methods such as the firing squad, the electric chair or lethal injection, all of which are still used today. The guillotine continued in use during the Napoleonic era, and in fact lingered on into the twentieth century. The last person to be executed by guillotine was the two-time murderer Hamida Djandoubi, who was guillotined on 10 September 1977, so within living memory.

Canada Remained Loyal to Britain during the American Revolution

You may read the above title and think, well, of course, in which case you are falling for that old trick of hindsight. Looking at things another way, the key cities of Montreal and

Quebec were seceded by the French in the 1760s, at the end of the Seven Years War. Fighting for the American Revolution started just a dozen years later. That isn't enough time to ensure the loyalty of any colony, not to mention that there were still people in those key cities who would rather not be British. Equally, in the 1770s, there were no firebrands in Canada preaching revolution as was happening in the American colonies. Add to this mix that the French speakers of Canada should naturally have been pro-French, and France was America's main European supporter in the American Revolution. Put like that, Canada, too, should have erupted into revolution. And yet it didn't.

This set of circumstances reveals two things about the realities of the American Revolution. First, it is easy to think that everyone in the thirteen original colonies was a diehard rebel; they weren't. Places like New York were loyalist bastions throughout. At the end of the war, about 100,000 'newly freed' Americans moved to Canada to remain part of the British Empire. There may also have been practical motives behind the decision to move as Canada was doing well economically; it was part of a growing empire with access to international trade, while America, by contrast, was forced to ask for international loans.

The American rebels recognised the potential to spread their revolution, which led to the forgotten invasion of Canada in 1775. This invasion reveals the second thing about the realities of the revolution: the rebels had very limited resources and, at times, were prone to bouts of optimism rather than military pragmatism.

How many troops do you need to do the trick? In 1759, the British needed about 4,500 to take Quebec – and that was just one city and one battle. So, did the American rebels send two or three times that number? No. At the start of Canada's famously harsh winter, they sent north two columns, numbering less than 3,000. The theory was that the attack would come as a complete surprise with regard to both location and time of year, which would enable the rebels to sweep through local militias before Britain could do anything about it. Great in theory, but they underestimated the Canadian winter, which would be a fiercer enemy than anything the British could throw at them.

To be fair to the rebels, they did achieve the anticipated surprise and managed to overrun several towns and forts. Round one to the rebels. But with cold weather coming and no sign of a popular uprising in the air, they needed to take Montreal and Quebec quickly to have any hope of holding onto their gains. A tall order.

Montreal was attacked in the most half-hearted manner, with just ninety-seven men (the majority were Canadians, so there were a few dozen rebels in the country fighting on the side of the Americans), who were comfortably beaten by the mixture of a few British regulars and nearly 200 local militia at the Battle of Longue-Pointe. The battle showed, yet again, that most locals wanted nothing to do with this foolhardy attempt at revolution.

Quebec was a bigger affair, but even then the Americans could only muster around 1,200 men for the attack on 31 December 1775. Compare that to the British Army's need for four times that number to succeed. To the rebels' credit, they did breach the city's defences, but that was as good as it got for them. This utter failure resulted in about half the force being killed, wounded or captured.

The failure to take either of the two key towns meant the Americans could not consolidate their meagre successes. They were forced to retreat in freezing conditions to the comparative safety of the colonies, a retreat in which more men died of the savage cold. Although peace would not be ratified between America and Britain until 1783, no further attempts were made by the American rebels to take Canada.

Literal War Games

There is a long history of simulating battles as a tabletop game of strategy. The oldest is most likely chess. The earliest predecessor of the modern game probably originated in India around the sixth century AD. From India, the game spread to Persia, then through the Muslim world and on to Europe via the Islamic Iberian Peninsula. By the Renaissance era, chess had more or less evolved into its current form.

Chess is sometimes called the 'game of kings' (quite literally, for there are many famous leaders who are known to have played, including Napoleon, Queen Victoria, Abraham Lincoln, Churchill and Lenin), and in terms of strategy and logic, it is peerless. However, as a battle simulator, it is poor. How often have two armies fought on a featureless plane with identical forces of exactly equal size? My research reveals ... never. So, in the period spanning the sixteenth and eighteenth centuries, many variations were created in attempts to make the game more realistic.

Then, in Prussia in 1780, Johann Hellwig invented Kriegspiel (literally 'war game'), in which the board's topography was completely altered to reflect a more realistic landscape that included fields, towns and woods. As well as a huge array of different troop types, the game took into account that troops travel at different speeds through different terrains. It also made things more abstract as blocks of colours and symbols were used to represent clusters of troops. But it would take more Prussians a few decades later to really get to grips with a war simulator. Georg Leopold von Reisswitz and his son Georg Heinrich Rudolf Johann von Reisswitz, who fought in the Napoleonic Wars, brought realism and first-hand experience to the simulation. They used accurate maps and abstract colours to denote the different troops and armies, and they called this new game ... Kriegspiel (why improve on suitability?).

Now the military had something that could more accurately simulate a real campaign and, as such, it was used as a learning and training tool in Prussian military schools before spreading throughout Europe. Wargaming the Prussian way introduced two key elements to the rules: an umpire to help with rule interpretation, and dice to introduce an element of luck ... as in, y'know ... how real life works.

Kriegspiel became an essential simulator of war and tactics throughout the nineteenth century and beyond to become the format still widely used to understand and plan battles. Arthur Wagner and Eben Swift made it part of the curriculum for the military academy that would later become the US Army Command and General Staff College. They even kept the German name until the First World War.

The ultimate evolution of the game became the legendarily complicated Campaign for North Africa. Likely to be the most complex board game ever commercially produced, it takes into account the minutiae of logistics from fuel evaporation to the water requirements of troops. The board is 10 feet long

Above: 1. The ancient apex predator Jaekelopterus. (Courtesy of Ghedoghedo under Creative Commons)

Right: 2. *Papaver somniferum* or the opium poppy, the source of all naturally occurring opium. The flower has been harvested for thousands of years. (Courtesy of the Wellcome Collection)

3. Shang dynasty bronze vessel, thirteenth to twelfth century BC. (Courtesy of Saliko under Creative Commons)

4. Bastet, the cat goddess of Ancient Egypt. (Courtesy of Einsamer Schütze under Creative Commons)

Right: 5. An example of the intricate bronze working from Luristan, eighth century BC. (Courtesy of the Metropolitan Museum of Art)

Below: 6. Deir el-Bahari, the 3,500-year-old complex built by Hatshepsut, the first female Pharaoh. (Courtesy of Kairoinfo4u under Creative Commons)

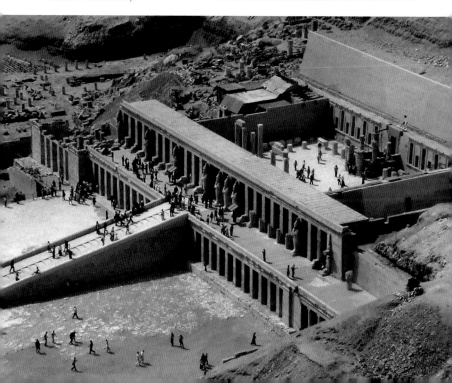

7. Kali, slayer of demons and gods but also bringer of life and new beginnings. (Courtesy of the Metropolitan Museum of Art)

8. The terracotta warriors that guard the first emperor of China's tomb. They were a complete surprise when discovered in the 1970s as all the chroniclers of the time had been so in awe of the riches in the tomb that they didn't think to mention the gigantic army of statues buried outside it. (Courtesy of Larry Koester under Creative Commons)

9. Hannibal, famous for his war elephants and crossing the Alps in 190 BC. He used another animal – snakes in jars – to win a naval battle. (Courtesy of the Rijksmuseum)

10. A marble bust of the murderous Roman Emperor Caracalla. (Courtesy of the Metropolitan Museum of Art)

11. The ruins of Pumapunku, a sixth-century AD site in modern-day Bolivia. (Courtesy of Psyberartist under Creative Commons)

12. The beautiful Fanjingshan rock formations, where the highest peak houses a Buddhist monastery. (Courtesy of Mande5255881 under Creative Commons)

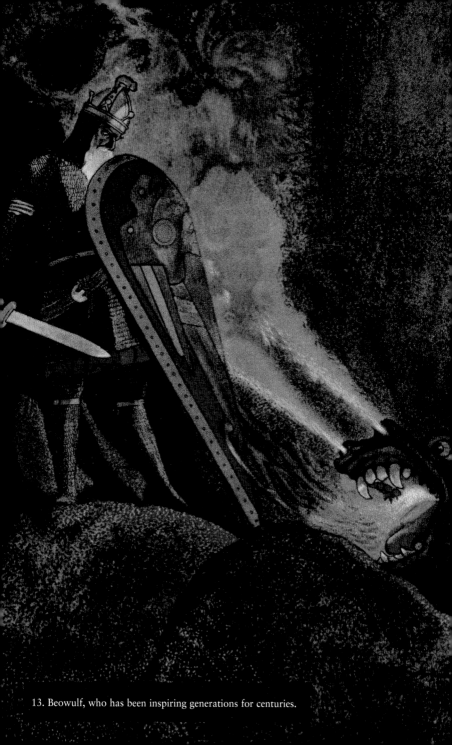

13. Beowulf, who has been inspiring generations for centuries.

14. Krak des Chevaliers, the formidable Crusader castle in modern-day Syria. This was the pinnacle of military defence prior to gunpowder. (Courtesy of Arian Zwegers under Creative Commons)

15. The resting place of William Marshall in the Temple Church, London. (Courtesy of Ben Paulos under Creative Commons)

16. The Temple of Kukulkan in Mexico; it is neither a pyramid nor a castle. (Courtesy of Stopardi under Creative Commons)

17. Reproduction of a contemporary portrait of the fabulously wealthy Jakob Fugger. (Courtesy of the Rijksmuseum)

18. A dancing mask depicting La Malinche. (Courtesy of Wolfgang Sauber)

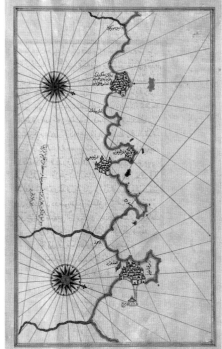

19. An Ottoman map of the coast of Algiers at a time that barbary pirates rampaged around the Mediterranean. (Courtesy of the Walters Art Museum)

Above left: 20. King James I of England was obsessed with the idea of witches, leading to him even writing a book on the subject. (Courtesy of the Yale Center for British Art)

Above right: 21. Queen Anne of Britain, the last Stuart monarch. (Courtesy of the Smithsonian Institute)

Left: 22. The exquisitely detailed interior of the Tomb of I'timad-ud-Daulah, nicknamed 'the baby Taj'. (Courtesy of Tim Moffatt under Creative Commons)

23. Alexander Hamilton as the founder of the National Bank was not only on the money but at times on food coupons too. (Courtesy of the New York Public Library)

24. Ira Aldridge, the greatest black actor of the nineteenth century, was American born but forged his career in Britain. (Courtesy of the Smithsonian Institute)

Above: 25. Note the reversed US flag on the right shoulder of the American soldier. (Courtesy of the US Army)

Left: 26. A Japanese card depicting a battle in the Russo-Japanese War, distributed so civilians could understand that Japan was winning. (Courtesy of Vintage Queensland)

27. Pilates is not ancient Asian activity but was created in the twentieth century by the German Joseph Pilates while he lived in England. (Courtesy of J. Vilchez under Creative Commons)

28. The crash-landing of the first successful non-stop transatlantic flight.

29. King Zog of Albania, who survived dozens of assassination attempts. (Courtesy of the Library of Congress)

30. Virginia Hall, a one-legged American woman, worked for the British Secret Service during the Second World War. Here she is receiving the Distinguished Service Cross for her contributions to the war. (Courtesy of the CIA)

(just over 3 metres), needs ten players, and the rules come in multiple volumes (compare that to the fold-out sheet that comes with Monopoly). It's estimated to take 1,500 hours to play to completion. As a commercial game, it didn't sell well.

Today Kriegspiel has evolved into fantasy tabletop gaming. So, even games like Dungeons & Dragons and Warhammer owe a debt of gratitude to the Prussian game creators. The original game of Kriegspiel can still be played online (it takes less than 1,500 hours), so it looks like this war game simulator will continue to evolve and live on.

The Incompetent Thomas Mifflin

Any history about the birth of a nation always muddles fact with legend. National pride means certain realities are neatly glossed over and others are exaggerated. Depending on the age of the country, some of these myths are easier to untangle from the facts than others. Because events are relatively recent (in historical terms), one of the best case studies is America and its War of Independence.

For starters, the rebels had one giant problem in a lack of competent military leaders. In the words of John Adams after watching yet another defeat of the Continental Army, 'In general our generals were out-generalled.' The myth that the rebels fought a guerrilla war against the British redcoats does not stand up to scrutiny. Similarly, the rebels did not lurch from victory to victory but, instead, suffered multiple humiliating defeats against either local loyalist militias or well-drilled regular army units.

All of these defeats led to the story of the birth of the nation at Valley Forge, when an attempt to hide the less-than-palatable facts was turned into something far more heroic. There is, perhaps, no greater embodiment of the terrible military leadership of this time than Thomas Mifflin. Major Mifflin became the army's first Quartermaster General, the man in charge of supplies. For a supposed pacifist Quaker, he did rather enjoy fighting on the front lines, which later earned him a promotion to Major General, *but that wasn't the job he was supposed to be doing*! He was meant to be looking after the army's supplies – and it wasn't like the Continental Army had many supplies to begin with.

The hardships at Valley Forge have become the stuff of legend because the rebel army nearly starved and froze to death. Some men boiled their shoe leather just to have something to eat. That desperate situation was created, at least in part, by Mifflin's incompetence. He is even known to have sold supplies at that encampment to the highest bidder – hardly the stuff of revolutionary zeal.

To be fair to Mifflin, he recognised his shortcomings and asked to be relieved of his role of Quartermaster General but was persuaded to stay because Congress was having difficulty finding a replacement. So a man who was terrible at his job kept it because he was better than nothing.

So, what was Mifflin's reward for his incompetence and near destruction of the rebel army? He became the first Governor of Pennsylvania after the war, and today there are counties, towns, schools and streets named after him. Having read this, they may want to consider a name change.

Hamilton Is on the Money

Rachel Faucette is a name you are unlikely to have heard, but she played an important role in the foundation story of the

United States. In 1745, when still a teenager, Rachel Faucette and her mother left their home on the island of Nevis (in the Caribbean) to visit relatives on the island of St Croix. While she was there, Rachel was forced to marry Johann Michael Lavien, a foul man who made a disaster of his finances and their marriage. When Rachel refused to live with her husband, she was imprisoned so that she might come to her senses. (Really?) In the legal documents of the time, she was accused of being a whore, but there is no evidence of this, and she was eventually released.

Unsurprisingly, Lavien's entirely monstrous actions did not endear Rachel to him. She abandoned the marriage and took her young son Peter with her when she returned to her home on Nevis. At some point after this, she met James Hamilton, fell in love and married him. Except she hadn't divorced husband number one, making the marriage to Hamilton null and void. Their two sons were illegitimate. When her youngest son was twelve, the Caribbean was hit by an outbreak of sickness. Rachel died along with her first-born, but the second son survived. His name was Alexander Hamilton, and he would become one of the founding fathers of America.

The debate about which historic figures should appear on national currency is an argument that never pleases everyone. Because Hamilton was undoubtedly a key figure in shaping America and its Constitution as well as its financial system, the country owes him a huge debt of gratitude. Prior to the musical *Hamilton*, however, he was not that well remembered in America.

Hamilton had been on the $10 bill since 1928, but by the new millennium, he was seen as a rather unfashionable choice, and the decision was made to replace him with a woman.

However, the currency decisions were taking place at the same time as *Hamilton* the musical was becoming a monster hit. So, in 2016, it was announced that Alexander Hamilton would remain where he had been and that Harriet Tubman, a former slave and freedom fighter, would appear on the $20 bill instead. Bad news for Andrew Jackson ... unless he scores a smash-hit musical.

America after the Revolution

The Grand Union flag was an early attempt at an American flag during the revolution. What it demonstrates is the fact that the colonists couldn't help but look back at the motherland for inspiration. The design of that flag strongly resembles the current American flag except that the Union Jack, the flag of Britain, is in the corner where the stars now appear. That was the wrong association for the new nation, so it was scrapped.

As mentioned in an earlier article, not all colonists were ardent rebels, and some 100,000 crossed the border to Canada to remain part of the British Empire. Meanwhile, thousands of men who had fought on the British side during the revolution remained in America. Men who were well known to have fought for the Crown were sometimes surrounded by gangs and beaten in the streets. Others simply moved away to start afresh. The South had an unusual concentration of ex-British militiamen, and this may have been one of the factors behind the idea of the fiercely independent 'Southern Gentleman'.

The America of the 1780s and '90s was not a nirvana that had shrugged off colonial rule to become a place of peace and prosperity. This was an uncertain time, with frequent outbreaks of violence and mob rule. Only a decade after the

War of Independence there was a full-scale revolt, not over loyalties to the motherland but over taxation on whisky, which sometimes led to shootings (the Americans *really* hated taxes). Over time, things settled down, but this is a period of American history that isn't much talked about and shows that the past is complex and rarely a clear case of good *versus* bad.

The story of post-revolution America tends to focus on the establishment of new institutions. This is important but should not side-line the wider story, which includes men being beaten by groups of their fellow countrymen for the crime of having fought on the losing side.

The Fate of the Chartists

In 1838, the People's Charter was narrowly defeated in the House of Commons. This was a bill that would have created universal suffrage (for men). Its rejection led to the formation of a group called the Chartists, whose movement lasted for twenty years. (Please wake up, it's about to get interesting.) While major changes to suffrage did eventually take place in the 1850s, the movement also led to the biggest armed uprising in British history.

The Newport Uprising of 1839 began as a protest march. In November of that year, John Frost, William Jones and Zephaniah Williams led the roughly 3,000 Chartists in a march on the Westgate Hotel in Newport, Wales. Quite why this hotel was chosen remains unclear, but there was a rumour that Chartists were imprisoned there.

Those on the march were largely miners and working men from the area who had armed themselves with a variety of home-made weapons. They weren't professional soldiers but they were strong, motivated and angry. The men demanded the release of the prisoners, but the sixty soldiers stationed in the hotel had their orders and told the crowd to disperse. Exactly who shot first is much debated (much like some of the early clashes in the American Revolution), but the well-trained and well-equipped soldiers held off the 3,000 Chartists. Lives were lost and some twenty-two Chartists lay dead at the end of the clash.

In the aftermath, about 200 Chartists were arrested for their involvement in what was termed a riot, and twenty-one were charged not with public order offences but, somewhat overdramatically, with high treason. All three leaders of the march – Frost, Jones and Williams – were found guilty and were sentenced to be hanged, drawn and quartered. They were the last people sentenced to this punishment (the first was William Wallace in the early 1300s), but after a nationwide campaign and, extraordinarily, direct lobbying by the Home Secretary, the government commuted the sentences to transportation for life.

Nostalgia Isn't What It Used to Be

Yes, it's an old joke, but it turns out to be true. That's because from about 1680 to 1870, nostalgia was considered to be a disease. It was a regular cause for concern by doctors on Royal Navy ships who noted men pining for a return to what they knew (so homesickness, really), a serious matter for the navy as it impacted the effectiveness of some of its crews.

In mainland Europe, the condition became known as the Swiss disease because Swiss soldiers were felt to be particularly prone to it (Toblerone isn't what it used to be, either). In his 1688 medical dissertation, Swiss physician Johannes Hofer coined the term 'nostalgia', from the Greek *nostos*, homecoming, and *algos*, pain, and described it as 'a state of moral pain associated with the forced separation from family and social environment'. So it wasn't a good thing.

Over the years 'cures' have included leeches, purges, bullying and – incredibly – being buried alive, which is enough to scare anyone out of the condition. The last time it was taken seriously as an illness was during the US Civil War when more than 5,000 Union soldiers were struck down by nostalgia, and seventy-four were said to have died of it. The situation got so bad that the Union Army banned the song 'Home Sweet Home' in case it debilitated any more troops. At the time, military doctor Theodore Calhoun thought nostalgia was something to be ashamed of and ordered the men to be slapped and shouted at.

Fortunately, those days have passed and today we are likely to diagnose severe cases as depression and/or PTSD. But for most of us, there are fleeting feelings of nostalgia evoked by sights, such as old photographs; smells, such as the cooking scents of childhood; and sounds that evoke musical memories. So the next time someone whines that songs or TV shows or films aren't what they used to be, best not to call them a coward and scream in their face. It won't help and may make things worse!

American Marines in Africa

If I said this article is about Americans fighting in North Africa, you might think it's about the Second World War, but you'd be wrong by over 100 years. In the late eighteenth and early nineteenth centuries, Tripoli (in modern Libya) and the surrounding region, which included the port of Derna, held the bases of Barbary pirates who had been the scourge of the Mediterranean for centuries. US President Thomas Jefferson was fed up paying tribute for safe passage and furious over Tripoli's seizure of American cargoes and crews, which were ransomed for their return. So, Jefferson (who had been in office just nineteen days) ordered a naval squadron to the Mediterranean, and the United States went to war in March 1801. The scenario that resulted feels surprisingly contemporary as this was America's first war abroad, its first against terrorism and its first against a Muslim power.

Early efforts in the war amounted only to minor confrontations and did little to stop Barbary harassment. In 1804, diplomatic consul to Tripoli and US Army Lieutenant William Eaton realised that by backing the claim of Tripoli's deposed ruler, Hamet Karamanli, America could not only have influence in the Mediterranean and neutralise what was, in effect, a terrorist pirate base, but could also show America to be an emerging power in the region. After meeting with Jefferson and presenting his idea, Eaton got the go-ahead and returned to the area in 1805 with three small warships and a dozen US Marines. On arrival in Egypt Eaton hired 400 Berber mercenaries and marched them 500 miles across the desert to confront the pirates along the North Africa coast.

Believing the majority of the population would prefer to be ruled by Hamet, Eaton's mission was to depose the ruling pasha of Tripoli, who had seized power from his brother, the very same Hamet Karamanli. When Eaton observed that the defending fort at Derna had eight guns, he ordered the American ships in the nearby harbour to open fire and bombard Derna's batteries. When Eaton's mercenary army failed to storm the fortifications, he personally led the charge and was shot in the wrist in the process. The defenders fled in haste, leaving their loaded guns, which Eaton turned on the city, and it fell later that day.

US Marine Corps First Lieutenant Presley O'Bannon raised the American flag over the fort and performed so heroically that (according to US Marine legend) Hamet Karamanli, now restored as ruler of Tripoli, presented him with what is known as a Mamluk sword. This became the model for the swords carried by US Marine officers today.

For the first time, an American flag flew over fortifications on the other side of the Atlantic Ocean. This was the first land battle fought by the United States on foreign soil and put America on the map of global affairs, albeit in a very small way. Eaton received a hero's welcome when he returned to the US, but he never fully paid the Berber mercenaries he left behind (he might have felt that, in failing to storm the Derna fort, they had not earned full pay).

This whole bizarre chapter has been immortalised in the 'Marines' Hymn' with the line, 'To the shores of Tripoli', commemorating events that unfolded in the Battle of Derna.

The History of the Banana

Trust me when I say there is a lot of history to this fruit from the berry family (see, you've already learned something). The standard yellow banana with its trademark curve is part of the genus *Musa*, botanically berries, called plantains, the vast majority of which are usually cooked, rather than eaten raw as is usual with the 'dessert' banana we know.

Farmers in South East Asia and Papua New Guinea were the first to domesticate the banana, and it seems we've been eating them for a long time. Recent archaeological evidence at Kuk Swamp in the Western Highlands Province of Papua New Guinea suggests that banana cultivation there goes back to at least 5000 BC – that's the Neolithic era! They were brought west by Arab conquerors in 327 BC, moved from Asia Minor to Africa and finally carried to the New World as it opened up to explorers and missionaries. It was Portuguese colonists who started banana plantations in the Caribbean, Brazil, and western Africa. They were thought to be a cheap and nutritious foodstuff, perfect for slaves and peasants. Eventually bananas made their way to North America where people began consuming them on a small scale at very high prices shortly after the US Civil War.

The name 'banana' is neither from the Papua New Guinean language nor Portuguese but may have origins in West Africa, arriving in English via Spanish or Portuguese traders. The yellow banana so familiar to us is called the Cavendish banana, named after William Cavendish, 6th Duke of Devonshire. Though this was not the first known banana specimen in Europe, Cavendish cultivated them in the greenhouses of Chatsworth House from around 1834. This British stately home in Derbyshire, a beautiful area of the English countryside, is about as far removed from the steamy tropical jungles of Papua New Guinea as it is possible to imagine.

The Cavendish bananas were shipped off to various places in the 1850s, and some of them ended up in the Canary Islands. In 1888, bananas from the Canaries were imported into England by Thomas Fyffe who grew wealthy from the trade (the company is still a major player in the banana market). Cavendish bananas entered mass commercial production in 1903, but along with many types of plantain, they were attacked by disease in the 1920s. As a result, banana plantations were moved every ten years in order to avoid what was known as the Panama Disease before researchers developed a banana that was immune to the mould that caused it. The Giant Cavendish, the variety that has come to dominate current global consumption, appeared in the 1950s.

Bananas are grown in more than 150 countries although 80 per cent are grown in South America. It is widely believed there are more than 1,000 types of bananas of which almost half are inedible. They come in all colours, sizes, shapes and tastes, but the Cavendish is the most common today.

Laskarina Bouboulina, Greek Freedom Fighter and Admiral of the Russian Navy

Laskarina Bouboulina is one of the key names associated with the Greek Independence movement in the early 1800s, and one of few women remembered for their contribution. She was born in a prison in Istanbul in 1771 because her father had fought for the Russians against the Ottoman Empire, and his pregnant wife was also imprisoned. Russia always supported the Greeks and the Slavs in Ottoman territories, partly because they were 'brothers' through the Orthodox Christian Church, but mainly because it was an easy way to create a fifth column inside the realm of an enemy empire (more on that later). It is fair to say that Bouboulina grew up with no love for the Ottomans.

Laskarina's early adult life was nothing exceptional: her first husband died, but by 1811, she was a wealthy woman following the death of her second husband. Because of his maritime business, she inherited a small fleet of merchant ships which, in 1816, the Ottoman authorities tried to take from her. When she went to Istanbul to meet Russian Ambassador Grigori Stroganov and request his protection, he responded by exiling her to the Crimea for three months. Later, she met with the Ottoman sultan's mother (showing she had powerful connections in the court), who, afterwards, reportedly convinced her son Mahmud II to leave Bouboulina's property alone. The sultan agreed, probably because he recognised that the empire needed major reforms to stop its terminal decline, and the confiscation of personal property was part of that.

At this time, the Ottomans and Mahmud II were facing the spreading threat of nationalism, a new concept in which primary allegiance was no longer to the local tribe, town or leader, but to the wider community or country. When an empire was as diverse in cultures, languages and religions as the Ottoman Empire, it was only ever going to shatter, but the Ottomans were in an even trickier situation than most other empires. If ancient Greece was the starting point of Western culture, according to many European powers, why was it not independent or, at least, under the control of one of the great Western powers? Why was it in the hands of decadent and corrupt Muslim sultans? This was an idea that grew in the West even as the idea of independence began to take hold in Greek-speaking areas of the empire.

In 1814, Filiki Eteria, the Society of Friends, was founded in Odessa (Russian territory at this time) along the same lines as the Freemasons, but this secret society was dedicated to the overthrow of Ottoman rule. Within five years its message had spread like wildfire until there was an extensive secret network of associated organisations not only in Greece itself, but in virtually every Greek community in Europe, both in and outside of the Ottoman Empire. When there had been rebellions by Greeks in the past, the Ottomans simply allowed bandits from Albania to descend on their towns and cause enough chaos for the rebels to put down their arms. The Ottomans didn't have to raise a formal army to suppress the unrest, and the Albanians could return home with carts groaning under the weight of their plunder. It was a win for everyone except the Greeks who, to this day, often believe that the average Albanian is a crook and is not to be trusted.

Albania wasn't a very powerful country, and the fact that a few bands of its outlaws could keep the Greek rebels in check shows how badly Greek freedom fighters needed outside assistance to stand any chance of achieving independence. As in the case of the American War of Independence, during the Greek War of Independence, there was a remarkable number of foreign troops (and, critically, equipment and weapons) floating around to help the cause. All of this was a little ironic as Mahmud II was the great reformer, the first sultan in centuries to make radical changes that lasted. As part of this rising voice of anger and demands for independence, Laskarina Bouboulina used her ships to move men and ammunition for the coming revolution. She also built a large 'merchant vessel', which was no such thing; it was a warship, the *Agamemnon*, which would end up being the rebel Greeks' biggest ship. Things were going exactly to plan … until 1825.

Greeks are passionate people who have a reputation for family feuds. So even in the middle of a war against an empire that had stood for 500 years, this national characteristic of inter-family bickering and vendettas came to the fore. A daughter of the Koutsis family eloped with Bouboulina's son. Seeking the return of his daughter, Christodoulos Koutsis went to Bouboulina's house with armed members of his family. Infuriated, Bouboulina confronted them from the balcony. Tempers frayed, and someone shot her in the head. She was dead before she hit the ground. The killer was not identified, but it was a Greek and not an Ottoman soldier.

After Bouboulina's death, Emperor Alexander I of Russia granted her the honorary rank of Admiral of the Russian Navy, which showed not only the importance of her role in the fight for independence, but also how much Russia loved rubbing events in the face of the Ottomans. Her legend has only grown in Greece, where she is well remembered as a national hero.

The Americans Didn't Always Pay Their Bills

The French contribution to the rebel cause during the American Revolution wasn't just another excuse for the French to annoy the British. The help came at a cost. Therefore, after independence had been achieved, France expected America to pay for the guns, provisions, ships and more that had been essential to the American war effort. It should be remembered that in the pivotal siege of Yorktown, the navy that blockaded the port was French, and in total, there were almost as many French soldiers, sailors and military personnel involved as American colonists. The French had a point, and as the first Secretary of the Treasury, Alexander Hamilton ensured that America honoured its debts.

However, by 1798, two things had changed. First, Hamilton was no longer in charge of the treasury; but second, and more importantly, the French regime that had come to the aid of the rebels had changed. Even after the French monarchy had been overthrown, the United States had continued to pay its debts. Revolutionary France received money from revolutionary America, a brotherhood forged in blood and their shared belief that a republic was better than a monarchy. But by 1798, it had dawned on America that it was honouring a debt that, technically speaking, didn't exist anymore. The incurred debts were, after all, monies owed to the French Crown as it had been French royal troops that had done all the fighting. But the French Revolution had made it clear that the new France was absolutely not the same thing as the old France.

Unsurprisingly, the French saw things differently and, when the money stopped coming, French protests were met with delaying tactics and a certain amount of sabre-rattling from America. This started the so-called 'quasi-war' between the two nations, a period (1798–1800) under the presidency of John Adams when French and American ships fought unofficial naval battles in the Atlantic. This occurred at a time when France was at war with pretty much everyone else in Europe and beyond.

The situation was taken seriously by America. Although he saw no action, Alexander Hamilton came out of retirement and was one of the leaders of the American forces during this period of uncertainty and violence. The reality was that France had bigger fish to fry (like fighting the Royal Navy threat in the Mediterranean) and hostilities petered out by 1800 when it was Napoleon who wanted to end what had become an annoyance. The conflict came to a close when both sides signed the Convention of 1800. Incredibly cheekily, America claimed that the hostilities had cost them $20 million in maritime trade. So a war that had started over not paying their debts to France turned into a demand for money from France. This was largely ignored in the articles of the Convention although the American government was forced to reimburse American shipping firms out of its own pocket. Amazingly, payment was delayed for more than a century until 1915, when the US government finally handed over $3.9 million to the heirs of the firms affected.

In 1858 France and Spain Attacked South East Asia

In the nineteenth-century game of imperial dominance, European powers cast around the globe looking for new territories to conquer or places to establish new colonies. France went to the peninsula south of China, and, after four years of fighting, gunboat diplomacy and threats, was able to found Cochinchina. This would form the base from which the French would eventually create French Indochina, which is Vietnam today. They would then go on to conquer the neighbouring countries of Laos and Cambodia.

From the Vietnamese point of view, the so-called 'Vietnam War' (called the American War in Vietnam as, from their perspective, every war they fought could be called the Vietnam War) was the last phase in a century of shrugging off the imperial yolk of multiple overlords. France never quite finished the job of cowing the indigenous Vietnamese. From

the 1880s to the 1940s, the country was ruled with an iron fist by the French. The Vietnamese despised their colonisers – though elements of French culture (including some words and the 'baguette', both the word and the bread) seeped into Vietnamese culture – and the French were never fully able to subdue the resistance. Part of this was due to the vast coastline with its many inlets, which made it easy for smugglers to avoid French taxes and/or to bring in arms and supplies for rebels. Added to this was the interior of the country, a nightmare of mountainous regions covered in thick jungle, perfect territory to hide rebel bases and carry out hit-and-run operations on French positions.

The French struggled with this for the best part of a century, and then in the 1940s, during the Second World War, Vichy France ordered the local forces to yield to the Japanese. In response to this, Vietnamese freedom fighters, led by Ho Chi Minh, were backed by the American OSS (the precursor to the CIA) to rise up against the Japanese. After the war, the French tried to recapture the country which already had declared itself independent. America had supported the Vietnamese freedom fighters during the war but didn't want to fight a Western ally, so it adopted a neutral stance. However, cutting a complicated story to the bones, once the French were defeated and Ho Chi Minh declared himself to be a communist, America felt obliged to intervene to stop the spread of communism, which had recently taken the whole of China. By 1975, Ho Chi Minh was dead, but all of Vietnam was at last free, unified and communist. The Western intervention that had begun when Napoleon III was Emperor of France was at an end.

Mail-order Brides in the Media

Today the phrase 'mail-order bride' implies old, lonely guys exploiting poor women from the developing world. While the research on arranged marriages in the twenty-first century suggests otherwise, the origins of the custom are even more counterintuitive. Britain had a version, consisting of lonely-hearts adverts in local newspapers from as early as the 1690s; they had only limited success because, at the time, a significant part of the population was illiterate. However, the need to advertise for companionship evolved to a whole new level in the second half of the 1800s in America, when the appeal was not meant for women from other countries, but for American women.

Two key events in the nineteenth century created the need, and a steady increase in literacy made it possible. The first event was the expansion of the American West. This part of the country was lawless and dangerous, so far more single men than families headed west to establish a homestead and/ or seek their fortunes. There were constant threats, including possible attacks by Native Americans, wild animals and those who might challenge your claim or rob you of your wealth. The men who struck out on this lonely life were surrounded almost exclusively by other men; the only single women were those who worked in the local bars and saloons. So, there was not a lot of choice for an honest, hard-working lad from West Virginia.

The second event was the US Civil War, in which 2 per cent of the population of the country died, the vast majority of them men. This may not sound like a lot, but the result was a shortage of men in a country where there were, literally,

thousands of women who wanted to marry, but for whom the concentration of men of marriageable age was out of reach. So, adverts began to appear in newspapers back east. Here is an example from the times:

> Bachelor, aged 42, considered good looking and affectionate wishes to marry suitable spinster or widow of Christian principles.

Clearly, this man was not looking for a casual liaison but had come to a time in his life when he wanted the companionship of marriage and, probably, a family. Interestingly, religion was important enough to get a mention. In the normal course of events, correspondence would follow (some of the letters were surprisingly intimate) and photos were exchanged (everyone looked their best, naturally) in long-distance courtships that were not dissimilar to the rituals of today's internet dating – although, of course, much slower.

The women who replied to these lonely-hearts messages tended to be spirited and independent and might have found the men around them to be crushingly patriarchal. Their hopes might have been that the men on the frontier were less traditional and more adventurous, but whether the expectations of the parties were based in reality was something that could only be revealed when they met. Both parties were taking their chances, and, as in all circumstances, some of these marriages worked well and some didn't.

The research into this most delicate of Victorian-era scenarios uncovers a universal truth: we all want to love and be loved, and sometimes unusual circumstances require unusual measures. I have to add that I find the topic touchingly sweet and very human.

Thousands of Men Died in the Middle of Nowhere for No Real Reason

One of the most appalling and shocking things about the American Civil War is how bloody it was. All wars and all civil wars experience carnage, but the clashes in this conflict were titanic; the Battle of Gettysburg saw more American dead in one battle than in any other battle in American history (the dead on both sides are counted in this instance). While Gettysburg is famous, all across the south-east of the United States there are hundreds of plaques to commemorate almost innumerable battles. The fighting was incredibly fierce and continuous.

In May 1864, the American Civil War was still being fought across the hills, fields and towns of a divided country. General Ulysses S. Grant was now in charge of the Union (US government) Army after a long list of staggeringly incompetent and lacklustre generals (I'm looking at you, Mead, McClellan and Burnside). For those arguing that General Robert E. Lee (leader of the Confederate or rebel army) was one of the greatest generals in history ... well, you have to beat some stiff opposition to get there. The three in brackets were military minnows, so, in my opinion, Lee was good and did a lot with not much, but to lose to Mead at Gettysburg was not a sign of one of the greatest-ever military leaders.

Grant was far more aggressive than Lee by this point in the war; he realised that he could afford losses the southern Confederates simply could not. He kept the pressure on by pushing at Lee, knowing that even a defeat could be seen as a victory if it cost Lee too many men. However, this mentality led to some bloody and pointless encounters. The worst of these was the Battle of the Wilderness, where nearly 200,000 men clashed for three days in the scrublands and woods of Virginia, far from anywhere important. The battle wasn't fought to gain access to resources or important transport hubs but was just one example of the attritional warfare that Grant was waging on Lee.

Grant had a two-to-one superiority in men, but as usual, Lee was careful in positioning his troops. While the fighting was hard and bloody, what struck both the fighting men at the time and, later, the historians researching it was the terrible fate that befell hundreds of the wounded on both sides. The cartridge system of the guns and the dry scrubland made for a lethal combination that led to bush fires. Men too badly hurt to move could be heard screaming in the midst of the battle as they were roasted alive. It was a slow and painful way to die, and their cries chilled the men on both sides.

The Union Army suffered more than 17,500 casualties, and the number suffered by the Confederates is believed to be over 11,000, with around 1,500 killed, 8,000 wounded and 1,700 captured or missing. Based on these numbers, the Battle of the Wilderness was the fourth-bloodiest battle of the US Civil War.

So, what was accomplished? Grant retreated, having taken far higher losses, but Lee felt his losses more keenly and had to reposition closer to the Confederate capital at Richmond, Virginia. It could, therefore, be argued that it was a Confederate tactical victory but a Union strategic one. Ultimately, though, it was a bloody engagement that led to an unnecessarily cruel loss of life for little, if any, gain on either side.

Nakano Takeko, the Female Samurai

Nakano Takeko was a Japanese woman born in Edo (now Tokyo) who came to fame during the Boshin War of 1868–9. This was a civil war between the ruling Tokugawa Shogunate, which had been in power for about 250 years, and those who wanted a return of the emperor as the primary power in Japan. The cause of the war was the widespread fear and disgust triggered by the Tokugawa Shogunate when it made the decision to open Japan to the rest of the world and allowed foreigners into the country. Ironically, it had been the founder of this very dynasty, Tokugawa Ieyasu, who had sealed Japan off in the early 1600s.

The fighting was the first serious violence in the country for over 200 years, and the war raged in a number of areas across the Japanese islands as local lords joined one side or another. In October 1868, the war came to Takeko, who lived in Aizu in the east of Honshu, the largest island in the Japanese archipelago, and an area renowned for the martial prowess of its inhabitants. Not much is known about her up until this point; however, she was likely to have had basic martial training if she was the daughter of either a local landowner of status or a samurai.

Takeko was on the side of the Tokugawas and took up arms to lead a contingent of exclusively female warriors called *onna bugeisha* (because 'samurai' is an exclusively male term) in the Battle of Aizu. Takeko did not invent the term *onna bugeisha* as there had been rare instances, going back hundreds of years, of women fighting in battles. Like many of the women, Takeko wielded a *naginata* (imagine a staff with a *katana* blade from a traditional samurai sword on the end; nasty, isn't it?), but thanks to the crushingly misogynistic and patriarchal rules of the time, the female detachment had to fight independently from the men.

Takeko's bravery was not in any doubt. While leading a charge against Imperial Japanese Army troops, she was fatally shot in the chest. Rather than let the enemy capture her entire body, she asked her sister to cut off her head and have it buried. Her sister reluctantly carried out Takeko's dying wish and took her head to Hōkai Temple where she buried it under a pine tree.

Although Takeko was ultimately on the losing side of the war, her bravery has been commemorated. A monument to her was erected to mark the place where her head was interred.

The Greatest Black American Actor of the Nineteenth Century

Ira Aldridge was a black American, born a free man in New York in 1807. He realised early on that he wanted to be an actor, and soon joined the African Company. He later joined the African Grove Theatre, the first resident African American theatre in the US. The theatre faced blatant racism, and so did Ira. Slavery had been abolished in the state of New York (it was not abolished throughout the US until the end of the Civil War in 1865), but racial prejudice was very much alive and well. So, perhaps a little counterintuitively, Aldridge decided to move to Britain in 1824 at the age of just seventeen. Britain was racist and accepted the concept of white supremacy, but with an empire that covered a quarter of the globe, there was, compared to other countries including America, more open-mindedness about people of colour having careers beyond menial servitude.

Aldridge initially settled in Liverpool, a bustling port and one of the mightiest industrial cities of the age. A year later, he was regularly performing around the country. Early in his career, Aldridge introduced a direct address to the audience on the closing night of his engagement at any given theatre. In the years leading up to the Slavery Abolition Act of 1833, which abolished slavery in Britain and its colonies, Aldridge spoke about the injustices of slavery and the passionate desire for freedom of those held in bondage. What's interesting is that his audiences didn't throw things at him or hurl abuse – they listened.

In 1831, Aldridge successfully performed in Dublin and at several other locations in Ireland (the entire island was then part of the British Empire), creating a sensation wherever he went. The small-town locals had simply never seen anything like him, and he was a hit. He continued to tour in Scotland, including Edinburgh, where some praised his skills and, inevitably, a few attacked his race. Since he was an American black actor from the African Theatre, *The Times* called him the African Roscius, after the famed actor of ancient Rome. Aldridge used this to his benefit, embellishing his African ties in advertising for his plays; he had in fact never been to Africa.

He successfully toured Europe in 1852, performing for Frederick William IV of Prussia; he also performed in Budapest. An 1858 tour took him to Serbia and to imperial Russia, where he met many of the great writers and artists of the day. Tolstoy became a friend and the Ukrainian poet and artist Taras Shevchenko sketched his portrait. He was well regarded wherever he went. While it's true that part of his attraction was in the novelty of seeing a black man on stage, novelty alone won't keep people in their seats for a two-hour play; it was his skill as an actor that kept them there. Of course, successful tours playing to large crowds earned Aldridge a healthy income. He purchased some property in England, toured Russia again and applied for British citizenship in 1863.

In 1856, Ira's private life was hit by scandal when one William Stothard accused Ira of having an affair with his wife, which resulted in the birth of an illegitimate child. Aldridge was found guilty and fined all of £2. He wasn't present for any of this as he was busy touring. Had this happened in the US, particularly in the American south, it's hard to think he would have come out of it alive.

Aldridge married twice, once to an English woman and the second time to a Swede. Both women were, of course, white, but contrary to common perceptions of the era, nobody seemed to care. With all of the racist ideology behind imperialism, anyone might assume that he would have found it impossible to be taken seriously in the royal courts of Europe, but it seems he was accepted for what he was: a damn fine Shakespearian actor.

Aldridge kept going until, at the age of sixty in 1867, he died while touring Poland. Apparently, he had just signed a contract for a 100-night tour of America, now that the civil war there had ended. He never returned to his country of birth, but African American actors for generations have regarded him as a great role model and inspiration.

Imperial Botany

The Wardian case is, in essence, a tiny, portable glasshouse. It's not much to look at, but it changed the entire global economy in the nineteenth century. The case was invented by Dr Nathaniel Bagshaw Ward in approximately 1829. The reason for the vagueness is because the significance of the invention was not obvious at the time. It only took off in the 1840s, when it changed the world forever.

Moving seeds from one place to another is easy, but they need the right conditions to grow and thrive. It might not be apparent how much water they need, the temperatures they require and the optimum soil acidity levels to make new life spring from the earth. In other words, shipping seeds is easy; growing them into plants is hard. One solution might be to wait and move young plants, but they tend to be fragile, so shipping them over long distances is extremely difficult. But it was the invention of this portable greenhouse that allowed young plants to flourish in a safe environment. The Wardian case made it possible to safely ship plants from Britain to places as far flung as Australia with a minimal amount of maintenance.

Somewhat frivolously, this did lead to some light-hearted uses; for instance, the Victorian upper classes used them to grow and show off orchids and ferns. It was quite the craze for a time. Far less frivolously and much more significantly, the case enabled Britain to break other countries' monopolies on important plants and provided a massive competitive advantage in the Victorian era. It also made Britain the epicentre of botany in the nineteenth century and was instrumental in creating centres of study like Kew Gardens in

London, a place of outstanding beauty and variety but also of vital botanical preservation and research.

The two most important examples of how the Wardian case changed the world are rubber and tea. Rubber originally came only from Brazil, part of the Portuguese Empire, so Portugal had the global monopoly. Using Ward's cases, British agents managed to smuggle young plants and ship them to Sri Lanka and Malaya, where they thrived. Portugal no longer had a stranglehold on the rubber exports of the world, and Britain could not only produce its own rubber but sell it to others at a profit. Rubber was vital for all kinds of machinery (not least car tyres), and all of this could now be sourced from within the empire. Britain no longer has an empire, but 150 years later, rubber is still vital to the economies of both Sri Lanka and Malaysia (as Malaya is now).

Most critically, however, there was tea. 'I wouldn't do X for all the tea in China' is a commonly heard phrase because, up until the middle of the nineteenth century, that's where all tea came from (green tea is not from a different plant but comes from the young buds of the tea plant). Tea was not known in medieval Britain; it was drunk by the aristocracy of the Iberian Peninsula and introduced to England when Catherine of Braganza came from Portugal to marry Charles II in the 1600s. After her arrival, Catherine fell ill and asked for some tea, but the English courtiers at the time had no idea what she was talking about and offered her some warm ale instead. This was clearly not an acceptable substitute, so the queen rectified this by having tea imported. It was introduced to Britain as a herbal remedy, but once it was seen as the must-have drink at court, it gained popularity through the aristocracy and then in wider society among those who could afford what was then an expensive commodity. (There was even a time when compressed tea bricks were used as currency in China.)

Fast-forwarding to the nineteenth century, 20,000 young tea plants were smuggled out of China and planted in India. It's hard to believe, but India was not a tea-producing country prior to the invention of the Wardian case; today, India is as synonymous with tea as China. Nothing better illustrates the impact of this little glass case. These new plantations created a huge new source of revenue at the time and are still generating huge sums of money today in modern India. The Indian tea plantations broke China's monopoly and allowed Britain to produce it under its own terms, which led to lower prices and is why, today, tea is relatively inexpensive.

The Real Frankenstein

Mary Shelley's *Frankenstein* is a work of fiction, but it was inspired by a certain kind of experiment being conducted in the early 1800s. Front and centre was Giovanni Aldini, an Italian physicist who studied the connection between muscles and electrical impulses. What form did these experiments take? He hooked up dead animals to rudimentary batteries and made them twitch by allowing an electrical current to flow through their musculature.

If you think that's gross, it gets worse. Aldini's most famous public demonstration of the electro-stimulation technique of deceased limbs was performed on the corpse of the (human) criminal George Forster, who was executed at Newgate Prison in London in 1803. The *Newgate Calendar* (a monthly bulletin of executions published by Newgate Prison – yes, really) describes what happened when the galvanic process was used on the body just hours later:

> On the first application of the process to the face, the jaws of
> the deceased criminal began to quiver, and the adjoining muscles
> were horribly contorted, and one eye was actually opened. In
> the subsequent part of the process the right hand was raised and
> clenched, and the legs and thighs were set in motion.

Nobody knows if Mary Shelley was present at any of his demonstrations (it's not implausible). She would have been a child when Aldini was doing most of his work, but his experiments were widely reported and discussed. Famously, it was one evening in 1816 when Mary came up with the concept of the artificially animated monster created by the mad scientist Dr Frankenstein. The inspiration struck when she was with her husband Percy Shelley as well as Lord Byron and John Polidori (who would later write the first book about the modern concept of the vampire, predating Bram Stoker's *Dracula* by sixty-eight years).

Whether or not Mary Shelley was channelling memories of stories she read as a child is complete conjecture. What is indisputable is that Aldini's work was groundbreaking, helping anatomists further understand how the human body works. However, it's safe to say that his experiments and his methods would certainly be repudiated in the scientific world today.

Why Did Eighteenth- and Nineteenth-century Armies Fight in Long Lines?

Packed formations, bright colours; battle formations both before and after the Napoleonic era seem so counterintuitive and, to the modern observer, so likely to result in mass casualties. But the military had their reasons, and some of these had to do with the musket. In the 1600s, musket men positioned themselves in solid square formations alongside pikemen (soldiers with pikes, essentially spears) so they could be deployed against the enemy while the musketeers paused to reload. This all changed in the late 1600s when the bayonet was introduced. At first they were 'plug' bayonets which were stuck *in* the end of the gun, removing the ability to fire so that the weapon became little more than an expensive spear. Let's not forget that this was a time when most firearms could only fire two or three rounds a minute, and only when it wasn't raining. Next came the 'socket' bayonet, which clipped around the gun barrel. This negated the use of pikemen, so now everyone could have a gun.

Gustavus Adolphus II was King of Sweden from 1611 to 1632 and is credited with establishing Sweden as a great military power. A large part of his success was his revolutionary rethink of battle formations. He recognised that in deep ranks of musket men many weren't able to fire, so he made his ranks longer and thinner so that more men could fire simultaneously. The result was that while the Swedish military had considerably fewer men than others, it was able to beat back the massed ranks of countries like Russia. Obviously, after armies were beaten by this tactic, they started to copy it.

But why were the men packed so close together? The answer is because the guns were smooth bore; there was no rifling in the barrel. Rifles and virtually all modern guns (even pistols) have a series of spiral grooves cut into the barrel, which makes the bullet spin as it passes through. A spinning projectile is less likely to drift off course and is far more likely to hit its mark. Because smooth-bore muskets were so inaccurate, the only chance of hitting anything was to have massed volley fire from a concentration of musket men. That way, there was a better chance of hitting some of the oncoming enemy soldiers.

As for the bright colours, there was so much smoke from cannons and muskets that colourful uniforms were needed so the generals knew whose army was where. Countries had a tacit agreement about who had which colours, so the British had red, Austria had white, France had dark blue, etc. There wasn't much point in wearing another country's colours to surprise them because in all the smoke and confusion your own artillery were just as likely to fire on you, thinking you were the enemy. Once the reasons behind seemingly ludicrous battle formations are explained, they're not so ludicrous. In fact, they are quite logical.

The Origins of Morse Code

Samuel Morse is world-famous as the inventor of Morse code, a simple way to transfer information using a telegraph or heliograph (a signalling device by which sunlight is reflected in flashes from a movable mirror) or even a lantern. The code has lasted into the digital era although it is no longer taught as standard in the navies of the world. Morse was one of the most influential men in the history of mass communication, and yet, that's not what he ever intended.

Samuel Finley Breese Morse was born in April 1791 and brought up in a strict Calvinist family in Massachusetts, where his father, the rather brilliantly named Jedidiah, was a clergyman. In the early 1800s, Morse studied horse anatomy, mathematics and religious philosophy at Yale University, where he supported himself by painting portraits and went on to establish himself as a talented portrait painter (although he preferred to paint historical events).

By 1826, Morse was established enough and wealthy enough to help found the National Academy of Design in New York City, where he served as the academy's president from 1826 to 1845. If you asked who Samuel Morse was in 1830, people would know of him as an artist, and that's it. However, during this period, while he was in Washington fulfilling the commission for a portrait, he received a message from his father that read, 'Your dear wife is convalescent.' Morse was heartbroken. The next day it got worse when he received another letter detailing his wife's sudden death. Morse left immediately for home. He was riddled with guilt that for days he was unaware of his wife's failing health. Surely, in this amazing age of science, there must be some way to send messages quickly over great distances. The guilt and desperation for a solution to the problem provided the spark Morse needed to explore a means of rapid, long-distance communication.

Now, as a middle-aged man, Morse's life took a very different direction. He contributed to the invention of a single-wire telegraph system (based on earlier European telegraphs), and later invented the code which bears his name and became the primary language of telegraphy around the globe. Remarkably, Samuel Morse used personal tragedy to make the world a better and more connected place.

The Forgotten Riot in a Forgotten Film

The Martin Scorsese film *Gangs of New York* is set during the US Civil War. Most agree that it's not his best film, but it is sumptuous and dripping in authentic period detail. As the story unfolds, a battle takes place in New York City, but it has nothing to do with the civil war raging in America at the time. Instead, the film portrays a series of violent riots that protested the federal government's proposed military draft in 1863, a proposal that met unexpected opposition.

On Monday 13 July 1863, at the Ninth District Provost Marshal's office at Third Avenue and 47th Street in New York City, an angry mob of around 500 men turned up to protest the local draft. The North had more manpower, more industry, more commerce and more manufacturing, so why was it struggling against the Confederate South? The threat of the draft being used to bolster the North's Union Army had been coming for some time, and as this was less than two weeks after the Union's success in the pivotal Battle of Gettysburg, it seemed to President Abraham Lincoln that the time had come to put the whole of the Union on a war footing and end this civil war once and for all.

But the president and his cabinet had not accurately read the mood of the men in the cities, and the news of the draft was greeted with anger as the poor of New York believed that the burden of the draft would fall heavily on them (which it would). Further, many of the rioters were recent Irish immigrants who feared having to compete for labouring jobs with emancipated slaves, a somewhat racially biased view we'll put to one side.

The stakes were high and it is therefore unsurprising that frustrations erupted into violence. Paving stones were hurled through the windows of the Provost Marshal's office, and later the rioters broke into the building and set fire to it. This was completely unexpected as the mob was led by the volunteer firemen of Engine Company 33, doing the opposite of what they usually did. When fire brigades turned up to put out the blaze, they were stopped and their vehicles were destroyed. Telegraph lines were cut so the police couldn't respond effectively, and the rioting continued as streetcars were pushed on their sides and, somewhat unnecessarily, horses pulling carts and buggies were slaughtered. The rioting went on for four days. Reporters at the *New York Times* saved the paper and the building by firing a Gatling gun (a precursor to the machine gun) into the mob. It's not known how journalists got their hands on a then state-of-the-art military-grade weapon.

The situation was clearly escalating at a time of national crisis, so Lincoln sent in troops to quell the violence and restore order. When the anarchy was over, about 120 New Yorkers had died (five of them black men who were lynched by the mob) and dozens of buildings had been gutted by fire. After all of this, the draft was implemented anyway.

The Most British Story You Will Ever Read

Queen Victoria was famously 'not amused' (an apocryphal tale), but she *was* quite the literary critic. In 1882, Roderick Maclean was so happy with his new poem he thought he would send a copy of this masterpiece to Her Majesty (he was a huge fan). Unbelievably, despite the thousands of letters she received every week, not only did she read the poem, but she disliked it so much that she took the time to send him a reply, which required (we are told) a considerable effort on her part. Mr Maclean thought the response was unnecessarily curt. Taking this literary critique to heart, he went a step further than most on the receiving end of a poor review and decided to counter her criticism in the most extreme way possible: Roderick Maclean set out to assassinate Queen Victoria.

On 2 March 1882, Queen Victoria was being driven through the streets of Windsor in an open horse-drawn carriage when Maclean drew a pistol and attempted to shoot the monarch. There are several contradictory accounts of what happened next, but one source claimed the gun was a toy and that no actual harm was intended. Others, however, were adamant that a shot was fired. One version has Chief Superintendent Hayes of the Borough Police thwarting Mr Maclean by wrestling him to the ground. Another account has it that (and this is a wonderfully British description) some Eton schoolboys grappled with Mr Maclean using the only thing they had to hand: their umbrellas.

Regardless of the details and conflicting aspects of the reports, it is, of course, undisputed that Maclean failed to kill the monarch. He was caught, imprisoned and tried. It was revealed in the trial that he had been in an asylum just two years earlier, and his extreme reaction to Her Majesty's review was another sign that he was not of sound mind. He was found 'not guilty but insane' after just five minutes of deliberation by the jury. The judge sentenced him to life in Broadmoor Asylum.

Interestingly, Queen Victoria was not happy about that verdict and requested a change in English law to allow those implicated in future similar cases to be found 'guilty but insane'. Her request led to the change in the Trial of Lunatics Act of 1883. This remained the law until 1964 when it was superseded by the introduction of the Criminal Procedure (Insanity) Act.

There is one more bizarre twist to this moment in history. The whole chain of events started with a bad poem, but it did not deter one William Topaz McGonagall from writing his own poem about the attempted assassination. McGonagall was infamous for his poor acting and terrible poetry. Fortunately for all concerned, he was also famous for not caring about the reviews he received. What Queen Victoria thought of this new poem is not recorded.

Modern

The Young Ioseb Jughashvili

Ioseb Jughashvili was born in 1878 in Georgia (then part of the Russian Empire), the son of an abusive, alcoholic cobbler. When the family fell on hard times, the boy and his mother left the family home and drifted from rented room to rented room, trying to escape the poverty that enveloped them. The boy grew up to be the man Joseph Stalin.

Joseph is the anglicised version of Ioseb, and the surname Jughashvili is typically Georgian, so in the context of the times, it was a surname that had to go. Joseph chose 'Stalin' because it means 'man of steel' and was very much in step with the contemporary concept of communist industrial output ... besides which, it is also kind of cool. For the purposes of this article, I will call Stalin by his famous moniker although he did not adopt it until well into adulthood.

It's easy to label the most appalling despots in history as 'monsters', but this lets both them and us off the hook. The term monster dehumanizes despots and makes them 'other,' when the reality is that each one is flesh-and-blood human being who likely experienced a relatively innocent childhood. How that child turned into a tyrannical murderer makes for interesting speculation. Was it possible, looking back, to see the warning signs?

Joseph Stalin is, undeniably, one of the most evil men in history. While the Soviet Union suffered 80 per cent of the Third Reich's casualties in the Second World War, that doesn't exonerate Stalin of his incompetent military strategies or the 1939 Molotov–Ribbentrop Pact, which made Nazi Germany and the Soviet Union allies. That alliance led to the carve-up of Poland in the same year, followed by Stalin's labour camps, the mass executions, the secret police and the man-made grain famine in Ukraine which, in turn, led to the starvation of millions in the 1930s. None of this is in serious dispute by anyone other than his most myopic fans. However, none of this could have been predicted based on what we know about the young man. Indeed, his early life evokes only sympathy.

Stalin suffered severe health problems in his childhood but was the only one of his parents' children to survive beyond infancy. In 1884, at the tender age of six, he contracted smallpox, an illness that has killed millions over the centuries and which left him with pockmarks and permanent facial scarring. After the period in which mother and son wandered from place to place, they found refuge with a family friend who employed the mother as a housekeeper and cleaner and helped the ten-year-old Joseph to enrol at the Gori Church School in his native Georgia. Places in the school were normally reserved for the children of clergy, but young Stalin excelled academically and shone in the arts, displaying talent in painting and drama, and singing in the church choir. That's right – Joseph Stalin was a choirboy. But that didn't mean he didn't get into fights, and a childhood friend noted that Stalin 'was the best but also the naughtiest pupil' in the class. Quite frankly, he sounds like an endearing child, a cheeky little boy who was both smart and talented.

Aged twelve, Joseph had his second health setback and was seriously injured when he was hit by a carriage in the street. This resulted in a lifelong disability to his left arm. At his teachers' recommendation, the boy proceeded from the church school to the Spiritual Seminary in Tiflis. He was enrolled in August 1894, enabled by a scholarship that allowed him to study at a reduced rate. Once again, he was academically successful and achieved high grades. At this point, Joseph was on his way to becoming a priest, pretty much the exact opposite of a tyrannical dictator with more blood on his hands than Hitler. But it gets even more counterintuitive.

It was during his time in the seminary that Stalin developed his love of poetry and had a number of his poems published under a pseudonym. The poems were regarded as so good they were taught in Georgian schools into the 1970s because even then nobody knew they were by *the* Joseph Stalin. Once the connection was made they were removed from the national syllabus.

Had things stopped there, we might have had the story of a young man who dragged himself up from poverty and hardship to become a priest and a poet, but the longer he remained in the seminary the more disenchanted he became with his religious studies, and he was frequently confined to his cell for rebellious behaviour. Among other things, he joined a forbidden book club where he read the books that would influence his socio-political leanings, including *Das Kapital* by Karl Marx, and he began to embrace Marxism, which was on the rise in Georgia at the time. Attendance at the book club turned into attendance at secret meetings (the Tsar's authorities were not inclined to tolerate socialist political theories) until, eventually, Stalin declared himself to be an atheist and walked out of the seminary in 1899.

This departure was the turning point that launched his career as a revolutionary firebrand and set him on a path that would lead him to become a bloody dictator. Stalin is a reminder of Pitt the Elder's famous quote: 'Power corrupts; absolute power corrupts absolutely.' The more power Stalin tasted, the more he wanted; the more he gained, the colder he became, and the poet priest turned into one of the most malevolent tyrants in human history.

The American Flag on Uniforms

You may have seen US soldiers in news footage with a rather unusual American flag emblem on their uniforms. I'm talking about the one that's black and grey (rather than red, white and blue) with the field of stars on the wrong side. It looks like an insult to the stars and stripes, but it isn't. The reason for this is all to do with history.

Up until the early 2000s and the War on Terror, American soldiers rarely had flags on their uniforms. GIs in the two World Wars and Vietnam did not have flag emblems. (A famous exception was the normal, full-colour flag worn on the uniform shoulder of paratroopers in the Second World War.) American flags had also been added for clarity during some joint manoeuvres with other countries, but that was all. So, what changed? In today's world, with so many nations fighting regularly together in coalitions, most fighting units now have a patch with their national flag on the uniform.

It also differentiates regular soldiers from mercenaries who may have similar weapons and equipment.

The reason for the apparently reversed flag goes back to the time of the US Civil War and before. In those days, a standard-bearer would hold aloft the flag as they marched towards the front. If they were to charge towards the enemy, the field of blue stars would fly backwards, making it appear as if the stars – that is, the flag – was running away. So the position of the stars was reversed. It's the same concept on today's uniforms: the stars are reversed on the right shoulder so that when the soldier moves into battle the stars are facing towards the enemy, rather than moving backwards if they were in the usual position.

Until the Americans fought in the Middle East, the colours of the flag emblems were the traditional red, white and blue, but in Iraq, it was agreed that bright colours didn't help camouflage the troops and muted tones were chosen. So, the legacy of nineteenth-century troop deployments and standard-bearers can be seen in the reversed flags of the American forces today.

The Samurai Myth

The samurai have been mentioned several times already in this book, so it may seem odd now to have an article with the above title; however, there is a legitimate reason for this. If I were to say that the samurai were, in a way, invented in 1900, you are likely to think not only that I'm contradicting previous articles but that I have wandered off into fantasyland. The truth is that the way the West thinks about the samurai can be traced directly back to the 1900 release of the book

Bushido: The Soul of Japan by Inazo Nitobe. (*Bushido* itself first emerged in the seventeenth century as the code of conduct of the samurai class in Japan.)

Nitobe was a Japanese immigrant to the West Coast of America. He wrote in English and it was his book that mythologised the samurai and brought them into popular culture. The samurai of the (roughly) one-thousand-year tradition in Japan were very different men to those described by Nitobe. While samurai bravery was already revered in Japan, the almost supernatural view of their nobility and skill came from Nitobe's interpretation.

There is a useful comparison with the knights of medieval Europe, who were respected at the time but whose image grew after their era as tales were embroidered and facts ballooned into legends. The image of 'a knight in shining armour' is probably about as historically inaccurate as the image of 'a noble samurai'. They both existed, but not quite as we think.

Nitobe's book was a smash hit, and suddenly, the samurai, the *katana* and *bushido* became famous and widely admired in the West. This admiration is particularly important to mention as Asia was heretofore seen as barbaric, with the Western sense of 'inherent supremacy' having been underlined by the existence of mighty Western empires. However, through a quirk of fate, just a few years later (1904–5), Russia went to war with Japan and lost both on land and sea. Japan was the first Asian power to defeat a Western one, which only enhanced the image of Japan's martial prowess.

Ironically, it was only years later that Nitobe's book was translated into Japanese and was, once again, a publishing sensation. The image of the samurai in the West undoubtedly starts with this book, but even though samurai history goes back centuries in the motherland, Japan has picked up the Western baton and run with it. With works by Akira Kurosawa such as *Yojimbo* and *The Seven Samurai*, as well as hundreds of other films that portray these warriors as almost supernatural in their skills, the myth of the samurai has become well entrenched across the globe (although, for the record, these films are cinema classics, no argument there). *Bushido: The Soul of Japan* is still in print and still historically inaccurate ... and still contains suitably cool images that perpetuate the samurai myth.

The Fate of the Millionaires' Ship

The RMS *Republic* was launched by the White Star Line in 1903 (the company that also launched the *Titanic* a few years later). It became known as the 'millionaires' ship' because it was famous for carrying rich passengers in great luxury. During a routine trip from New York to Gibraltar, in the early morning of 23 January 1909, it sailed into a thick fog off the coast of Massachusetts and collided with the SS *Florida* (the *Florida* ploughed into the side of the *Republic*, to be precise). The *Republic* had the latest Marconi radio technology on board and was able to signal for help as it took on water. The quick signalling and the fact that the ship was located close to shore meant that the passengers and crew of both ships, numbering about 1,500, were all saved. This was the first significant marine rescue using the new communication technology, which vindicated its use and brought it worldwide attention.

Unfortunately, the ship itself could not be saved, and twenty-four hours later, the RMS *Republic* sank into the waters of the Atlantic. However, unlike the story of the *Titanic*, this is not a tale of human tragedy; instead, it is the story of the *Republic* shipwreck that is of interest. What might still lie within its bowels? Remember, this was a luxury liner and rich passengers took not only cash but jewellery when they travelled. Aside from all the personal wealth of those on board, it is thought that the *Republic* was carrying a large number of gold coins. Nobody is sure quite why. The most popular but least plausible explanation is that the money was intended to go to the relief effort for a recent earthquake in Italy. Or perhaps it was pay for the US Navy (unlikely as sailors aren't paid in gold). Or maybe it was a loan intended for the increasingly threadbare Russian government (considered to be the best explanation). Whatever the reason for the gold being on board, naval salvage experts are generally confident it exists. Who knows? Maybe this is just another old mariner's tale.

Whatever its intended destination, the supposed gold on board the RMS *Republic* is estimated to be worth around $5 billion on today's gold market, which would make it the richest wreck in history. There's just one problem: nobody has found the gold. The wreck itself was discovered by Captain Martin Bayerle in 1981 at a location approximately 50 miles south of Nantucket Island, just off the coast of mainland North America, in approximately 270 feet of water. But just as Captain Bayerle started to survey the wreck, he was distracted by personal matters. (I'm being polite; he went to prison for murdering his wife's lover.)

After this, things went quiet for decades. Despite the ridiculous amount of gold supposedly lying somewhere on the ocean floor, no one was looking for it … until the late

2010s, when the wreck was located again and searched by a salvage team. There was even a TV documentary about it, but – spoiler alert – nobody has found even one gold coin, let alone $5 billion worth. However, the salvage work is set to continue, so watch this space!

The Iceland Worm Monster or Lagarfljót Worm

Many countries have a mysterious creature: the Yeti in Tibet, the Loch Ness monster in Scotland, the Sasquatch in North America, and so on. Iceland is no exception, and there they have stories of a giant, worm-like monster that lives in the icy waters around their volcanic island. It is said to live specifically in Lagarfljót, a freshwater, below-sea-level, glacier-fed lake which has very poor visibility due to silt. The creature is described as roughly 39 feet (12 metres) long, and has also been reported outside the water, lying coiled up or slithering into the hinterland. This worm monster is truly the stuff of nightmares.

Tales of the creature are first mentioned in the Icelandic annals of 1345. Sightings were considered to foreshadow a great event such as a natural disaster. A folk tradition was recorded by Jón Árnason in the mid-1800s:

> The great serpent in Lagarfljót grew out of a small 'lingworm' or heath-dragon; a girl was given a gold ring by her mother, and asked how she might best derive profit from the gold, was told to place it under a lingworm. She did so and put it in the top of her linen chest for a few days, but then found that the little dragon had grown so large, it had broken open the chest.

Frightened, she threw both it and the gold into the lake, where the serpent continued to grow and terrorized the countryside, spitting poison and killing people and animals. Two Finns were called in to destroy it and retrieve the gold said that they had managed to tie its head and tail to the bottom of the lake, but it was impossible to kill it because there was a still larger dragon underneath.

That's a great story, but what of reality? The worm has been sighted several times recently, in 1963 by the head of the Icelandic National Forest Service and in 1998 by a teacher and students. In 1983, contractors laying a telephone cable measured a large shifting mass near the eastern shore; when the cable failed to function they found that it was broken. In 2012, the Icelandic National Broadcasting Service aired a video thought to show the Lagarfljót Worm, an ancient creature now captured by modern technology.

But why is this information in a book about history? It's because all of these legendary creatures are a reminder that our brains haven't evolved from beyond the Stone Age. The unknown is scary, and something seen out of the corner of the eye sends a chill down the spine because our ancestors really were preyed upon by large predators. It's better to think we see a monster in the shadows and run away from something that might be harmless than to miss the lurking monster and be eaten.

Have a look at the worm video online and see what you think. It's definitely something, but it could be a cable or a large eel or a tree root. Whatever it is, it's nothing like the epic beast described in the legend. These stories of mysterious monsters are the echoes of our survival instincts from prehistory.

The Largely Forgotten Russo-Japanese War of 1904–5

The Russo-Japanese War of 1904–5 sent shock waves around the world. For the first time since the Industrial Revolution, an Asian empire had beaten a European one in modern warfare. It was an epic conflict that had everything: sea battles, artillery duels, machine guns and titanic clashes on the ground.

The contemporary German empire could empathise with Japan's fear of encroachment by a powerful competitor in its natural sphere of influence. It was Germany's fear of such an encirclement that would become one of the triggers for the First World War. But in this case, ten years earlier, it was Russia's encroachment into the Far East that triggered a war with Japan. Russia had recently started using Port Arthur and Vladivostok as warm-water ports, and had also been working with the Chinese government, which worried the Japanese. Japan therefore came up with a reasonable compromise: it would recognise Russian influence in Manchuria if the Russians recognised Japanese influence in Korea.

The Russians refused, presumably due to Western arrogance and the assumption that they could push around an Asian empire. What Russia failed to realise was that compared to the other Western empires, theirs was the least industrialised and had the poorest troops with the worst equipment. On the other hand, since the mid-nineteenth century, Japan had been forging ahead with industrialisation and modernisation. It had also completely restructured its military according to modern Western principles. All of this preparation paid off. Throughout the war, which lasted about a year and a half, the Japanese largely got the better of the Russians.

One of the most important clashes was at Mukden in February and March 1905. Mukden (now Shenyang in China) was then the capital of Manchuria, and the Russians and Japanese were fighting over who should control this part of the crumbling Chinese empire. The result was a major land battle with more than 600,000 men involved. The Japanese were attacking a larger, firmly entrenched Russian force. The received military wisdom is that whenever attacking a fortified enemy, the attackers should have at least two-to-one superiority in forces. In this case, however, the size of both forces was so great and spread out over such a large area that it wasn't pure folly.

Initial attacks met stout resistance and casualties on the Japanese side were heavy, but then the Russian left flank began to be pushed back. The Russians then made a mistake that they would repeat during the Revolution and in both World Wars. They decided to reposition their forces and retreat, but did so with poor coordination. What started as an orderly retreat turned into chaos, and the Japanese used it to gather momentum.

Field Marshal Ōyama understood what was happening and ordered the army to 'pursue and destroy'. The Russian army was shattered. By the end of the battle, there were over 150,000 casualties (killed and wounded), and the Japanese ejected Russia from the entirety of southern Manchuria.

The grand naval battle of Tsushima came in late May 1905. Although Britain and the other Western powers were technically neutral, there was a general unease about Russia's expansion, so Britain did not allow the Russian fleet to sail through the Suez Canal. The Russian fleet were thus forced to sail from northern Europe, down past Spain and along the whole of Africa before sailing east across the Indian Ocean. This meant that Admiral Zinovy Rozhestvensky led the Russian Baltic fleet 18,000 nautical miles to engage in battle with the Japanese.

You would think that after all that effort Admiral Rozhestvensky would have won a well-earned victory. The Russians had eight capital battleships to Japan's five, but in every other category they were fewer in number. What happened next was one of the most crushing defeats in naval history. In fact, with it happening a hundred years after the Battle of Trafalgar, many British experts considered it every bit as important. By the end of the second day of fighting, more than 10,000 Russian sailors had been killed or captured and six of the eight battleships had been sunk, with most of the rest of the armada either destroyed or captured. Admiral Rozhestvensky was knocked unconscious during the fighting, but even so, he was court-martialled in 1906. His death sentence was commuted by the Tsar, but he left his post in disgrace.

This battle and the war in general had lasting political impact. There was outrage in Russia, which further weakened the Romanov dynasty. It made the Central Powers (Austria-Hungary, Germany, Bulgaria and the Ottoman Empire) realise that despite its vast resources, Russia was weaker militarily than they had thought, and it emboldened Japan to continue its conquests in Asia which would go on for another forty years.

Peace was declared in the Treaty of Portsmouth (Maine, USA) where US President Theodore Roosevelt was instrumental in the negotiations and won the Nobel Peace Prize for his efforts. The signing of the treaty settled immediate difficulties in the Far East and created three decades of peace between Russia and Japan. The treaty confirmed Japan's emergence as the pre-eminent power in East Asia and forced Russia to abandon its expansionist policies there.

The Russo-Japanese War was huge in scale and decisive in nature. It is, therefore, a shame that it is utterly forgotten today.

Pilates Isn't Old

I don't know about you, but to the extent that I've thought about it at all, I assumed Pilates came from some Eastern branch of movement and meditation, maybe linked to yoga. I would have guessed that it comes from a practice that stretches back centuries and probably involved bald monks in saffron robes doing slow-motion aerobics on mountain tops. But that would be completely wrong. For starters, the term 'Pilates' doesn't sound very Asian, and that's because it's the surname of Joseph Pilates. He doesn't sound like he came from the East, and that's because he didn't.

Joseph Pilates was born in 1883 in Germany. He was a sickly child who suffered from all kinds of ailments but built himself up through exercise and martial arts training, a bit like Teddy Roosevelt. However, Pilates took things much further, and by the age of fourteen, he was fit enough to pose for anatomical charts. While still a teenager, he formulated a programme of healthy stretching and developed exercises designed to improve not only the body but the mind as well. This was revolutionary for the time. Unusually, his exercises didn't involve any gym equipment because even back then he looked to the animal kingdom as a source of inspiration for physical fitness.

Pilates moved to England in 1912, where he boxed, trained and even became a self-defence teacher at police academies. He was devoted to his work; for him, health and fitness was all that mattered. Nevertheless, political events loomed large whether he was interested or not. As a German living in England, the power-playing between empires caught up with him when the First World War broke out. At the time Britain had a policy of interning civilians from enemy countries. So, along with other German nationals, the British authorities held him throughout the war in several different locations, including Lancaster Castle. This was where Pilates turned his theories into a core concept, one he called Contrology, now known as the Pilates Method.

Pilates' confinement in the castle meant that no gym or exercise equipment was available. This recalled the exercises of his youth, and worked well with his belief that the key to health and fitness lay in humans imitating the movements and stretching of animals. Rather than reliance on special equipment, then, only a mat was needed. The upshot was a programme that could be done anywhere. Pilates was able to promote his ideas and exercises among his fellow inmates, and as a result, they left internment stronger and in better shape than before they entered, something that was virtually unheard of. There weren't many good outcomes to the First World War, but one small positive was this new fitness regime.

After the war, Pilates returned to Germany for a few years before he immigrated to the United States around 1925. On the ship to America, he met his future wife Clara. He would remain in New York for the rest of his life, perfecting Contrology and writing books about it. He became a multimillionaire, but money didn't change his ethics or his commitment to health and fitness. He died in 1967 at the age of eighty-three, knowing that the Pilates Method of physical fitness had become an international phenomenon.

The Female Canaries in Factories

With most of the young men of working age off fighting in the First World War, the women on the home front had to start doing all kinds of jobs that were traditionally regarded as masculine work. While much has been said about how this led to universal suffrage and women getting the vote, there were some strange and unexpected side effects.

One of these could be seen in the women employed in the munitions factories. This was hard, back breaking and, of course, highly dangerous work. It's also worth remembering that women were doing this in an era when they were supposed to be wives and homemakers, not factory workers (oh, and they couldn't vote on any of this either). The work had a bizarre side effect. Some of the explosive materials (including TNT) acted like bleach, and over a period of time, the chemicals bleached the women's hair blonde. Once this was recognised, some women saw this as a desirable perk and stole small amounts of these high explosives to bleach their hair. NOTE: USING HIGH-EXPLOSIVE CHEMICALS TO BLEACH YOUR HAIR IS VERY, *VERY* DANGEROUS. DO NOT TRY THIS AT HOME.

The overarching problem was that continued use of the chemicals led to the women's skin starting to turn yellow too. It wasn't jaundice, but the physical reaction of the chemicals bleaching the skin. As a result, the women were known as 'canaries', a term that became something of a badge of honour.

It was clear to everyone that these women were sacrificing their appearance for the greater good of the war effort and the men at the front.

Unusual side effects to one side, had it not been for the tens of thousands of women creating munitions for the front line, Britain would simply have run out of ammunition not just for rifles, but more critically, for the millions of artillery shells used in the attritional trench warfare. The canaries might not have been songbirds, but they were vital to Britain's war effort.

The Forgotten Bloodbath of the First World War

Tsarist Russia didn't do very well in the First World War. In fact, the war was to be the trigger for a revolution that destroyed the 300-year-old Romanov dynasty and knocked Russia out of the war completely. One of the first battles between Russia and Germany was near Tannenberg, where the Teutonic Knights suffered a humiliating defeat about 500 years earlier. The German victory in August 1914 led to 150,000 Russians being killed, wounded or captured and allowed the German powers to call it the Second Battle of Tannenberg. The battle resulted in the near destruction of the Russian Second Army and the suicide of its commanding general, Alexander Samsonov. It was just one more humiliating defeat inflicted on the crumbling Romanov dynasty. Despite all of this, there was one moment of important success for the great Russian bear.

The Brusilov Offensive in the summer of 1916 was one of the biggest clashes of the entire war but is rarely mentioned. This is probably because the main combatants – Tsarist Russia and the Austro-Hungarian Empire – no longer exist. At the same time, Britain and France were preoccupied with the Western Front where all the talk was about the Somme and Verdun. In contrast with the tactics employed at the Somme, Brusilov tried something new: a short and highly accurate artillery barrage. At this point in the war, a barrage might have been devastating, but it also signalled days of pounding, so everyone settled in their bunkers to wait it out. However, on this occasion, the barrage could be measured in hours before it suddenly stopped, and the Russian infantry quickly advanced, catching the Austro-Hungarian forces by surprise.

The numbers involved were eye-watering. The Central Powers (Austria-Hungary, Germany, Bulgaria and the Ottoman Empire) had about 1.5 million men, and the opposing Russians had amassed an army of 1.7 million. The fighting took place in an area of present-day western Ukraine and led to a breakthrough by Russian forces, something that failed to materialise on the Somme. A total of at least 1.5 million men were killed, wounded or captured by the end of the offensive, numbers that dwarf those of the Somme. And finally, a Russian general, in this case Aleksei Brusilov, hence the name of the offensive, was able to say afterwards that he had won a significant strategic victory, a feat that had eluded all the generals of France and Britain. But it had come at an appalling loss of life.

Brusilov's operation achieved its original goal of forcing Germany to halt its attack on Verdun as well as pulling German forces off the Italian border and relocating thousands of soldiers in the east. It also broke the back of the Austro-Hungarian army, which suffered the majority of the casualties. Afterwards, it was forced to rely increasingly on the support of the German army for its military successes. On the other hand, the German army did not suffer much from the operation, managing as it did to retain most of its offensive power, but it was now stretched thin, its main ally fatally weakened.

There was an interesting lesson from this campaign. Up to this point, the Russians had deployed massed formations of thousands of peasant troops, which led to terrible casualties. However, prior to the offensive, Brusilov had trained small units of specialised troops to attack bunkers and work their way through trenches. These specialist units performed very well, but with Tsarist Russia sliding ever further into chaos, knowledge of the tactics fell by the wayside. It was the Central Powers, Germany in particular, that took note. In 1918, during Germany's last great offensive, the Kaiserschlacht, stormtroopers were used in the very same way. They, too, performed well.

There was one more notable moment in this forgotten offensive: the early successes convinced Romania to enter the war on the side of the Entente Cordiale. It was another front that the Central Powers had to defend at a time when manpower was increasingly scarce. This applied yet more pressure but came at a huge cost to Romania, a forgotten ally of Britain and France in a forgotten campaign.

Who Made the First Transatlantic Flight?

No, this isn't about Charles Lindbergh. The answer is the rather forgotten duo of John Alcock and Arthur Brown in 1919. Both had been airmen in the First World War: Alcock had been shot down and had been a prisoner in Ottoman lands, and ironically, Brown had also been shot down but on a different continent and was a prisoner in Germany for years.

Their flight took place barely six months after the end of the war in a converted Vickers Vimy British heavy bomber. It was not unusual at the time for decommissioned RAF planes to be used for civilian purposes. (It's a forgotten fact that the first civilian flight for the company that would become British Airways was also in a decommissioned RAF bomber, flying one passenger from London to Paris.) In this case, the two men decided to take the shortest Transatlantic route possible and flew from St John's, Newfoundland to Clifden in Ireland.

It was not an easy flight. While the Vickers Vimy had been stripped of all its weapons and military apparatus (including bombs, obviously), it was still heavily loaded with all the fuel they needed, and they had difficulty taking off from the rough runway (it was a field) in Canada, only just missing the tops of the trees as they gained height. Early on, the wind-driven electrical generator failed, which prevented them from sending or receiving radio signals; the aeroplane was so noisy they could only easily communicate with each other via electronic intercom, so that too was lost. Most critically, the heating was also electrical. The flight may have taken place in June, but up in the sky over the Atlantic, there was a very real danger of exposure.

So far, so bad, but then an exhaust pipe burst, causing a 'frightening noise', the source of which took time to locate. The damage wasn't fatal to the flight so they pressed on. The noise, however, made conversation even by shouting impossible.

So the mechanical issues, while aggravating, weren't fatal, but then the weather became their greatest adversary as they were forced to fly through thick fog. The situation was serious because it prevented Brown from being able to navigate using his sextant. Blind flying in fog or cloud should only be undertaken with gyroscopic or electronic instruments, which they didn't have. Alcock twice lost control of the aircraft and nearly hit the sea after a spiral dive before they had to deal with yet more mechanical failure when a broken trim control made the plane nose-heavy as fuel was consumed. It is fair to say that things were not going well – but then it got worse.

About eight hours later, they flew into a large snowstorm. They were drenched by rain, the carburettors and their instruments froze over, and the plane was in danger of icing up. This condition added a dangerous amount of weight, creating excess drag and making the plane potentially unflyable. They managed to get through that by wiping away frost particles and, in some cases, smashing chunks of ice off the parts of the plane they could reach. Onwards they flew through the night, cold, miserable and deafened.

They finally made landfall in County Galway at 8:40 a.m. on 15 June 1919, not far from their intended landing place but not exactly on target. Their last bit of bad luck came when the aircraft was damaged in their attempt to land on what appeared to be a suitable green field, but which turned out to be a bog. They (crash)landed near Clifden in County Galway, but almost miraculously, neither of the airmen was hurt. Brown said that if the weather had been good, they would have pressed on to London.

Their altitude had varied between sea level (remember the dive) and 12,000 feet (3,700 metres). They had spent just over fourteen hours crossing the North Atlantic, having flown 1,890 miles (3,040 kilometres) in 15 hours 57 minutes at an average speed of 115 mph (185 km/h).

Charles Lindbergh made headline news when he crossed the Atlantic flying solo from New York to Paris eight years later in 1927. While that was a great achievement, the Alcock–Brown flight of 1919 was equally memorable for different reasons and deserves its place in history.

Some Really Strange Ideas

The Thule Society is mentioned in all kinds of occult novels and counter-historical novels about the Nazis. The society was founded in Germany in 1918 by Rudolf von Sebottendorf, an occultist and eccentric who believed in a pan-global Aryan super-race from pre-history (this idea would obviously influence the Nazi ideology). He started the society in order to promote his own occultist theories, but as time went on, the society was forced to reflect the politics of the era and to promote German nationalism and anti-Semitism.

Belief in the occult was fashionable both before and after the First World War and séances were regularly taking place in the parlours of respectable people who believed they were communing with spirits in the afterlife (Houdini, among others, spent years debunking these). This widespread fervour for the occult happily incorporated many bizarre ideas, not least of which were those of James Churchward and his theory of a lost continent.

In his 1920s book *The Lost Continent of Mu: Motherland of Man*, Churchward claimed that there was a lost continent in the Pacific Ocean. He also claimed to have gained his knowledge from an Indian priest who taught him to read an ancient language, spoken by only three people. The priest was conveniently dead, but Churchward had preserved this oral tradition, supposedly going back thousands of years, in his book. According to Churchward, Mu 'extended from somewhere north of Hawaii to the south as far as the Fijis and Easter Island'. He claimed Mu was the site of the Garden of Eden and, at its peak, the home of 64 million inhabitants known as the Naacals. According to Churchward, this civilization, which flourished 50,000 years ago, was technologically more advanced than the West of the 1920s, and the ancient civilizations of India, Babylon, Persia, Egypt and the Mayas were the decayed remnants of its colonies. If all this sounds similar to the theory of Atlantis, it's because Churchward's writings influenced later pseudoscience including that theory.

Easter Island, according to Churchward, was a remnant of Mu and 'proof' of its existence ... except that the statues on Easter Island are centuries old, not millennia, and there is no geological evidence of a lost continent in the Pacific Ocean. There is also the issue of the huge gap in time between 50,000 years ago and the oldest of the ancient civilisations; even ancient Sumeria and Babylon only date back some 4,000 to 5,000 years. Also, and unknown to Churchward at the time, the Mayan civilisation was much later and is roughly contemporary with medieval Europe. The archaeologist Stephen Williams perhaps best summarises Churchward's theories in his book *Fantastic Archaeology* (1991) by describing them as pseudoscience: 'His translations are outrageous, his geology, in both mechanics and dating, is absurd, and his mishandling of archaeological data, as in the Valley of Mexico is atrocious.'

In other words, it's all made up, the delusions (or mischief-making) of a clever self-promoter. However, it's important to bear in mind that Churchward's writings were persuasive enough to influence the theory of the lost civilisation of Atlantis that lingers today – and, more chillingly, Nazi ideology.

Ahmet Muhtar Zogolli Had Quite the Political Career

Ahmet Muhtar Zogolli was born an Ottoman subject and a minor member of the Albanian aristocracy in the 1890s. When his father died in 1911, the sixteen-year-old Ahmet became governor of a region called Mat. In 1912 he was one of those who signed Albania's declaration of independence from the crumbling Ottoman Empire. The collapse of both the Ottoman and Austro-Hungarian Empires brought years of brutal conflict in the boiling cauldron of violence that was the First World War, which meant that it was also a time of considerable turmoil in the new state of Albania.

But it's after the war that Zogolli's career really took off. He served as Governor of Shkodër (1920–21), Minister of the Interior (1920–24) and chief of the Albanian military (1921–22). In 1922, he changed his surname to Zogu to sound more Albanian, but the instability in the country became personal when, in 1923, he was shot by a would-be assassin in Albania's parliament.

In the following year, Zogu was forced to flee the country with 600 political allies. He quickly returned with the backing of Yugoslavia and a White Russian army, and was Prime Minister before 1924 was out. His rise didn't stop there. Zogu was officially elected the first President of Albania by the Constituent Assembly on 21 January 1925. He continued in this role as he consolidated power, becoming a virtual dictator.

In 1928, the stage was set. He took one final step to transform Albania into a kingdom, and President Zogu became King Zog I. The other European royal houses ignored him because he was a self-proclaimed monarch.

During the global economic depression of the 1930s, Albania was almost entirely reliant on economic aid from Mussolini's Italy (you know things are bad when you need Italy to help you economically), so Zog was pro-fascist ... which did not help him when Mussolini's Italy invaded Albania. The Albanian army was no match for the Italian army (you know things are bad when your army is worse than Italy's), and while there were pockets of resistance, it was said that many Albanians cheered the arrival of the Italian forces. Realising that their lives were in danger, the 'royal' family fled into exile, taking with them most of the country's gold. This ended King Zog's reign as monarch and curtailed his nearly thirty-year political career.

Zog was known to have smoked over 200 cigarettes a day and took some pride in calling himself the world's heaviest smoker. He died in exile in 1961 at the age of sixty-five, having survived around fifty-five assassination attempts. He was mourned by few.

Good Intentions Gone Wrong

It's comforting to know that in the First World War there were people in Britain doing things that had nothing to do with the war. In 1917, Major Rupert Penny was shopping in a London department store when he came across a young male highland gorilla which had been orphaned by hunters. Of course, Major Penny did what anyone would have done in the circumstances; he bought him for £300 (about £20,000 in today's money) and named him John Daniel. Major Penny took John Daniel to Uley in Gloucestershire and gave him to his sister Alyce Cunningham, who decided to raise the gorilla like a human boy.

John Daniel was adored by everyone and clearly saw himself as human, like everyone around him. He had his own bedroom and knew how to turn on the lights and use the toilet. He made his bed and helped with the washing up. He attended the local school at the kindergarten level (although he did not learn to read and write). People remember him walking around the village with the local children who used to play a game that involved pushing him in a wheelbarrow. One charming fact was that he liked to go into gardens and eat the roses. He also got a taste for cider and knew which houses had it, often turning up to beg a mugful. He was fascinated by the village cobbler and liked to watch him repairing shoes.

Sometimes Cunningham took him to her London home on Sloane Street, where he would drink cups of tea in the afternoon and attend her dinner parties. However, after about four years, John Daniel had grown to be a full-size male gorilla and was starting to display the territorial behaviours of an alpha male, such as urinating on men and preferring the company of women, especially if they were in groups. Nature was taking its course. So Alyce sold John Daniel to an American for a thousand guineas, believing that he would be sent to a home in Florida where they were better equipped to deal with a full-size gorilla. Except that's not where he went.

In fact, John Daniel was bought by PT Barnum's circus (Barnum had died some thirty years earlier). He travelled around in a cage and was put on show as a curiosity because of his human-like behaviours. The circus later sold him to the zoo at Madison Square Garden in New York, where his health deteriorated, and it was believed he was pining for his 'mother'. When Alyce Cunningham received a telegram warning of John's deterioration, she took a steamship to New York to rescue him. Unfortunately, John Daniel died of pneumonia before she arrived in America. I'm sorry this story doesn't have a happy ending.

The Hawthorne Effect Originated in Cicero, Illinois

The Hawthorne Works, a factory making telephone equipment outside of Chicago, commissioned a study in 1924 to see if its workers would become more productive in higher or lower levels of light. Workers who participated in the studies were told that they were in a 'special test group'; they knew they were being observed. The study later expanded to include other variants in conditions of work such as the regularity of breaks, their length and the foods consumed in the breaks. These became known as the Hawthorne studies, which revealed what is known as the Hawthorne effect.

The studies found that in general, no matter what changed, there was an increase in workers' productivity as a result. The term 'Hawthorne effect' didn't come into use until the 1950s, by which time more studies had been conducted to corroborate the original finding that it doesn't matter what you do to a group; if you tell them they are in a 'special test group', people generally work harder.

However, in more recent years the findings have been contested. The received wisdom of the Hawthorne effect has been challenged because of the conditions in which the studies were carried out, the leaps in logic and the errors in the collation of data. The studies were simply not up to the standards that would be required today. Saying that, there are those who believe that the data, while flawed, still stands. After all, telling someone they are special and seeing a boost in productivity as a result makes sense.

Now, by reading this, you have been selected to participate in a special test group. Have a productive day!

The Cute Girl Was a Cute Boy

Ernest Hemingway was dressed as a girl until about the age of six; there are images of him at the age of four looking unmistakeably like a little girl. While researching this, I discovered that the dress and the long hair weren't uncommon in the Victorian era (Hemingway was born in 1899). Similarly, there are pictures of the very young Winston Churchill who, again, looks like an adorable little girl. At the time there was a fashion for preschool children of both sexes to wear their hair in long curls and dress in fussy clothing. When the time came, usually when the boy went to school, there was a certain ceremony to cutting off the curls as a way of showing that the child was no longer a baby. While all of this is true, it was taken to the extreme with Hemingway.

Young Ernest had to pretend to be the twin sister of his real sister because his mother didn't want a boy; the pretence went on until he was six. This early upbringing would later backfire spectacularly because Ernest Hemingway is regarded as one of the toughest, manliest writers in history. In his late teens, he enlisted to fight in the First World War; he drove an ambulance and was seriously injured, experiences that would inspire one of his classics, *A Farewell to Arms*.

Later he would become a reporter on the Spanish Civil War where he got a little too close to the action and was in the thick of the fighting at times. He continued his career in journalism throughout the Second World War but developed a sideline in running a resistance cell and became the *de facto* leader of a small band of village militia in Rambouillet outside of Paris. Of Hemingway's many exploits, historian Paul Fussell wrote, 'Hemingway got into considerable trouble playing infantry captain to a group of Resistance people that he gathered because a correspondent is not supposed to lead troops, even if he does it well.'

There are many stories about Hemingway's bravery, hard drinking, multiple affairs and macho toughness, so it's only logical to wonder if all of this was the result of the way he was dressed and treated when he was young. Was his later behaviour the ultimate overcompensation and rebuke to his mother? We will never know.

The Obsolete Symbol of Modern Warfare

The Junkers Ju 87, better known as the Stuka, was a remarkable piece of 1930s technology. This two-man ground-attack plane could dive-bomb a target, acting as a kind of aerial artillery support for ground troops. It first revealed its potential in the Spanish Civil War.

In September 1939, Germany showed the world *Blitzkrieg* – lightning war – when the fast-moving armies of the Wehrmacht raced across the fields of Europe. It took Poland in six weeks, and then, in 1940, it successfully invaded Denmark (which capitulated in just six hours), Norway and the Low Countries; finally, and famously, it took France in a matter of weeks.

The Stuka was ubiquitous throughout these campaigns, tearing holes in enemy front lines, which allowed the infantry and the Panzers to keep moving. Its weapons were potent, but so was the built-in Jericho siren, which gave out a terrifying shriek as the Stuka dived towards its target. Even if it missed, everyone learnt to keep their heads down when they heard this sound. It provided a vital psychological edge in battle.

The Stuka became the poster child of both Allied and Nazi propaganda as a weapon of war. The Germans loved it; the Allies loathed it. So, it's ironic that as soon as it became famous, the Stuka was pretty much obsolete. Along with other German aircraft, scores of Ju 87s were sent to fight in the Battle of Britain, and it was here that the Stuka's limitations were revealed to horrifying effect. It was fast compared to ground vehicles but slow and not very manoeuvrable when compared to the Hurricanes and Spitfires of the RAF. The Stuka failed to shoot down RAF fighters and carried too few bombs to be considered a useful bomber by the Luftwaffe. Dozens of Stukas were shot down and the casualties were piling up to no real advantage. It was eventually taken out of service in the Battle of Britain campaign because, quite simply, it wasn't good enough.

The Stuka got a new lease of life in Operation Barbarossa (the code name for the Axis invasion of the Soviet Union in 1941) when the Soviet air force was woefully behind its German counterpart, but even that didn't last. Once again, the Stuka became little more than artillery support for the army. Whenever the Allies had air superiority, the famous Stuka was a sitting duck. Even though it became rapidly obsolete, it was a symbol of modern warfare. The reality is, on closer inspection, the Stuka was outdated even for its time.

Lydia Vladimirovna Litvyak Was Russia's First Female 'Fighter Ace'

Lydia Litvyak was born to a Russian-Jewish family living in Moscow in 1921, so she had two very good reasons to fight the Nazis after they invaded the Soviet Union in 1941.

Lydia learned to fly as a teenager, and after the annihilation of the Soviet air force in the first few weeks of Operation Barbarossa, the Red Army needed everyone they could get. This explains why a woman found herself serving as a combat pilot in the Second World War. Lydia was assigned to fly a Yakovlev Yak-1, a Soviet version of the British Hurricane (whose chassis was also largely wood and canvas). She started in a female regiment but was later assigned to a male one; she was better than most pilots, male or female, so why not?

In September 1942, she was assigned to fly over Stalingrad, then under attack by the Germans. On 13 September, three days after her arrival, she became the first woman fighter pilot to shoot down an enemy aircraft ... actually, two in that one patrol. Her first kill was a Ju 88 Mistel bomber, followed by a Messerschmitt Bf 109 fighter. The Battle of Stalingrad was the biggest in human history, and Lydia was in the centre of it.

This fearless young woman kept being deployed to the front lines and was involved in another titanic clash at the Battle of Kursk (the campaign involved around 3.5 million soldiers and was the biggest tank battle in history). With five solo victories (Soviet propaganda claimed up to twelve) and two to four shared kills in sixty-six combat sorties, she was declared an 'ace'. In two years of operations, she became the first female fighter pilot to shoot down an enemy aircraft, the first of two female fighter pilots to have earned the title of 'fighter ace' and the holder of the record for the greatest number of kills by a female fighter pilot.

In 1943, she failed to return from her fourth sortie of the day. Since there was no immediate evidence that she had been shot down, it was assumed she had been captured, but there was no evidence of that either. Persistent searches for the next thirty-six years finally yielded the wreckage of her plane with the remains of a female pilot, later confirmed to be Lydia. At the age of just twenty-one, she had been shot down and killed near Orel (Ukraine). On 6 May 1990, USSR President Mikhail Gorbachev posthumously awarded her the title Hero of the Soviet Union.

The Baedeker Raids

In March 1942, the RAF bombed the picturesque town of Lübeck in Germany. This was the RAF's first concerted attack on a city, selected because it had a strategic port. It was also lightly defended, so the choice was not arbitrary. While there would be, undeniably, collateral damage to the city itself, the goal was to deny the Axis powers the use of Lübeck's dockyards. It would be a rich prize for a relatively low cost.

The raid damaged three of the city's large medieval churches, which caused outrage in Germany. In response, Hitler carried out what became known as the Baedeker raids (named after the famous travel guides). The operation concentrated on cities in England, chosen not for their military or industrial importance but for their historical and cultural significance. Luftwaffe bombers flew over places like York and Canterbury in an attempt to destroy their centuries of culture and historical significance.

While the raids were conducted mainly in April and May 1942, throughout the war there were occasional raids on towns and cities that were guilty of nothing more than being tourist destinations. The effects were minor. Germany never developed a heavy bomber, and the Luftwaffe never had the equivalent of a fleet of Lancasters or B-17s. Their medium bombers could only cause limited damage, and meanwhile, the dwindling numbers of Luftwaffe aircraft meant that Germany could ill afford a militarily pointless raid against cities such as Bath (another target).

While this isn't even in the top ten of heinous crimes carried out by the Third Reich, there is a special revulsion for any force that deliberately attacks places of historical and cultural importance, with complete disregard for human life.

The One-legged Spy

Virginia Hall was born in Baltimore, Maryland, in 1906. By the 1930s, she had already travelled the world and spoke several languages. She was a resourceful, nature-loving woman who enjoyed fishing, hunting and hiking. Unfortunately, in pursuit of her interests, she climbed over a barbed-wire fence and accidentally discharged her shotgun into her foot in 1932. As a result, she had her leg amputated just below the knee and replaced with a wooden appendage she called Cuthbert. What is truly remarkable is that this terrible accident didn't slow her down.

Hall made several attempts to become a diplomat with the United States Foreign Service, but women (let alone disabled ones) were rarely hired in those days, so in 1939, she resigned from the Department of State, where she worked as a consulate clerk, and joined the British spy network known as the Special Operations Executive at the start of the Second World War, before America joined the fray. It was in this role that her language skills were to prove invaluable.

Hall was something of a pioneer in the early days of the SOE. Due to the leg situation, she couldn't be parachuted in, so she went by ship to occupied France where she was the first female operative to take up residence. She set up a number of resistance cells and became an expert in all areas of support. She was also instrumental in starting a network that helped downed RAF crew evade capture by the Germans and smuggled them over the Pyrenees to neutral Spain.

In her youth, Virginia had learned how to make cheese. Completely unexpectedly, this became an important part of her espionage work as she took on the role of an elderly peasant cheesemaker. Dressed in her scruffiest clothes, she would hobble into town and position herself near German soldiers who paid her scant attention, assuming the old cheese seller couldn't understand them. But Virginia was fluent in German as well as French and made mental notes of everything they said that could help the French Resistance. It was a low-tech yet genius way to gather intelligence. Although she never saw any action, she did have to flee to Spain in 1942, when she knew the Germans were after her.

In March 1944, Virginia returned to France to continue her work in support of the French Resistance, working in German-occupied territory until the liberation in September.

The Germans gave her the nickname Artemis, and the Gestapo reportedly considered her to be 'the most dangerous of all Allied spies'.

Her outstanding service earned her the British Distinguished Service Cross (one of the highest awards available to both men and women), which was presented to her by the American General William J. Donovan in recognition of her supreme efforts and her nationality. She was later made an honorary member of the Order of the British Empire (MBE) and was awarded the Croix de Guerre avec Palme by France.

By the end of the war, Hall had moved to the American Office of Strategic Services, later renamed the CIA, where she worked into the 1960s. In 1957 she married former OSS lieutenant Paul Goillot, and they moved to a farm in Maryland when she retired in 1966. She died in relative obscurity in Maryland in 1982, aged seventy-six.

Weird Tanks

In the Second World War, Germany was at the apex of tank technology, right? Yes ... however, the quest by German designers to create evermore effective tank designs meant they went down some curious cul-de-sacs. One of these dead ends produced a strange armoured vehicle known as the Kugelpanzer or Ball Tank. It was nearly spherical because it was thought that anything other than a direct hit would make the projectile bounce off its relatively thin armour.

The tank consisted of a cylindrical centre compartment with a single direct-vision slit and an access hatch at the rear. The vehicle moved via two rotating hemispheres that made up the sides of the vehicle. These hemispheres were powered by a single-cylinder, two-stroke engine, which moved the vehicle at a meagre 5 mph (8 km/h), a speed that would have been on the slow side for the first generation of tanks in the First World War. It's believed that it used the smaller wheel on the rear of the tank to steer and keep it stable. Although the driver could, in theory, put a gun through the vision slit, the tank didn't have any armaments, so it was not a well-thought-out design for a vehicle of war.

Although the idea that a perfectly spherical tank would be hard to destroy put the Germans on the right path, the Kugelpanzer was not a perfect sphere so lacked that chief advantage. Add to that the slow speed of a pre-war design, and we have a tank shrouded in mystery. The only existing example is in the Kubinka Tank Museum in Moscow, and Russia has never released any more data about the captured vehicle. There aren't any internal photos, so nobody's sure where the crew sat or even if it was a one- or two-man vehicle.

Because the Kugelpanzer had no major gun emplacement, it is thought it might have been a reconnaissance vehicle, but this is all guesswork. What's clear is that the design never caught on as the battlefields of the Second World War were not exactly heaving with Kugelpanzers. It is, however, a fascinating dead-end to tank design.

Then There's the Ironically Named Maus

The Germans produced more than 1,300 of the famous Tiger tank, a war machine that outclassed almost anything the Allies had. There were instances of just one Tiger taking on a convoy of Allied vehicles, armoured or otherwise, and laying waste to the lot. While the Americans and Russians had inferior tanks, they had a lot more of them; Germany, on the other hand, focused on producing fewer tanks of greater quality and size.

This approach reached its zenith with the Panzer Mark VIII, known as the Maus (German for mouse). Only one was ever finished and it came in at a ridiculous 207 tons. When it was realised that no bridge could support its weight, it was fitted with various attachments to allow it to go through rivers. The turret armour was hardened steel 46 centimetres thick, and it had a 150 mm main gun. For comparison, the Tiger was 60 tons and armed with an 88 mm cannon, and a modern battle tank weighs closer to 50 tons and is relatively streamlined.

The heaviest tank ever made, the Maus was a monster. It was as if the designers (including Mr Ferdinand Porsche) had turned the idea of a tank up to 11. The Maus was impractical in pretty much every way: it was sluggish, ridiculously thirsty for fuel, and while it was virtually indestructible, how could it be supplied? How could it be kept in formation with the rest of the army? The only working model was captured by the Soviets in 1945. Having made absolutely no contribution to the German war effort, it is now on display in – you guessed it – the Kubinka Tank Museum in Moscow.

A Brave Woman Pilot

On 7 December 1941, 414 Japanese attack aircraft bombed the US naval base at Pearl Harbor in Hawaii. The Japanese caught the Americans by complete surprise and destroyed multiple warships. In excess of 2,000 people were killed in the attack. As the Japanese first wave flew in, they found only one American aircraft in the air. It was not a US Navy spotter plane; instead, it was a civilian training plane flown by civilian pilot instructor Cornelia Clark Fort. Fort inadvertently became one of the first witnesses to the Japanese attack while in the air near Pearl Harbor teaching take-offs and landings in an Interstate Cadet monoplane.

When Fort saw a military aeroplane flying directly towards her, she swiftly grabbed the controls to pull up and over the oncoming craft. It was then that she saw the rising sun insignia on the wings. Within moments, she saw billows of black smoke coming from Pearl Harbor and bombers flying in. When a Japanese Zero fighter plane began hunting her down, she quickly landed her plane at the civilian John Rodgers Airport near the mouth of the harbour. The pursuing Zero strafed her plane and the runway as she and her student ran for cover. The airport manager was killed and two other civilian planes did not return that morning. Fort was able to outmanoeuvre a then cutting-edge military aircraft with no chance of retaliation. Quite a feat.

The next year, Fort signed up as the second member of what became the Women's Airforce Service Pilots. These women transported aircrew from one base to another and also flew newly built aircraft to their intended destinations. It was long hours and hard work and the closest American women pilots got to combat during the war.

Fort was working as a pilot ferrying crews when a mid-air collision made her the first female pilot in American history to die on active duty. She was just twenty-four. Although there is a small airfield in Tennessee named after her, to date, there have been no official commendations for her bravery and service.

Cornelia Fort, we salute you.

The Battle of Dubno

In late June 1941, Operation Barbarossa was in full swing as Hitler's men and Panzers swept boldly across western parts of the Soviet Union … until German forces came across the five mechanised corps of the Soviet 5th and 6th Armies at Dubno.

The Germans had around 750 tanks; the Soviets had a colossal 3,500. The German panzers were outnumbered roughly five to one at the start of the Battle of Dubno (or Brody, as it is sometimes called), but the Germans were confident. They had been up against a poorly equipped infantry and an obsolete air force, and they were bringing their cutting-edge tanks to the fight. So, while the German amour had the technological advantage, they faced the most up-to-date tanks the Soviets had, and in plentiful numbers.

While the Battle of Kursk was to become the biggest tank battle in history, that happened over a large area. The Battle of Dubno, for its part, could be classed as the most 'intense' tank battle in history because so many tanks battled it out in such a comparatively confined place. Those June days in what is now a location on the Ukrainian border would have been filled with the thunderous, ear-splitting sounds of thousands of armoured units blasting away at each other.

The Germans weren't stupid and were prepared to use every available weapon to break this tide of steel, and the Luftwaffe, with complete air superiority, showed how vulnerable tanks can be to air power. However, with all of the frantic activity, giant dust clouds were kicked up by the tank tracks of both sides. Some air sorties missed their targets or were unable to correctly identify enemy tanks and flew back to base with full payloads.

On top of air superiority, the Germans also had better leaders. This was the Wehrmacht in its prime, so decisions were made and orders were executed quickly and efficiently while the Soviet generals dithered, delayed and watched their units being picked off by Panzer, plane and artillery. It didn't help that only a few years earlier Stalin had purged the officers of his armies, leaving loyal lackeys rather than effective commanders in place. In the end, the Germans lost around 200 tanks; however, the Soviets lost more than 800, with hundreds more captured and tens of thousands of men killed or captured. As the Germans advanced, the shattered remains of the two Soviet armies were forced to flee to the east. Epic in its own way, the Battle of Dubno should be better remembered.

Foyles, the Amazing Bookstore in Central London

The famous bookshop Foyles was founded by William and Gilbert Foyle in 1904, but getting into book sales was not the original plan. The brothers both wanted to join the civil service, but when they failed, they were left with a pile of redundant textbooks. They were surprised how easy it was to sell them – and a bookshop was born. By the 1930s, the brothers had built a successful business and were taking a back seat as William's daughter, Christina Foyle, was joining the family business. She took over complete control in 1945 and would go on to run the shop for decades.

Christina was appalled by the Nazi book burnings in Germany and sent a letter to Hitler saying that she would be happy to buy all their books (at a reasonable price) and so there was no need to burn them; Hitler could get rid of the unwanted books, Christina would save them from destruction, and everyone would be happy. Simple. Her offer was declined in a letter from Hitler himself.

Then, in an attempt to create a better understanding, she invited Hitler, Stalin and Mussolini to do a talk at her bookstore. At the time it was a highly sought-after honour to do so as the cream of literary and political society would attend. Hitler politely declined and Mussolini said he would be interested when things 'quietened down'. Stalin never replied. During the Blitz, the bookshop protected its building by stacking unsold copies of *Mein Kampf* on the roof. Christina took great satisfaction in the knowledge that if it took a hit, the Germans would be destroying Hitler's very words.

By the time Christina entered the business, the talks were usually accompanied with lunches. She was usually seen with a champagne in hand. A well-known raconteur and a famous character in the book world, she was, by all reports, a nightmare to work for. Mercurial in nature, she could be charming or cruel in the same meeting. She refused to introduce any modern methods, and her accounts and inventories were a shambles. Because she refused to invest in the store, the business stagnated but survived at a time when many others did not.

After seventy years working in and later running one of one of the world's most famous bookstores, Christina Foyle died in 1999 at the age of eighty-eight. For the charitable foundation established in her will and for her responses to Hitler, she deserves to be remembered.

Hobart's Funnies Were Deadly Serious

Major General Percy Hobart (affectionately known as Hobo) was the commander of the British 79th Armoured Division in the Second World War. While he didn't personally design the so-called 'Hobart's Funnies' (that would be the Royal Engineers), it was his division that deployed them. So what are they?

Tanks come with certain specifications, depending on their design and use. For instance, the Churchill tank has certain equipment, and the Sherman tank is outfitted in another way, and so on. The Funnies were major variations on standard tank designs. The 'crab' was a Sherman tank which used the drive power of the engine to spin a flail at the front of the tank to detonate mines. It could fire at the enemy and clear a path for friendly troops at the same time. The more normal 'crocodile' was a converted Churchill tank which had the standard machine gun replaced with a flame-thrower. While this was perfect for bunker clearing, it still had its main gun for long-range shooting at enemy armour.

Perhaps the most unusual of these variations was the DD (for Duplex Drive) tank. An amphibious Sherman tank fitted with water-tight canvas housing, it was able to float towards the shore after being launched from a landing craft a considerable distance from the beach and was intended to give support to the first waves of attacking infantry. Of course, if anything went wrong, Sherman tanks didn't float well, which makes this writer think that anyone brave enough to try it should get a medal before even entering combat.

If you are spotting something of a theme, you would be right to conclude that many of these tank variants were devised to be used specifically for the Normandy landings on D-Day. Indeed, the brutal fighting on Omaha Beach was exacerbated when all of the DD tanks sank. The terrible irony was that the tanks floated as planned ... until they tried to correct course, which led to the flooding that sank them. Had they simply stayed on their current path, they would have made it to a different beach and could have made a real difference. They are still lying there at the bottom of the English Channel.

Churchill's 'Fake'

I was genuinely shocked by this fact when I unearthed it. It sounds completely unbelievable, so if you need corroboration, look at the website of auctioneers Bonham's where you can find out more.

Winston Churchill was a master orator. If you haven't been moved by his 'Finest Hour' and 'the Few' speeches, then you haven't got a soul. So, it's hardly surprising that these pivotal moments from the Second World War have been preserved for future generations. But it's not as simple as that. While we know the content of the speeches absolutely comes from the wartime era and was printed in the newspapers, the problem is that there was no sound recording equipment installed in Parliament – or the other relevant venues – until after the war.

So, what are we hearing? Churchill was approached by the record label EMI to record his great speeches in 1949. By then he was semi-retired and enjoying life at Chartwell, but he agreed; the royalties were to be distributed to Churchill's favourite charities, and EMI went on to produce a classic series of Churchill's most famous speeches. Among the fourteen major speeches in this collection, spanning October 1940 to March 1944, are his speech to France in October 1940 and to Italy in December 1940. 'On Japanese Treachery' is from December 1941, as are the address to the US Congress and the address to the Canadian Parliament. The second address to Congress is from May 1943, and 'The Hour is Approaching' is from March 1944. The recordings from this era include all of his most famous speeches from the war, except for one: as EMI stopped at March 1944, there is no final victory speech. Nobody knows why.

This information shouldn't take anything away from the content of the speeches; it is a matter of record that Churchill gave them when he did. It's just that we are listening to the great man recording them when he knew the outcome of the war. It takes a little of the gloss off these key moments of history. Sorry to be the bearer of bad news.

Meet the Schicklgrubers

Adolf Hitler's father was called Alois, but he was born Alois Schicklgruber. He changed his surname to gain an inheritance when a relative's will stipulated the change in order to keep the Hitler family name going. While this turned out to be an appalling decision for that family name, it also means that the German Führer was just one piece of paperwork away from being known as Adolf Schicklgruber.

There is another Alois in this story. Alois Hitler Jr was Adolf's half-brother. Just before the First World War, he moved to England where he fell in love with an Irish woman called

Bridget Dowling. The newlyweds settled down in Liverpool where they had a son, William, in 1911. When the First World War broke out, Adolf Hitler served in the German army, after which he began building his political career. By the 1930s, Alois and Bridget had separated, and young William went to Germany to see if he could benefit from Uncle Adolf's rising power.

Throughout the 1930s, William made a living doing various jobs in Germany, none of which he found satisfying. He wanted something better and threatened his uncle with blackmail unless things changed. The crunch came in 1938 when he was asked to renounce his British citizenship in return for a high position. This seems to have been the tipping point for William, who promptly fled the country and became a fervent anti-Nazi.

William ended up in America as the Second World War broke out, and it was here that he tried to join the US armed forces to fight against his uncle. The problem was that when he tried to enlist and gave his name, William Patrick Hitler, it made things difficult. In frustration, William wrote a letter to US President Roosevelt asking him to intercede so he could sign up. (The letter has been preserved to this day in the Library of Congress.) Finally, in 1944, he was able to join the US Navy, sailed to the Pacific theatre of war and served as a pharmacist's mate. He earned a Purple Heart when he was wounded, but more than anything, William was proud to have fought against the evils of fascism and everything else that his uncle stood for. Following his discharge from the navy, William finally erased his connection to Adolf Hitler by legally changing his name to William Stuart-Houston.

The Slinky Is a Toy ... of War!

Richard James was a naval engineer in the Second World War. He wasn't a key designer; no great wartime inventions can be attributed to him. But he did come up with something harmless and fun. He was working with tension springs for the US Navy when he noticed that certain coils acted in a peculiar way. When he accidentally knocked some off a shelf, they didn't fall, they 'walked'. James didn't do anything about it then, but after the war, he went back to these springs and developed a toy called the Slinky.

While James invented the toy, he knew nothing about promotion and marketing. Step forward Betty, Richard's wife, who came up with the marketing plan, the price point (she was very keen to keep the price affordable) and even re-mortgaged their house to finance her plan to take it to market. She stopped at nothing to get the toy in front of the right distributors to take it to the next level – and it worked. The Slinky went to market in 1945 and sold well from the start, but it was hard to produce, so in the end, James not only patented the Slinky toy, but also the machine to mass-produce it. This had the advantage of protecting his patent while also ensuring the quality of toys with the Slinky brand name. Once the Slinky took off, many other companies created their own, cheaper versions, but none of them could get the tension and the materials quite right. Slinky was simply the springiest toy on the market – and the most fun! Over the decades it has sold over 350 million, making it one of the most popular toys ever.

Unfortunately, in the midst of his success, Richard had a breakdown, joined a religious group, went to Bolivia and left the business (plus six children) for Betty to get on with.

Richard now communicated with his wife only by letter, telling her to repent of her sins and come to join him in Bolivia. She declined. This capable and talented woman had a family to manage and a business to run – and she did both spectacularly well. It was Betty who invented the Slinky Dog, famous for decades and given a more recent boost in the *Toy Story* films. Confirmation, if it were needed, that behind every great man, there's a great woman.

It was, however, another war that took this children's toy into a real combat situation. The Vietnam War involved a lot of American infantry patrolling the jungle. In these conditions, radio antennae had a limited range, but some enterprising radio operators worked out that if they connected the standard antennae to a Slinky and threw the rest of the spring into a tree, the Slinky stretched out for several extra feet/metres and greatly boosted the effective range of the radio, potentially saving the lives of men who had grown up playing with the toy.

So, the Slinky. One toy, two wars – and a great story!

The Ongoing War in Vietnam

For Americans, the Vietnam War ended in 1975. It was arguably one of the saddest chapters in American military history. The wanton destruction, the divisive nature of the war at home and the treatment of its veterans are the topics of innumerable books, documentaries and films.

Just over 58,000 Americans lost their lives, and up until the war in Afghanistan, it was the longest war in American history. But the numbers of American casualties pale in comparison to those of the Vietnamese at a little over 1.3 million ... and rising. If America will forever remember this tragedy, so will the Vietnamese, who still have to live with its lasting effects.

Thanks to America's massive technological superiority, there were numerous extensive bombing campaigns. Some of these involved smaller aircraft like Skyraiders (propeller aircraft) and Banshees (jet fighter aircraft), but huge amounts of ordnance were dropped by B52s. By the end of the war, more bombs were dropped on Vietnam (in terms of tonnage) than were dropped by the Allies in the whole of the Second World War. The plan to bomb the country into submission didn't work; even 388,000 tons of napalm (a petroleum jelly that burned everything it touched) couldn't do the job.

Horrific as all of this was at the time, just as horrific is that fact that after the war, these bombs continue to be a threat. There is an occasional disruption in London when an unexploded Second World War bomb is found, but that's nothing compared to what happens in Vietnam. Today, about 20 per cent of the country still has unexploded ordnance buried and unseen in the landscape; around 1,500 people die every year when they accidentally disturb these hidden bombs and mines. This means that since the fall of Saigon in 1975, more Vietnamese people have died from this forgotten ordnance than the total number of Americans killed in the entire war.

The US government does continue to pay in part for the ongoing operation to clean up the Vietnamese countryside.

The Forgotten Soviet Hero

Russia is quite often seen as the 'bad guy' in terms of East–West politics. Make no mistake, poisonings, computer hacks and an ongoing war in Ukraine make that narrative easy to reinforce, particularly when it was the 'bad guy' for the second half of the twentieth century during the Cold War (from the late 1940s to the early 1990s). However, as in any country, it has good and bad people.

Enter Lieutenant Colonel Stanislav Petrov and the Soviet Oko ('eye' in Russian), the country's nuclear early-warning system. Oko was a satellite-based observation system designed to detect launches of ICBMs from the West. The satellites were being launched in the early 1970s but weren't fully operational until 1982. This was cutting-edge stuff for the times, and in 1983, Petrov was in charge of the Soviet system. His main responsibility was to assess any data relayed by the satellite and to notify his superiors of any impending nuclear missile threat. On 26 September 1983, the system indicated an ICBM launch from the United States; even worse, it subsequently identified five more.

At the time, relations between the Soviet Union and the West were particularly strained due to the Soviets having recently shot down a passenger aeroplane by accident. Given ongoing Cold War tensions, the incident looked to many like the spark that could set off the Third World War. According to his orders, Petrov was to alert his superiors immediately, which would inevitably have led to a retaliatory launch of Soviet nukes. However, contrary to the usual Western image of Russian officers blindly following orders, Petrov made one of the biggest assumptions in history: Oko had a glitch and he was seeing false data. Imagine yourself in that situation: would you have so easily made the same assumption when the new, state-of-the-art system was telling you that your ideological enemy was doing what was expected? It was one hell of a call, but it was, of course, the right one.

The report from the investigation into the incident revealed that 'the false alarms were caused by a rare alignment of sunlight on high-altitude clouds and the satellites' Molniya orbits', an error later corrected by cross-referencing a geostationary satellite. In explaining the factors leading to his decision, Petrov followed his training and cited his belief that any US first strike would be massive, 'so five missiles seemed an illogical start'. Stanislav Petrov died at the age of seventy-seven in May 2017. Thank you, Stanislav, for keeping a cool head.

A Strange Museum

Places like the Louvre in Paris and the British Museum in London are home to internationally important collections, but such treasures are not usually available to museums in smaller cities and towns. While they don't have collections that might attract global visitors, they like to accumulate and display collections of their own. The need to fill such display cases has led to some weird and wonderful acquisitions, and Kentucky can claim to have one that is truly unique.

The marvellously named William Shakespeare Berger wasn't a ventriloquist, but he loved the art so much that he became the president of the International Brotherhood of Ventriloquists. In his work for the organisation, Bill identified a genuine need: what to do with the dummies of ventriloquists who retired or died. Why, of course! Create a special museum for the hundreds of now 'homeless' dummies ... dummy!

Vent Haven Museum is the world's only museum dedicated to ventriloquism (as far as I know). While the recognition and appreciation for the dummies is ... er ... admirable, some of the inhabitants, with their grotesque smiles and exaggerated features, can create a sinister atmosphere. While these characters are not from horror films, they are for many (including this writer) the stuff of nightmares.

Sleepover, anyone?

What's the Closest We've Been to Nuclear War?

It's not a cheery topic, but the answer isn't the Cuban Missile Crisis. To understand the term 'close to war' we have to define what we mean and that takes us to the DEFCON (Defense Readiness Condition) scale. Created by the American Joint Chiefs of Staff during the Cold War, it's a system the Americans used to assess the likelihood of nuclear war (and other extreme events) and was used to measure the state of alertness of American defences in a time of emergency. The scale has five graduated categories. The first statement in each category describes what is needed; the second statement is an assessment of how the armed forces should respond.

DEFCON 5 Lowest state of readiness. Normal readiness.
DEFCON 4 Increased intelligence watch and strengthened security measures. Above normal readiness.
DEFCON 3 Increase in force readiness above that required for normal readiness. Air Force ready to mobilize in fifteen minutes.
DEFCON 2 Next step to nuclear war. Armed forces ready to deploy/engage in less than six hours.
DEFCON 1 Nuclear war is imminent. Maximum readiness.

During the Cuban Missile Crisis, the majority of US forces were at DEFCON 3 (although their nuclear forces were briefly at DEFCON 2). However, eleven years later, all US forces were put on DEFCON 2. The reason? The Yom Kippur War of 1973, when it was Israel versus Egypt and Syria. The Arab states, backed by the Soviet Union, wanted to destroy the state of Israel, which was backed by the USA and was, therefore, a tough nut to crack. It had already resisted several massive assaults and, despite its small size and population, had acquitted itself extremely well against its much larger neighbours.

The Soviets feared that if Israel started losing too much ground they might launch their nukes (which, officially, they didn't have, but everyone in military intelligence knows they had them then – and now). Briefly, the Soviets brought nuclear weapons to the port of Alexandria in Egypt, reasoning that if Israel launched, then a nuclear response from Egypt would be proportional. This was the trigger for America to go to DEFCON 2. Fortunately for planet Earth, the initial attacks by Syria and Egypt got bogged down, and Israel ultimately won the war. After initial gains by the Arab states, the situation quickly reversed so that Israel was never going to lose and, therefore, the nuclear option was never on the table. After the humiliating defeat of Egypt and Syria, the Soviets quietly removed the nuclear weapons.

This little-known moment in history is, in some ways, the most important in all of history. Had things panned out another way, we could have all been wiped out by an obscure war. You will be pleased to hear that at the time of writing, we are at DEFCON 5 ... for now.

Fake Archaeology

There is an ideological war in archaeology that isn't much talked about. On one side we have the archaeology mainstream, and on the other side we have the fringes that take finds out of context to 'prove' more unusual theories. These may support religious beliefs or ideas about ancient civilisations, which invariably drags aliens into the story.

An example of one of these more far-flung notions is the so-called London Hammer. Found in London, Texas, in 1936, it's a hammer-like tool embedded in some rock. The rock is said to be Ordovician, a period before even the dinosaur roamed the earth, which would make the hammer about 485.4–443.8 million years old. This pre-dates even the earliest hominids by a staggering 440 million years. So this hammer must be conclusive proof of an incredibly ancient human civilisation, right?

In fact, it's so wildly off known history/geology that any serious geologist would recognise that this has to be an error. The theory that this is an ancient hammer embedded in Ordovician rock is dismissed even by someone with only a rudimentary grasp of archaeology and geological time. In reality, the hammer is a nineteenth-century mining tool that fell into some limestone sediment which hardened over a few years. You can look at photos online where there are usually accompanying articles explaining how it proves one pseudoscientific idea or another.

To Creationists, the London Hammer is regarded as evidence of the human civilisation they believe existed before the Great Flood, and unsurprisingly it is held at the Creation

Evidence Museum. All reputable archaeologists challenge these findings and maintain that it's just a hammer that fell in some mud. A radiocarbon test of the wood would provide definitive proof; however, the museum has refused to carry out any such test.

The London Hammer reflects the way of the world today. Humans love agreement; it's why we seek like-minded individuals to call friends. But consensus on its own doesn't validate anything. Social media is full of echo chambers, groups of people who feel passionate about a certain topic and support each other in their agreement, while yet other groups make it their purpose to attack any science that challenges their world view, whether we're talking about a flat earth, religious calendars or certain conspiracy theories. Not all views are equally valid. A scientist with a PhD and twenty years of experience in his field has a more valid viewpoint on his topic than Hank from Wyoming who read an article on Facebook that gave him a 'feeling'.

So, if you want truth based on hard facts and evidence, rely on trusted sources, educated opinion and common sense – and beware of facile explanations by nobodies on social media and elsewhere.

Is Sitting Too Close to the TV Bad for Your Eyes?

We have all been shouted at to move back from the TV because the screen is bad for your eyes or – my personal favourite – because it will make your eyes go square. Well, I can help with that one. Before the 1950s, television sets emitted levels of radiation that after repeated and extended exposure could have heightened the risk of eye problems in some people, according to Dr Norman Saffra, the chairman of ophthalmology at Maimonides Medical Center in Brooklyn. But those were some of the very first cathode ray tube televisions. Modern cathode ray sets are built with proper shielding, so radiation is no longer an issue. 'It's not an old wives' tale; it's an old technology tale,' Dr Saffra said. 'Based on the world our grandmothers lived and grew up in, it was an appropriate recommendation.'

Of course, cathode ray technology generally died out in the 1990s, and current flat-screens use all kinds of different techniques to transmit a picture – and none of them cause eye damage. While concentrating on a screen for hours on end may not cause blindness, however, it can lead to eye strain as would happen if staring at any moderate light source for extended periods. Keeping the room fairly well lit while the television is on and peeling your eyes from the screen for an occasional break can prevent this.

So yes, in the very earliest days of TV, it was a thing (you could call it a hangover from history), but now you can snuggle up in front of that 50-inch flat-screen monster and feel safe in the knowledge it's totally fine.

When Money Becomes Worthless

It has been admitted by the US Treasury that it costs more than one cent to make a one penny piece. The US government could save around one billion dollars if businesses made the one cent coin obsolete simply by rounding all prices to the nearest five cents. Studies have also shown that average-income Americans would not stop to pick up a penny because it's not worth it – and let's be honest, what could you buy with it? It seems the main group that support its continuation are the manufacturers of the coin and, of course, the copper suppliers who have a guaranteed market. So while there is mild lobbying pressure to keep it, there is no economic reason to do so. Why not just get rid of it, then?

This would seem to be the logical thing to do and there is a precedent. America used to have a half-cent coin, legal tender from 1793 to 1857, when it was abolished because ... it was uneconomical to make. That was nineteenth-century economics, so not as smart as contemporary economics you would think, but even back then they thought it senseless to produce something that's instantly worth less than the cost of making it.

Meanwhile, in Britain, we had the halfpenny until 1984, and as in the US, it was finally withdrawn because it was no longer economical to produce. The Americans were ahead of us on that one. While it did cost less than one pound to produce the pound note in the UK, it was withdrawn in favour of a coin because metal coins last so much longer than paper money and are, therefore, more economical. However, in America, the paper dollar seems to be in rude good health and shows no sign of being terminated even though a one-dollar bill is not the most economical way to present the value of one dollar.

Economics, eh?

In the 1980s Pepsi–Cola Could Have Been a Military Power

In the 1950s, the Soviet Union and the United States embarked on a cultural exchange. Both held exhibitions in each other's country to extol and promote the benefits of their different economic models. The purpose was to try and thaw the tensions of the Cold War, but Soviet leader Nikita Khrushchev claimed to be unimpressed with everything the Americans had to offer. When he was shown a colour TV he declared the Soviet Union would soon have one too, and it was the same show of bravado with any technology or engineering accomplishment that America presented to their political enemy ... except when he tried Pepsi-Cola.

At one point during his tour around the exhibition, Khrushchev declared he was thirsty and a quick-thinking Pepsi representative handed him a bottle of their cold, carbonated beverage. The USSR did not have anything like this. The closest thing the Soviets had was a beverage called Kvass, made out of fermented bread. The writer has tried it and can assure the reader that there is no comparison. Khrushchev was taken aback by this sugary soft drink, which he immediately liked. In fact, it seemed to be the only American invention he had no answer for. So, overnight, Pepsi gained a market that Coca-Cola had no chance of accessing.

To pay for this American import, Khrushchev gave Pepsi the rights to distribute Stolichnaya vodka in all markets except the USSR. This worked for decades, but by the 1980s, it simply wasn't paying the bills, and the Soviets still wanted their sweet, sweet Pepsi. So what did the Soviet Union offer? The one thing they had in abundance: military hardware.

Army units would be hard to deliver due to basic geography, and fighter aircraft were arguably a little too sensitive. So, instead, the USSR dug into its cache of obsolete naval vessels, and Pepsi was to get a total of seventeen submarines, a cruiser, a frigate and a destroyer. Had this acquisition gone through, it would have made Pepsi technically the sixth-largest navy in the world! Unsurprisingly, Pepsi had no interest in adding a military arm to the company. While this deal was mooted in 1989, the actual deal that materialised in 1990 was for non-naval tankers and freighters from the USSR.

So, for a brief period in the 1980s, an American soft drink company could have admirably acquitted itself against the Royal Navy. Coca-Cola is, of course, the world's biggest soft drink brand, but it can't claim to have ever been offered a navy.

Also available from Amberley Publishing

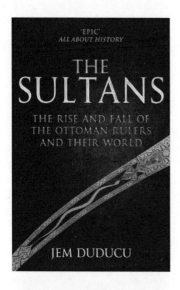

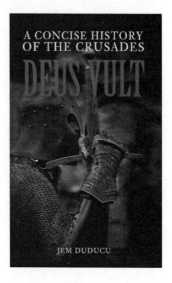

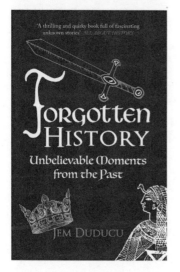

Available from all good bookshops or to order direct
Please call **01453-847-800**
www.amberley-books.com